PRAISE FOR
Journaling as a Spiritual Path

"I have toyed with the idea of journaling, tried it a number of times, but it was never long-lasting. As I move into the latter stages of life, I wish I had a better recollection of my significant experiences. Now that I'm journaling, I'm eager to share my experiences with my children and grandchildren. Jo-Ellen shares her personal journey and provides exercises and questions that have led me to deeper insights as to who I truly am. In my journaling, I find a greater love for others, for self, for all of creation, and the Creator of all."

~ **GEORGE MAUNZ,** M.A.

"While healing can occur on any level of our being, its source is primarily spiritual. *Journaling as a Spiritual Path* offers the reader a welcoming invitation to open one's journal, engage with it, and thereby discover the sacred Mystery that is the Self. The author gently guides the reader to support a path to healing."

~ **REGINA BOGLE,** Healing Consultant and author of *Feeling Our Way: Embracing The Tender Heart* and *Chiron's Light*

"Our mind is full of thoughts! Write them down. Then read these pages as Jo-Ellen Darling gently guides you through the transformative power of journaling. Her book is a treasure full of love, compassion, and honesty."

~ **LINDA KLOPP,** Spiritual Director

"Tonight a searchlight lit the clouds, a beacon that has always made me wonder. Seeing it again made me realize a searchlight can be a metaphor for self-discovery. Let Jo-Ellen Darling help you find your own metaphors on what she calls "the pilgrimage to wholeness."

~ **GREGORY D. COOK,** Writer, Editor, Organizer, Believer, Husband, Father, Grandfather, Friend

"If you've been in the desert with your journaling practice, this book is just the oasis you're searching for. Leaving no stone unturned, *Journaling as a Spiritual Path* will be a boon to the novice as well as the seasoned spiritual traveler. This book is pure journaling genius!"

~ **CATHERINE CAMPANARO,** Celebrant, Spiritual Director, Drum Circle Facilitator and Retreat Leader

"In *Journaling as a Spiritual Path,* Jo-Ellen takes her lifetime passion of writing and brings the reader along with her on a journey toward wholeness in God."

~ **KATHERINE FERRARA,** M.A., OTR

"Jo-Ellen Darling's *Journaling as a Spiritual Path* is a guidebook for spiritual seekers who desire to author and narrate the story of their lives, to find their own purpose and place in the world. Such will grant them the courage and muscle to live out their "spiritual humanity" as they excavate their longings, often buried beneath layers of time and events."

~ **SHERRY BLACKMAN,** author of *Call to Witness,* and *Tales from the Trail, Stories from the Oldest Hiker Hostel on the Appalachian Trail*

JOURNALING
as a
SPIRITUAL
PATH

JOURNALING
as a
SPIRITUAL PATH

*A Journey to Your
True Self and the Divine*

JO-ELLEN A. DARLING

Publisher's Cataloging-in-Publication data

Names: Darling, Jo-Ellen A., author.
Title: Journaling as a spiritual path : a journey to your true self and the divine / Jo-Ellen A. Darling.
Description: Includes bibliographical references. | Yachats, OR: Wild Ginger Press, 2022.
Identifiers: LCCN: 2021923604 | ISBN: 978-1-943190-32-4
Subjects: LCSH Spiritual journals--Authorship. | Spiritual life. | Diaries--Authorship. | BISAC SELF-HELP / Journaling | SELF-HELP / Personal Growth / General | SELF-HELP / Spiritual | LANGUAGE ARTS & DISCIPLINES / Writing / General
Classification: LCC BL624 .D37 2022 | DDC 291.4/46--dc23

Wild Ginger Press
www.wildgingerpress.com
Book & Cover Design by Bobbi Benson

A continuation of the Copyright page appears on page 265.

This book is dedicated
to the
Spirit of Unfailing Love,
full of abundant
mercy, compassion, tenderness, and grace –
and to all those who seek
a Spiritual Path.

CONTENTS

Chapter 3 - Journaling the Depths

Chapter 4 – Creativity and Journaling

Chapter 5: Journaling as a Spiritual Practice

PREFACE

Journaling as a Spiritual Path is a book for anyone who desires to journal. As you step onto the path, it's best to come as you are and do as you feel led. There is no right or wrong way to journal. Your encounter with the mystery of your own being, while at the same time encountering a compassionate Mystery beyond yourself, will provide the inspiration required for the journey.

In many ways, journaling is about *pilgrimage* because it is a journey to the inner self. There are vast places in you of which you are not yet aware, and also many parts of you that you are well aware. Journaling, in many ways, provides a chance to meet the unacquainted stranger within you, as well as to reconnect with the person you have always been.

I've written this book with both the novice and seasoned journal writer in mind. It is not a religious book, but it may help you find an authentic spiritual path. Ultimately, it encourages journaling as a way to discover *the divine and your truest self* in your everyday, ordinary, and extraordinary life.

The power of journaling cannot be underestimated. Besides aiding the process of spiritual illumination, studies in recent years show over and over how journal writing may positively affect or change our moods, our attitudes, and our physical wellbeing. Other benefits may include reducing stress and strengthening our emotional skills, such as our capacity to change. Discovering the good in our lives and living from that place may be challenging or difficult, but these self-discoveries can be life-changing.

This book has grown out of the challenges and joys I have lived through, the time I take to reflect and to be in the presence of

Spirit, and the writing I do in my journal each day. As you journal, you may choose to identify by name the source of your philosophical, religious, spiritual, or cosmic understandings. When we follow a desire to go deeper in our lives in the company of a higher power – however we understand or choose to name that – amazing things can happen.

I like to think journaling can help us to live into our spiritual humanity, which is the coming together of all the seeming contradictions in our lives: our frailty *and* our strength, our personality deficits *and* our creative and spiritual capacities, our woundedness *and* our intrinsic wholeness. Journaling our experiences from these perspectives, we come to recognize meaning and purpose as we become more awake, more intentional, more in touch with our better angels, and to a greater degree, more loving and willing toward all of life – perhaps especially in our stance toward ourselves.

Other gifts in the writing of this book have been to more fully understand my own need and motivations for journaling all these years, as well as the spiritual path I have taken. I look forward to sharing these understandings with you and hearing about your own journaling and spiritual experiences on my website at www.journalingasaspiritualpath.com.

The opening reflections for each chapter are designed to draw forth the possibilities of our own transformation. I suggest how journaling can play a significant role in discovering a healthier path to seeing ourself more wholistically – in mind, body, emotion and spirit. Both practical and sacred/spiritual suggestions are included for the reader – such as creating rituals for journaling – and various spiritual and creative practices, such as spending time in nature and making a vacation into a spiritual pilgrimage. I've included ways to try your hand at poetry and other writing and nonwriting experiences that tap into your creativity. Each chapter, and many subsections, begin and conclude with quotes and poetry by beloved spiritual authors and other writers to meditate upon, questions for reflection and journaling, and exercises that may expose readers to a more contemplative and meditative life.

As you begin or continue a pilgrimage to wholeness, I leave you with these lines from the poem "*For a New Beginning*" by Irish scholar, poet and author, John O'Donohue:

> "Though your destination is not yet clear
> you can trust the promise of this opening;
> Unfurl yourself into the grace of beginning
> that is at one with your life's desire."

Jo-Ellen A. Darling
The Lehigh Valley, Pennsylvania
November 4, 2021

INTRODUCTION

"When we commit to journaling, we will all be beginners to some degree. For all of us, it will be like meeting a new, exciting, and important friend."

In 1986, my life had plateaued to a wilderness of disappointment, and I could see no end in sight. Alcohol was problematic and my relationships were in shreds. Although I was living independently, attending graduate school and writing for a living, I was not nearly as fulfilled by these things as I had hoped. Everything looked fine on the outside, but I was empty and adrift on the inside. I now know that it was a kind of dark night of the soul, for I had, in fact, lost my way. Then unexpectedly, a spiritual experience changed the direction of my life.

Though I'd always been a spiritual seeker to some degree, I had not gone looking for a spiritual experience then. What I now know is, the spiritual experience had come to me – *unasked*. For many months, a bright and kindred Light had filled my soul, its presence powerful and often clearly pointing the way. And even though more disappointments came, the hope I received from that spiritual experience was like a new set of wings. Those wings have helped me to grow spiritually to this day.

In retrospect, it is clear to me that the devastating emptiness I experienced – accompanied by loneliness and *yet my full acceptance of it* – were the needed conditions of this "unexplainable" event of 1986. It seems to be common sense, for example, that space cannot be filled with something new without "making space." You cannot fill a room with new furniture if the room is already filled with furniture! Unbeknownst to me, this emptying of my soul had readied me for the spiritual floodgates to open and inhabit that space. The amazing thing was, I hadn't clearly known what to ask for then, or what I needed. Yet, the abiding Light was given – the gift of hope I so desperately needed.

Hope is a *spiritual* quality that is important to human development, an energy that takes us forward in a trajectory of something we long for, or desire that is possible. Hope is a belief in the possibility of attaining something good in our lives, even if it is met with challenges and delays. Hope can be a feeling or state of mind that is experienced on and off throughout our lives, or it can be an instant or series of flashes of confidence, or trust in something greater at work. Hope can simply be a question we keep asking ourselves, and have not yet lived the answer. Take some time to think about this, even if your life is clouded by darkness now.

What does hope have to do with keeping a journal? And why journal from a spiritual perspective? After all, we may have already found a spiritual path and are living deeply spiritual or faithfully religious lives. Yet so many of us – religious, spiritual, or not – have not yet found a path of sustained inner peace, or one of continued transformative growth. Maybe we haven't recognized an abiding purpose for our lives, or an ability to know or trust that it's there, even when it's not yet apparent. The more recently popularized phrase, "We are *spiritual beings* having a human experience" counters the way we've been reading this line for a hundred years *(i.e.,* "We are *human beings* having a spiritual experience"). We have long denied and then concluded, because of our cultural values and well-meaning but faulty spiritual or religious training, that our own spiritual condition – often pounded into us as a series of dos, shoulds, and don'ts – isn't that important. Tragically, we've come to believe that true inner freedom – to live the spiritual principles that can meet our needs and fulfill our deepest longings – is not within our reach.

The result is that many of us are still searching for a life beyond the immensely complex, secularized, or spiritually avoidant culture (and world) we live in. By looking at the state of things, there's a need to understand ourselves and each other more than ever. I'm convinced that without real spiritual underpinnings in our lives, we cannot get there. Nor can we fully experience our *spiritual selves*. The noted psychiatrist Carl Jung underscored this when he said that religiousness – a word which today could be easily replaced with *spirituality* – was a path that could support a process of becoming distinct individuals in our search for ourselves, and where we could come to a final appreciation of who we are. The goal for Jung was wholeness.

There are potential distractions in every moment of this complex age, resulting in so many of us experiencing an inner restlessness and desire for things to be different. I wonder if more than things being different, we have a burning desire for deeper purpose and meaning in our lives, that a deeper recognition or longing for "something more" is our true hunger. I believe this something more begins by forming a spiritual connection within ourselves.

Sometimes the longing for more is strong, like a current within which takes us in new directions toward mind and heart-altering experiences; sometimes it is weak and fleeting, like dreams that are unclear and escape our awareness upon waking. I have always had this longing, yet it has taken many years to unlearn many things and to have many new experiences. I've needed to revisit and even re-experience things from my past. Throughout this adventure, my sense of self has grown strong and Spirit has become a more stable presence and foundation in my life.

I've known many people who have found a spiritual path as a result of any number of personal crises: divorce, abandonment, job loss, death of a loved one, addiction, illness, abuse, financial ruin, or being a victim of crime. The list is endless. My own spiritual journey ignited at age 30 when I began to journal through an existential crisis with alcohol addiction. Now decades later, there's a history of perspective to draw upon, specifically to see the evidence and the fruit of my growth and healing. However, there also have been many gaps over the years when I drifted too far from soul care. This is normal and part of the natural course of spiritual growth over a lifetime. In recent years of journal writing, I've been consciously led to several ungrieved losses and my need to mourn them. And yet my hopefulness about life – and even death – have taken hold over this time. How has this happened? Part of my answer is that a foundation has been formed by tending to all aspects of my life through the process of journaling.

Some may say that paying so much attention to your own life leads to an overly self-focused existence, or to "navel-gazing" as some critics call it. I would say we can certainly become trapped along the way in self-centeredness, but in some measure, it's a normal part of the process in coming to truly know ourselves. It's similar to adolescents stuck in the narcissistic phase – most eventually grow out of it. When stuck as adults, we learn ways to detach from our selfishness with love and disengage from the ego or "smaller self" with compassionate self-awareness, as we humbly reconnect to our true spiritual path once again. It's not a perfect process, but it is one that takes into account the *value* of making mistakes, becoming derailed, and beginning once again.

Beyond all of our failures and mistakes, our past experiences, and our social, cultural and religious conditioning, each one of us is endowed with the qualities of creativity, authenticity, and most importantly, essential goodness. Think of encountering this essential goodness within you as an invitation to know your *true self*. Discovering ourselves may take all of our lives to unfold, to make things right, to forgive ourselves, and to find a semblance of sustaining peace in our hearts.

Yet, it is ultimately a journey worth taking and one with many graces along the way. One way to commit to journaling is to consider it as a spiritual path. But you might wonder: how is this done?

One of the key questions I ask in Chapter 2 is: What is *your* idea of a spiritual path? As you reflect on this question, it may be to identify the *transcendent* or supreme qualities of life that are most important to you, such as love, kindness, patience, generosity, or forgiveness. For some it will be living a life as a devoted follower of the God of your understanding, such as Jesus, the Buddha, or Brahma. For others it will mean to engage your mind, heart, body and soul in spiritual practices that will bring balance and steadfastness, such as mindfulness, yoga, prayer, or meditation. It may mean finding a meaningful career or vocation where your true self can flourish. It could be volunteering for causes committed to social change or helping others. For many more, it might mean allowing yourself to heal from a devastating childhood or traumatic events in your past.

Whatever your path includes, it may mean to embrace a spiritual or philosophical *mindset* toward your life. This mindset will help to move you from your particular circumstances and difficulties to a larger picture of life, a birds-eye view of your place in it, and its amazing possibilities. At the same time, a closer look at your circumstances can inform you of the changes and choices you need to make in the present that can enable you to live into your true self.

If we are committed, this process never ends and we will change as often as we attend to life. What we value one day may shift, slightly or greatly, as we go deeper into self-knowledge and spiritual wisdom. Therefore, a relationship with the "self" will be, perhaps, the first task for beginner journal writers. For seasoned journal keepers, it may be a renewed and deeper relationship with self. When we commit to journaling, we will all be beginners to some degree. For all of us, it will be like meeting a new, exciting, and important *friend*.

At the time of this book's publication, we are living in the Covid-19 pandemic and many of us have been forced into unwanted isolation. When I suggest that gifting our lives with times of solitude (i.e., being alone with yourself) is an important aspect of discovering our true self, I am speaking mostly about it in the context of life prior to the pandemic – when we would have had a *choice* to take that intentional break from long working hours, caring for our families and sick loved ones, or time away for rest, travel or retreat. Planned solitude can be a gift as well as a challenge. First, we may not feel we deserve it – our culture certainly promotes long hours and overworking. Second, we may feel fearful about spending time alone, even in a group setting such as a silent retreat. From experience, I can say that once our intention is set and our fears are faced and even minimally overcome, intentional solitude can be a source of both creative and life-renewing experiences.

As we continue to journal as a spiritual path, we may find new life sparking and taking root in us between the spaces of our living and our times of reflective journaling. The light of a spiritual Presence will likely become apparent, even if we are agnostic, atheist, or religiously unaffiliated. *Even times of darkness can be fruitful* when we establish ourselves with a daily spiritual connection. We will learn to navigate our lives from a more grounded, whole, and wise self rather than a fragmented, upheaved, and dispossessed self.

Even though at times it will be difficult and frustrating to face the pain and endure the stages of transformative growth, it will also be a joyful work: we can learn to trust ourselves, as well as the Cosmic Presence that is everywhere and available to anyone for the asking. These experiences may not only sustain your spiritual path: your journal will also hold the parts of you that are familiar – as well as those parts that are just coming to light – those unknown landscapes of self that you will want to explore even further.

We have often heard, "I am spiritual, but not religious." I agree that being spiritual and religious have their differences. Yet I believe there is much in common between deeply spiritual people without religion, per se, and religious people who have deep spirituality. For example, there are highly spiritual people who do not follow a religion, but they adhere to a philosophy or 12-step program or some other ancient or modern practice which includes fundamental principles that guide them into a life of peace, wholeness, and fruitfulness. In this way, you might say, they follow these principles *religiously*.

There are also people who follow a particular religion who are also deeply spiritual people because of how they live the fundamental principles of their religion. They do this not by the letter of the law (i.e., rigidly) or so much by their adherence to the religious practices that their institution teaches, but in the spirit of the Source of their religion (in heart-felt freedom and love). They do not necessarily focus on dogma and creeds, but instead focus on the practice of deepening their own spiritual journey, and in the way they offer those fruits to others in kindness, compassion, service, and love.

There is often a difference between the outward appearance of religious and spiritual experiences, but I believe that both are spiritual when there is an inward transformation of renewal, no matter how small or large the impact. In any case and for all people, spiritual awakenings can provide us deep connections to Spirit, to ourselves, to others, and to our planet.

Anyone can have a spiritual experience. So whether you consider yourself to be religious or nonreligious, spiritual or nonspiritual, or none of the above, it doesn't matter. The purpose of the journey is the journey itself. You will likely make new discoveries about who you are at your deepest core, which I call the true self.

The chapters build one upon another, so it may be best to do them in order. Some of you will want to go first to those sections that are calling your attention and then return to the other sections later. The many quotations from beloved authors – provided throughout the book and in the Meditation sections of each chapter – may inspire you. There are numerous questions for journaling and exercises that will help you flesh out the areas of your life that need your attention. However you approach the subject matter, the gems and rewards of being on this journey will require time and patience.

Chapter 1 suggests ways to set our intentions and create rituals that not only support our journaling practice, but invite us on the journey of self-discovery and divine connection.

Chapter 2 describes the importance of finding our metaphors on the spiritual journey. Besides developing a creative way of thinking, metaphor eases the soul into a deeper understanding of our ourselves and our lives.

Chapter 3 tackles the sticking points and challenges that keep us stuck, yet which also provide opportunities that are likely to yield profound wisdom for each of us.

Chapter 4 underscores the importance of creativity in our lives and provides suggestions for finding our creative pursuits, as we delve more deeply into the soul work of journaling.

Chapter 5 focuses on contemplative journaling as a result of our day-to-day experiences, as it supports the healing of our wounds, the feeding of our souls, and the deepening of our journey to the divine and the true self.

Throughout the book I share aspects of my own spiritual journey to provide context to the topics. Although you may not identify with my particular experiences, I hope that they will provide a bridge to your own life, as your journaling uncovers the sacred wisdom waiting to be revealed.

Meditations from the Introduction

In retrospect, it is clear to me that the devastating emptiness I experienced – accompanied by loneliness and *yet my full acceptance of it* – were the needed conditions of this "unexplainable" event of 1986.

I wonder if more than things being different, we have a burning desire for deeper purpose and meaning in our lives, that a deeper recognition or longing for "something more" is our true hunger.

In recent years of journal writing, I've been consciously led to several ungrieved losses and my need to mourn them.

A closer look at your circumstances can inform you of the changes and choices you need to make in the present that can enable you to live into your true self.

Even times of darkness can be fruitful when we establish ourselves with a daily spiritual connection.

It's not a perfect process, but it is one that takes into account the *value* of making mistakes, becoming derailed, and beginning once again.

Questions for Journaling

1. What went through your mind as you were reading the Introduction? Was it thoughts about family, friends, or your job? Was it something you've been wanting to do your whole life? Try to locate some of these thoughts and journal them now.

2. Where is your sense of hope? Is it in some of the words and ideas that you read in the Introduction? Or do you sense a

hopeful feeling in your spirit that makes you want to begin the process of journaling or to start over in your life? Or is it hope somewhere in your past? If so, when? What was the context? Who inspired it?

3. Which Meditations from the Introduction above resonate with you? Use your own words to repeat what each is saying to you. How does any of it relate to your own life?

4. The ancient Greek sages coined the phrase, "Know thyself." How well do you think you know yourself? Journal your thoughts and what it might mean to *truly know yourself*.

Exercise

Sit with the Introduction for a few days. Read it in the time you set aside to reflect and journal. Try to be alone and in a quiet space when you do this. What stands out to you? Journal your thoughts and take some of them into the day with you.

CHAPTER 1

Beginning or Renewing a Journaling Practice

Setting Intentions and Creating Rituals for Journaling

"Intention is defined as being conscious of what you want to experience."
~ ALAN WOLFELT, PH.D., UNDERSTANDING YOUR GRIEF

The human will is a beautiful gift. As human beings, we have much freedom to imagine our lives. Our *intentions* are the manifestations of the will and are the conscious choices we make about how we want to live. Being intentional can serve our life, our loved ones, and our work in the world. We have been given free will and it is up to us how we will use it, how we will choose to live, perhaps especially in difficult circumstances. Being conscious of our *will* can help us transcend the unfavorable circumstances in which we live. The tricky part is this: we will have intentions whether we are conscious of them or not — so the key is to be aware of them.

A key question for us might be: Am I acting from a place of fear? Or am I acting from a place of self-informed choices? If our intentions are always to protect ourselves from too much discomfort in life, we can be led away from our true purpose, and from being truly ourselves. Instead of avoiding discomfort, we will want to work with it, to invite it to the pages of our journal. Using our will to create intentions that lead to inner freedom — by taking risks and allowing discomfort — is one of the greatest fruits of the will.

Intention and ritual are two sides of the same coin. Intention is what I desire, wish, or long to happen. Ritual shows us how to nurture those intentions. Creating a time and place for my intention to stay connected to myself — by reflecting on my life — will be the initial focus to create a journaling practice. In this case, my ritual might be to rise early enough each morning to have this time before I rush into my day, or to find a quiet place on my lunch break, or a time in the evening when the house is quiet. Of course, it can be a combination of these times of day, as your schedule allows.

Creating a ritual can help us to be habitual in our commitment to honor the desire we have to create or deepen a journaling practice. It may be helpful to place yourself near a window in a comfortable position in a comfortable chair, or in lotus position on the floor. Or, you may decide to move outdoors onto your porch or in the backyard. You may also wish to light a candle, read a short poem or passage, tap a Tibetan singing bowl, or listen to background music. If you decide to journal later in your day, you may find that taking a walk, visiting a local park or wildlife refuge, shrine, or other place that attracts you, will help you keep your intention to reflect and journal later on.

One of the most important routines in my life is to rise at approximately the same time each day, and apply the same principle for going to bed. However, I have also read that the time we rise each day is more important to getting a good night sleep than the exact time we get to bed. This principle is not about being rigid, such as when you are out dancing the night before, attending a conference, or traveling home from a trip. This is about creating habits that can support a structured time to attend to your life.

When thoughts and feelings rise to the surface when you wake in the morning, it will be important to review whether attention needs to be given to them. You can jot them down anytime in your journal, to be fully explored at another time. These thoughts and feelings may be about an event from the previous day, how you are feeling about it now, or something you are anticipating in the day ahead. Perhaps you are going to give a group presentation and are experiencing some fear about your lack of self-confidence or how you will be perceived, or you have an upcoming parent-teacher meeting for your child about a behavior problem. You may be checking out part-time jobs and feeling anxiety about the interview or how to present yourself or your portfolio. Creating a ritual for journaling helps to set the tone and create a sacred space in which these realizations can be expressed and choices can be discerned – such as taking action – or taking no action at this time.

Once you've set guidelines around your intentions and rituals, it is best to follow them daily for at least a week. The first days may be choppy. One day nothing shows up that you think is worth journaling about. The next, something significant could surprise you. If nothing shows up, simply sit and enjoy your coffee or tea by candlelight. You could write yourself an encouraging note to start your day. You could – maybe for once – be your own best friend. Perhaps in a couple of days or a week, the journaling may start to flow a bit more as you have begun to create a habit of noticing what is going on inside of you. During this experience of taking time to reflect, you will want to go with the flow of your awareness. This flow will contain what has surfaced from the subconscious – such as thoughts, feelings, intuitions, hopes, dreams (both night dreams *and* daydreams) – as well as longings, fears, and other personal issues.

Like me, you may also experience periods of restlessness in your practice when your ritual feels dull and unproductive. When this happens, I have an opportunity to remind myself that the practice of journaling is not about productivity – it is about *process*. I might think I am disconnected from my deeper self and my life, but now I more often recognize that something just needs to shift, such as my attitude or some minor action I can take. Perhaps finding new and different rituals by changing our routines, such as reading inspiring passages from a book, or practicing a few minutes of silence, can reinvigorate our connection to ourselves when these restless periods come.

Early in my spiritual journey, it was difficult for me to know or feel that I was truly being heard by the God of my understanding. I needed to do something concrete to sense a new connection was being made. One day, I noticed an old red telephone on the top shelf of a closet. I took it down and set it next to the chair where I journaled each morning. Somewhat in a roleplaying spirit, I began picking up the phone and dialing in to talk to this very big, seemingly distant God. It worked: a conversation was set in motion that has never really stopped. This journey with Spirit has grown deeper and more consistent over the years. Although I do not use the phone anymore, I have been led to use many other prompts that still help make the connection. These will be offered throughout the pages of this book. There is not a day that I don't notice something shown to me spiritually. Gratefully, I have learned and experienced many different ways of knowing, sensing, and feeling how my true self and the divine are being revealed in my life.

Adding Prayer and Meditation

*"We are to remember that we are always beginning in the spiritual life.
When we think that we have it all 'figured out,' the further
we are from the spiritual path."*

~ CHRISTINE VALTERS PAINTNER, THE SOUL OF A PILGRIM

One of the purposes of journaling is to have a place to figure out what we need and what we want, primarily for ourselves. Oftentimes it will include the interactions and struggles in our relationships with others. Although our reflection time includes others, we are primarily making an intention to know ourselves better: our feelings, thoughts, and actions regarding a situation; how we are honestly responding internally to others and ourselves; and identifying our hopes and dreams going forward. In paying attention to our relationship with ourselves and others, we begin to build our lives on a foundation of spiritual insight and knowing.

Linking prayer and meditation to our intentions to journal can make our lives richer. Using prayer and meditation, we can ask a spiritual power greater than ourselves for support. This takes a measure of humility and courage as we acknowledge the possibility of the existence of a Universal Power, the Great Spirit, God, or the Divine – essentially a wise and advanced intelligence, but one that we can connect with nonetheless, whether we currently believe this or not. Perhaps the first step is to *trust the process.* If we are agnostic or atheist, we can imagine the existence of something larger than ourselves, such as nature or a philosophy we follow; or acknowledging that an energy, if not someone, is deeper at work in our lives. The key is open-mindedness.

Perhaps belief must be set aside. Instead, we can think of praying and meditating as the practices that help raise our consciousness and open our hearts. Many have found these two forms of soul connection to open doors that cannot possibly be opened without them. I found one such door when I was confronted with the possibility of letting go of a friendship many years ago – through the door of love and forgiveness.

Letting Go of a Friendship

I recall a friendship that I could not fix or save. We had become intimate friends, sharing our joys and challenges and supporting one another. But my friend had quite suddenly shifted and no longer shared the warmth or intimate conversation that had been growing over time. I realize that I, too, have been this person in other relationships in my life, needing space and releasing others for whatever reasons. It was difficult because we saw each other often, frequently in a group setting. When I brought up the subject, my friend said nothing was wrong. I was mostly perplexed, but for a time also sad and hurt. I processed it for weeks in my journal, asking for grace and compassion.

My intention in these weeks of journaling was to honor that our time had been precious, but that change had occurred and there was not a willingness to continue – for whatever reason. In the writing, I learned how to let go gracefully and without resentment; how to tend to the hurt I felt without judging her or myself; how to not interpret it as rejection or a personal failure on my part. Gradually, I chose to bless this person and see her as an equal who had done no wrong.

Eventually I processed this loss in prose that set me free:

Dear Friend,
Your path is not my path. But here is what I wish for you:

- *Freedom* to ask for what you want and need from others

- *Wings* to fly high and see the big picture of your life

- *Courage* to hone your gifts and break chains that keep you imprisoned in a lack of joy, smallness, and fear

- *Enough love* to turn some of it on yourself and sprinkle it on all those around you

- *Eyes clear enough* to see your own sparkle and the beauty in others
- *Deep faith* in Life itself, and in the One who's made it all possible
- I wish you well on your journey!

With love, A Friend

I never sent this prose to her, for this was not the purpose of writing it. I saw rather quickly that this was more so a letter to myself that expressed a great sense of self-understanding and self-love that had for so long escaped me. It was my higher self speaking to the small self, whom I could finally begin to embrace with compassion. It reflected a pivotal moment, the integration of my own soul and personhood, a transformation that had ripened in moments on a blank page of paper, revealing my own growth. It was also a roadmap of spiritual practices – namely the grace to let go and the openness to find gratitude for our relationship – that I would continue to weave into my imperfect yet expanding life.

Beginning Our Day

"Our tendency is to belittle ourselves when we lose the rhythm of our commitment. We should seek instead to embrace starting over with joy."
~ CHRISTINE VALTERS PAINTNER, THE SOUL OF A PILGRIM

Journaling gives meaning to our lives. On any given day, we can find something to be grateful for, or something we're struggling with that we desire to make peace with. But we may have to look back to yesterday's journal entries or yesterday's events for evidence that our lives are full of significant and meaningful learning experiences.

Because I journal early in the morning, I mostly begin my own daily entries by writing about the significant happenings of the previous day. This works well, as recollecting the previous day isn't too far in the past, yet gives time for things to marinate a bit. Essentially, I ask: "What do I remember as the significant parts of my day?" Perhaps for you it will be:

- A significant phone conversation with someone; an interaction at lunch or during the day with a coworker, or the people you serve; something that you were glad you expressed – or wished you hadn't; something your child or a family member experienced at school or on the job that affected you
- Moments with your partner or spouse
- Dreams you had recently, or the night before
- Thoughts that "came to you" as you drove, worked, walked, cleaned, or sat at the kitchen table
- Words you read, saw or heard on the radio, Internet, or in a video
- Strong feelings, a sense of something important that you now feel – *or could feel* – grateful for (now that it's in your awareness)

As I write, I include feelings, thoughts and perspective about these moments and events. I try to be honest, especially about my negative feelings or attitudes that I may be more likely to shove under the rug. This usually leads to a deeper exploration of my own life. Perhaps for you it will be:

- The many shades of your motivations, feelings and beliefs; your needs and desires or your hopes for the future
- The things you want to explore, change, or accept in yourself
- Your true values
- Concerns about people who are ill or have heavy burdens who you want to remember today

- Or perhaps those you want to reach out to, in some way

When you feel as though you've unearthed some treasure about your previous day, you can then move to acknowledge your thoughts about the present day:

- What are you anxiously or eagerly anticipating? Is there something or someone that challenges you, and where you can set an intention as to how you want to approach or respond to them?

- Is there someone you're scheduled to spend time with, someone you want to be more present to and mindful about *their* life, with an intention to listen well? Are there things you want to share with them about yourself, if given the opportunity?

- Where do you need help to let go of outcomes, let life unfold, and *accept things as they are?* Is there something else you need to do better or prepare for in advance, something you're intuitively sensing or knowing about what might be coming?

- Is there something you need to communicate to someone today, a subject that will require a humble attitude while perhaps being more honest with a spouse, friend or coworker?

As we review the previous and upcoming days, we do this not to project into the future or control the day ahead. Rather, we are practicing becoming more aware so we can be *intentional.* Journaling these thoughts will help move our concerns from the subconscious (or constant background chatter of our false self), to the conscious (or more intentionally aware) place in the true self. When we bring these thoughts to our conscious awareness, it's more likely we can weed out and identify fears that may be either hidden or are wreaking havoc in our souls. Journaling these thoughts, feelings, and perspectives will make us feel freer as we walk into our day.

Going Deeper with Touchstones and Anchors

In *Understanding Your Grief,* Alan D. Wolfelt describes touchstones as the "signs that let you know you are on the right path." He considers these markers also to be "wisdom teachings" – when relied upon and practiced consciously – that prevent you from getting lost on the journey. For example, one of Wolfelt's touchstones is "Nurture Yourself." During grief or any major upset in our lives, it is an important point to remember. Nurturing ourselves helps us value and find compassion for ourselves, no matter what has happened. Self-care strengthens our spirit as we find the courage to do whatever it takes to find support and make healthy changes. Caring about ourselves sends a signal to our souls that we are not abandoning ourselves, that we are worth the trouble, and that we won't let ourselves completely lose the way.

Being in a state of unknowing is not the same as losing our way. When we've lost our way completely, we probably have been abandoning ourselves for a long time. On the other hand, a place of unknowing can include waiting for clarity or the next thing to be revealed. We may or may not already have a sense of direction of where we're heading, but we may have a sense of trust and peace, nonetheless. In the frame of self-care, we're more likely to see our options more clearly: what we can and cannot do, what we need to surrender, and what we might decide to do now or later. Journaling our experiences and returning to their important lessons will provide a pattern of unfolding that begins to show us how the divine operates in our individual lives.

In psychology, an anchor traditionally refers to a memory that continues to illicit pain. In going back, you have an opportunity to see yourself with compassion instead of the old ingrained judgments that continue to speak and generate fear around that time of your life, such as: "You are bad" (i.e., you are stained for life); "You're not worthy of this love," (wait until they see the real me); "You really messed up" (I will never be whole); or "You will never get over this" (I will never experience freedom from this).

Let's say a negative memory about a situation at work or elsewhere frequently occupies your conscious mind. A place to start might be to validate your openness to change, your budding goodwill toward others, or your growing desire for personal integrity in spite of your errors being exposed. Working through this memory in your journal can help you take that step toward freedom, as you release yourself and continue to recognize *this memory no longer reflects who you are now*. When we take positive action to correct our judgmental attitudes towards others as well as ourselves, we become more vulnerable and honest. Using the journaling process as a spiritual tool, we come to be more in touch with our true self, the parts of us that are vulnerable, human, and willing to be changed.

Sometimes we are given opportunities to revisit a time in our life that has more wisdom to give us for the present. It may have been a time of depth and significance in your life that may need to be reflected upon, then celebrated or mourned. For example, perhaps something good happening in the present has a lot of fear around it, or something in the present is bringing up unusual sadness. Going back in time, what does this current event bring to mind? It could be a time in your life that brought you a deep sense of a grounded self, or a period of overcoming painful feelings. You may have experienced joyous love or deep sadness, extreme hope, or major discouragement or depression.

Each positive and negative memory that sometimes fiercely intrudes – or sometimes gently appears on our doorstep – may contain an important lesson for our lives:

- The good that came even from a painful memory
- A belief or certainty that you came to hold dear, but one that you now doubt

- A deep experience of "knowing" about yourself or the world, which revitalized your life and gave you hope

- A dream that symbolized something meaningful for you and may have provided new direction for your life

- A powerful or memorable visit or encounter you had with someone

- A strained or fond relationship and how that was resolved – or not

- Something you've said or done that still makes you feel uneasy, guilty, or ashamed

- Something you've come to feel completely at peace about, or that brings you frequent turmoil

- Some unidentified feeling that is gnawing inside and continues to hang around (usually accompanied by *thoughts* – so it's best to write those down, as well)

Exploring these memories can bring a deeper awareness to our present moments as we not only reimagine them from a new place, but reexperience them and gain a new perspective.[1]

Mourning a Time of Life in the Past

"Each opening of the door makes it worth the effort. We may not believe this initially, but with time we see and accept gratefully the wisdom our journey contains."

~ JOYCE RUPP, OPEN THE DOOR

In 2017, I was informed that a close friend of mine from high school had passed away. A class ahead of me, Richie and I had accompanied each other to one another's senior prom. We both also experienced difficulties at home. His brother took his own life in Richie's senior

---

[1] Please see "Author's Notes" for this chapter at the end of this book for sharing these experiences with a professional.

year, and it was Richie who had found his brother's body afterward. It was the early seventies, and alcohol, recreational drug use and partying had been a way of avoiding the pain in both of our lives. After high school, we saw each other occasionally for a year, but then lost touch.

When Richie died nearly 40 years later, I felt there was unfinished business between us. I journaled honestly about this, and I was perplexed by my deep sadness and what seemed a strong desire to attend his service. My husband encouraged me to go, as did a close friend of mine who asked, "What is your motivation for going?" I definitely felt a need for closure, but I wasn't clear as to what that was about. Wanting to trust this deep feeling inside, I made the 300-mile trip to attend Richie's wake and funeral.

What continued to astonish me was the level of grief that arose in me as I approached the eve of his wake. I wept a lot, no doubt fueled by the melodies and words of Rod Stewart and other classic rock that we had come of age listening to. His family and close friends, who I hadn't seen in 43 years, were sweet, open, and caring. We had all experienced so much life since the last time we were together.

When I returned to Pennsylvania, I journaled for several weeks on and off. At first, I thought the grief was solely about my relationship with Richie, and indeed it was partly about not having healthy closure with him after high school. But as I dug deeper during the weeks after the funeral, I realized I had not grieved this time of my life – when I was drinking, using drugs, and terribly confused about the direction, purpose, or meaning of my life. I was also aware that even back in high school, I longed to be free from my addiction.

After the funeral, I became aware that these difficult memories and feelings from those pre-adult and formative years had been sealed away and inaccessible, even years later when I made a vow to live a sober life at the age of 30. In retrospect, my relationship with Richie represented a time of life that had hurt me terribly by my own addiction, and yet it was a time I had also been comforted by his friendship and love.

13

Not fully conscious of my motivations for attending Richie's funeral, I had discerned to make this journey without fully knowing why, but trusting it would reveal something that needed to be faced, deeply known, and embraced.

The experience was amazing, and in retrospect I became grateful for following what seemed like an invitation from Spirit that led to inner healing and a great experience of love. I believe at the time – when I decided to attend his service – I was listening and honoring my truest self – and something deep in me that went unfinished. Much gratitude and peace came to my heart in the ensuing weeks, which helped me to say good-bye and to move through the tomb of buried pain from that period of time we had shared.

And then I had a dream. I stood in a very large building with many levels of floors connected by a spiral staircase in the middle. It was filled with mist and low lights with music playing. Standing on a mid-level floor, I searched high and low for someone, but unsure who I was looking for. When I turned around, Richie was there, tall and young like he'd been when we were younger. We held hands and looked into each other's eyes for a long time without speaking. I was both observer and subject in the dream, experiencing our connection directly, and yet observing the two of us meeting again. The spiritual connection of love and deep gratitude had been made.

After the dream, I thanked Richie often for his love and the time we had together that had helped me greatly through my personal challenges in high school and even afterwards. I also saw myself with a deep sense of self-compassion as the young woman who had succumbed to the use of mind-altering substances as a sadly mistaken way to deal with her life. Although no one else had been able to reach me during this period, Richie and I had been there to help each other get through the loneliness and pain during our turbulent passage into adulthood.

The anchors or events from which we have freed ourselves do not change themselves, but our perspective of them can and does change when we revisit them. Finding the positive aspects of memories and the evidence of our learning and growth can help us connect to those good feelings and thoughts in our present day, and to remember that our life – although hard and full of challenges – has also been blessed, and that more blessing will likely come when we search for it.

Journaling Is a Process

"Every moment and every event of every [person's] life on earth plants something in the soul. For just as the wind carries thousands of winged seeds, so each moment brings with it, germs of spiritual vitality that come to rest imperceptibly in the minds and wills of [people]. Most of these unnumbered seeds perish and are lost, because [people] are not prepared to receive them; for such seeds as these cannot spring up any-where except in the good soil of freedom, spontaneity and love."

~ THOMAS MERTON, NEW SEEDS OF CONTEMPLATION

As Merton brilliantly tells us, each day is a new beginning of things small and large. Even the mundane hours have some important quality within them; perhaps it is gratitude or contentment, or realizing on a bad day, *"This too shall pass."* Sometimes it brings a new chapter, or a new and surprising or subtle turn in the path of life that we did not expect.

At least in the beginning, journaling on a daily basis will help you become committed to keeping a journal. Avoiding the journal each day – especially if you're trying to establish a new or revived journaling practice, or trying to change your life in some significant way – is, in the end, simply passing up rich opportunities to discover the treasure in your life. And perhaps most importantly, daily entries, long or short, will help you develop the habit of journaling while raising your level of commitment to stay connected to yourself and to your own life.

15

An equally important aspect of creating a habit of journaling will be to spend some time alone each day. This may be quite challenging for people who carry heavy loads, such as raising children and working full time, working and tending to elderly parents, running a business, or caring for a loved one who is ill, among many other unnamed situations here. Yet, spending time alone can help you slow down, to notice how you feel and think – even though you truly think you don't have the time at this moment in your life. It's also important to remember to value yourself in the life you are living, to give yourself mini breaks, and even big breaks whenever you can. Try to spend at least 10 or 20 minutes each day in quiet by yourself, whether it's sitting in the car before you go into work, pulling into a public park on the way home, or getting up 15 minutes earlier each day for a cup of coffee in silence and reflection. During these breaks, you can certainly take your journal with you.

Dialoging Exercise: The False Self and the True Self

If you have been journaling for some time and are coming back to it, or you are just beginning to journal, you can try this dialoging exercise that may help you to distinguish between your false self and your true self. This is done by alternating between your dominant writing hand – or the hand you usually write with – and your nondominant hand. For example, if you are right-handed, your *dominant* hand is your right hand. The *dominant* hand may represent the ego or part of you that's in charge and resists doing the writing, or is wondering – with skepticism – what this true self is all about. Think of the nondominant hand – in this example, the left hand – as the part of you which is open to the treasure and possibilities of the *unknown self* – no matter how faint or fragile this part of you may be.

16

Guidelines

There are a few important guidelines for doing this exercise.

1. Write for as long as you can without stopping for more than a few seconds. This will help you to NOT edit the script as the words fall onto the paper.

2. It's helpful to set a timer so that you not only write what immediately comes to mind, but you continue to write past your conscious thoughts. Even if the words do not make sense to you, write them all down as they come.

3. Remember, it's not the quality of what is written that's important, such as vocabulary, punctuation, grammar, or clearly articulating your thoughts. The important thing is to capture the words, phrases, and ideas coming to you and then write them down as quickly and briefly as possible – and to keep writing.

Exercise

1. Using your **dominant hand**, write out any question that comes to mind, such as:

   Who are you, True Self? How long have you been around?

   What does my True Self have to do with the real me?

   Why am I feeling _____ ?

   Why did I think about _____ today?

2. Using your **nondominant hand**, respond to the question that you have just asked yourself.

3. Then with your **dominant hand**, continue the dialog by responding to what the **nondominant** hand just wrote, repeating

this sequence back and forth for as long as the responses are coming, or until your timer goes off.

4. If you get stuck, or it feels natural to stop, write another question with your **dominant hand** and repeat steps 1-3.

5. Try not to edit (change) what comes to mind. Rather, as you write, just *go with the flow*.

When You Finish

1. When you stop writing, take a short break, then read what has appeared on the page.

2. Use a **highlighter** to identify any words or phrases that resonate or those you feel a connection to, but **do not** try to figure out "why" or what it means yet.

3. Set it aside for 10 minutes, then go back and review the **highlighted** text.

4. Journal about these **highlighted** words, phrases or ideas. Notice and express your feelings as you journal about them. Do you find any connections as to how these self-truths fit into your life today?

The Power of Finishing a Sentence Stem

A sentence stem (also known as a writing prompt) is simply the first part of a sentence which you can use to get your journal-writing started on any given day. Let's say you identified an issue you want to explore or gain some insight about. Simply write a sentence stem – such as, "*What I want to know is….*" – and finish the sentence. Continue responding to this stem for as long as the answers are coming. For example, your page may look something like this:

What I want to know is how am I going to get through this day?

What I want to know is how am I going to pay the bills?

What I want to know is how do I even begin to talk to [name of person] about the problem we are having?

What I want to know is....

- how am I going to get through this day?

- how am I going to pay the bills?

- how do I even begin to talk to [name of person] about the problem we are having?

At a writing retreat I once attended, we were given the task of writing for five minutes without stopping, using this sentence stem:

"What I really want is ..."

What appeared on my paper showed I was absolutely in a stalemate with my job, which had been increasingly unfulfilling for a few years, and that I truly wanted a change. The way it came out was quite extreme and humorous in its own way. I wanted a new job – but I didn't care what it was. I told myself it could be working as a garbage collector and it would have been better than what I was doing. Upon more reflection, it wasn't a certain *type* of job I needed, but more so, a desperately needed change as to how I was spending most of my time each day at work. In large part, my job lacked creativity and demanded too many repetitive computer tasks. Moving to another position within the company was a rare thing, discouraged by strict rules and political maneuvering between departments. Amazingly, this timed exercise, using the sentence stem, planted the seed that helped me to make the decision to leave three months later. I could no longer deny that I was unhappy or even okay in this job. I needed to either make it work, or look elsewhere for a new position.

Whenever you feel stuck with the journaling process, use the sentence stems in "Writing Prompts for Tending the Soul" in Appendix B, or create your own.

Meditations

"More than we know, moments come that will make a difference to the quality of our lives. These are moments of choice that will never come again."

~ *Kabir Helminski, Living Presence*

"In retrospect, I can see in my own life what I could not see at the time – how the job I lost helped me find work I needed to do, how the 'Road Closed' sign turned me toward terrain I needed to travel, how losses that felt irredeemable forced me to discern meanings I needed to know. On the surface it seemed that life was lessening, but silently and lavishly the seeds of new life were always being sown."

~ *Parker Palmer, On the Brink of Everything*

"When the fruit appears, the blossom drops off. Love of [Spirit] is the fruit, and rituals are the blossom."

~ *Ramakrishna*

Questions for Journaling

1. Choose one of the meditations above and respond to it in your journal. What words or phrases resonate with you? Where do you sense some resistance in yourself? What is your life trying to tell you?

2. Who or what do you need to lovingly release or place in your Higher Power's hands today?

3.   Has something come up from your past that *wants to be acknowledged*? It could be something joyful or sad, or something important that just needs your acknowledgement.

   a.   If it's a difficult thing, is there someone *safe* with whom you can share whatever comes out in your journal?

   b.   Is there something you need to do for yourself – a ritual or celebration, perhaps – that would help you acknowledge whatever came up?

4.   While reading this chapter, what words, phrases, paragraphs or sections stood out for you, and why? Be as detailed as you can in your response.

5.   Do you need something *not mentioned* in this chapter to help you create your journaling practice? What does that look like for you?

6.   What fears or other feelings came up as you wrote about the significant happenings of yesterday, or the day ahead? What positive images or thoughts arose?

7.   Describe any recent experience of knowing, seeing, hearing, sensing, embodying or feeling how the divine or Spirit is being revealed in your life.

Exercises

1.   Make a commitment to try journaling every day for 30 days, even if you only have a couple of minutes, and even if you can only muster a sentence or two. It will more likely stick if you commit to going through the motions of opening your journal daily, especially at the beginning. Record the date and *anything* you notice upon waking, or from your previous day, or what lies ahead today.

2. Refer to Appendix A – Tools for Journaling to select the right paper and writing implements for your journaling practice. Appendix A also addresses writing in online journals.

3. If you are new to journal writing, or if you have attempted journaling before but it just never stuck, you may want to simply write about the happenings of your day or previous day, both significant and insignificant, in chronological order. Afterward:

    a. Go back and read the entry and notice what stands out – what draws your attention?

    b. Remember that it's not about how well you write but the *nuggets of truth* in what you have written that is of value. Try to answer the *why* of what you just wrote by asking: "Why is that which resonates in me, *important* to me?"

4. If this is your first week journaling or you are in a dry time with writing in your journal, sit quietly for several minutes of silence, then return to this step.

    a. Is there unfinished business that keeps showing up in your thoughts or interactions with someone else?

    b. Ask for what needs to be remembered or dealt with, then write down whatever comes up. Ask yourself: is this really what I need to explore? Wait a few moments. If it is an especially difficult memory or situation, you can set it aside before journaling about it, and schedule a time to talk with a trusted person about it first, if need be.

5. To help you focus on something you think needs to be explored from recent days or weeks, use the writing prompts in Appendix B. Doing all of the prompts on that worksheet may unblock the flow of energy (your thoughts and feelings). Some of the

prompts are similar or may sound repetitive, but doing the entire list may help you uncover some of the silver and gold (insights) that you are seeking to make contact with. Follow these guidelines:

a. Do the exercise quickly and don't take too long to think about each response.

b. Finish all the prompts before you go back and identify something that has now come into your conscious mind that *needs tending*. You'll usually know pretty quickly what it is that needs to be journaled – or acted upon.

6. Begin to notice your thoughts on a daily basis... Jot down any of them to explore later. For example, you may have a thought about someone that is judgmental. Those thoughts are always good to explore, no matter if we like the person or not. Where are these thoughts *leading*? To the same old ruminations, worries, comparisons, or fears that you've been recycling in your mind, or to a new awareness, new feelings, or a new perspective? Even the negative thoughts and feelings can lead to new possibilities if we take time to write about them and explore them.

CHAPTER 2

The Soul Work of Journaling

The Power of Metaphor

"You aren't writing with a particular goal in mind, but writing as pilgrimage, which means as a journey of discovery itself."
~ CHRISTINE VALTERS PAINTNER, THE SOUL OF A PILGRIM

Metaphor is a powerful spiritual tool that can feed our souls for our entire lives. Discovering our personal metaphors will be found in the many circumstances we find ourselves in, reflecting for us the wisdom we may need. Some metaphors may serve to represent the seasons of our lives, such as spring – when life is blossoming and glorious – or in fall, when we experience deep loss or letting go. Other metaphors will symbolize and serve as doorways that invite us to cross into new experiences, challenges, or significant changes in our lives. Ultimately, claiming these metaphors will be flashpoints that will inspire and sustain us.

A woman I met once on a pilgrimage in Ireland related a metaphor to our group about drinking wells. In essence, she said we can choose to create 10 shallow wells and move interiorly and exteriorly in many directions that compete for our time and energy. Or we can choose to live a more focused life by concentrating deeply in just one or two areas of our lives. Perhaps that focus can be to deepen the one well of our own spirituality for the first time – or by returning to it after being "off-road" for many years. Journaling is a way to give our lives this focus.

On a clear morning in 2018, where I was vacationing near Big Cypress National Preserve in south Florida, I woke early, hoping to begin some of the pages you are now reading. I sensed I needed a fresh spiritual connection before I could begin the task of writing my thoughts about journaling, so I did what works best for me: I went for a walk.

While hiking the park's nature trail, I came upon a sabal palm. Its trunk is thick and remains short and stocky for years. In time, however, it grows between 30 and 80 feet tall, and its root system travels up to 36 inches deep. It's considered to be the most wind-resistant tree in

26

south Florida. Yet during storm Irma that hit the Gulf Coast in 2017, thousands of these trees fell from the impact of the storm.

Directly centered behind the sabal palm grew a Jamaican dogwood tree: its limbs grew out of the base of the tree at ground level and spread in all directions. The two trees were beautifully balanced and I was struck that the image may hold symbolic meaning. Initially what came to me was the ancient teaching of the Buddha:

"When the student is ready, the teacher appears."

The True Self and False Self

"Metaphor is invariably more meaning, not less. Literalism is the lowest and least level of meaning. We must never be too tied to our own metaphors as the only possible way to speak the truth, and yet we also need good metaphors to go deep."
~ RICHARD ROHR, IMMORTAL DIAMOND

In the past several years, I have read about the *true self* and *the false self* with much interest. Many excellent books have addressed these concepts from a broadly religious and spiritual point of view. In 2016, I spent a year reading Christine Valters Paintner's book, *The Soul of a Pilgrim*. This collection of wonderfully meditative essays inspires an attitude of hospitality and compassion toward all the many aspects of our humanity, including our faults, our self-imposed limitations, and our wounds. I have found that these are the places in ourselves where the *negative ego* thrives because we have created defenses from the wounds and hurt we have experienced over time. These defenses work much like a crutch on our journey because they create a false sense of self.

These ways of responding and protecting ourselves block us from reaching all the treasure of the true self, and prevent us from accessing our character strengths, our vulnerability, and places where we can grow, heal and thrive. Paintner has been an important teacher for me because of her great encouragement to find self-compassion as I come to a place of self-acceptance and integration in many of these wounded and dysfunctional areas in myself. Soaking in her words as a daily discipline, I became more willing to regard myself with the same compassion I had for others.

As I sat and contemplated the image of the two trees, the palm seemed to symbolize the true self – the part of me that, among other things, is open to a higher power and aware of the connectedness of all things. This part of me bears fruit when I give my inner life time, attention, and opportunities to be nurtured. The palm's treetop branches were healthy and strong and flowing like a fountain in all directions, which expressed a deep freedom in my own soul. Its sturdy trunk reaching skyward resonated with my own experiences of desire for union with Spirit. These capacities in ourselves can grow out of the *healthy ego*: the areas of positive energy in us that are free and willing to take the risks in life that help us to grow and become who we are meant to be.

In contrast, the dogwood, with its many graceful branches splayed evenly behind the palm, initially seemed to symbolize the false self, which grows out of the unhealthy or negative ego. The false self might include some of the things I do out of guilt or manipulation to get what I want or need, or because of a negative self-image and low esteem. For example, using anger, charm, or passive-aggressive language can be unhealthy ways we've learned to make requests or negotiate with others. We can begin to see how we may not have integrated the parts of ourselves that include the old wounds, character flaws, and past failures that underlie the false self.

Upon a closer look, it seemed that at least some of the branches of the dogwood tree also represented my sincere attempts at doing good in the world to the best of my ability. These are some of the positive aspects of my *healthy ego* that are able to hear or notice Spirit and respond from that hearing in my life and relationships, in the service I offer to others, and the time I spend to nurture my relationship with the Spirit. I recognized that even these well-intended motivations are *both/and:* sometimes my responses come from a firm, spiritually centered place – what I know now to be the true self – and at other times these responses are my mistaken interpretation of where I think Spirit is pointing to, like when I may be responding to something out of fear. Maybe some of these branches of the dogwood tree represented other aspects of my life, including the many choices, opportunities, and experiences I am given on a daily basis. Going more deeply, however, I sense that even the healthy ego has its limitations. This has led me to realize that I also need the grounded, loving, and compassionate care of an inner teacher whom I shall continue to refer to as Spirit, God, the Universe and the Divine, among other names in this book. For some of us, connecting to the *Source* of our spirituality will be an important part of discovering the true self.

Of course, the image of the trees can be interpreted in an entirely different way, depending on the observer and the context of one's life at a given time. As I reflected at a later point, I was struck how the palm tree may represent a more masculine energy, whereas the dogwood felt much more feminine and yielding. The images of the palm and dogwood trees also suggest that we live life both vertically and horizontally: we reach for the stars (our hopes, longings and dreams) as well as ground ourselves in our daily, earthly life (doing dishes, running errands, and changing diapers). Metaphorically, both of these dimensions of life are needed for our wholeness, and both have gifts to bear and wisdom to impart. And that is the beauty of the teacher appearing when the student is ready: what you see is what needs to be seen now. It is truly gift and helps us take the next step to a new and more liberating stage of becoming one's truest self.

Reclaiming Our True Self

Scientists have observed that different species of trees can be rooted in the same place, sharing and protecting each other's resources for nutrients and water, as Peter Wohlleben so aptly describes this process in his book, *The Hidden Life of Trees*. Wohlleben describes a scenario in the forest in which strong trees, like humans, become diseased and unhealthy over their lives. Amazingly, however, they can be supported and recover from the help of their surrounding *weaker* neighbors. Yet when these weaker allies are no longer around, even minor insect invasions can lead to the destruction of these stronger giants.

Thinking about the palm and the dogwood trees, Wohlleben's findings led me to embrace the idea that our true self can emerge transformed from the roots of our false self. Examples of this might be when we're numbed-out and we suddenly awaken to a new awareness; when our resentment and anger turn toward an unexpected ability to forgive; when our woundedness and self-disparagement blossom into self-compassion and healing; and when the negative ego surrenders to the grace of divine love. Spend some time with an infant, for example, and you will experience the divine presence often emanating from them: they don't yet carry the baggage of a negative ego, the accumulation of life's hurts and wounds, or the severe failures of life. Later, when the child becomes an adult, her true self may not be readily apparent to her, but it will still be there, if sought.

In actuality, we have always had our true selves. When we survey our childhood and young adulthood, our dreams and passions and the recurring events over our lifetime, one can begin to connect the dots to the true self. The fact that we have become seriously lost or distracted or have avoided or covered our true self with many things, people, addictions or otherwise, does not mean the true self cannot be recovered. Reclaiming this true self by bearing compassionate witness to the struggles of the false self can lead to a seismic shift in our perspective, as the mystery of the palm and dogwood trees showed me one day. If we allow our roots to grow deep, we have a better chance of weathering and transcending the inevitable storms in our lives. We do this by *being present* to our life and our self.

Questions for Journaling

1. Do you have a sense of some aspect of yourself that is deeply true? Do you have a sense of another aspect of yourself that feels false? Be gentle as you journal your thoughts.

2. Notice as you go through your day, are there any symbols or metaphors that attract you? What are they? Be as specific as you can.

3. Perhaps you have a collection of photographs or objects that you've collected over the years or have kept from childhood. These can represent important or significant aspects of your life. Sitting in view of these artifacts, journal your memories. What did you take with you to the present, and what was left behind?

The Gifts of Journaling

Some say that our every thought, feeling, and interaction has been, in some way, previously shaped by our earlier experiences in life. It's also a spiritual axiom that our outer world – our relationships, our actions, and the path we have chosen in life, whether consciously or not – is a reflection of our inner world. Becoming conscious and aware of our inner world is the only way to be truly free from the negative thinking that can enslave and sabotage our lives. As we confront our demons and find the gold in the true self that awaits our discovery, we can begin to make daily decisions that are right for us and for those in our care. Reflecting on our own lives takes effort, yet I believe that daily journaling is one of the most powerful ways to awaken and liberate our true self and to savor the present moments of our lives.

In our pilgrimage toward a more spiritual mindset, mentors will be significant in our journey to wholeness. We highly value business and career-related mentors in our society. But when it comes to our spiritual lives, many of us may not be so well connected. Spiritual guides can be kindred spirits with whom we can share our vision of life, and our sense of God or a higher power. These guides can be psychotherapists, spiritual directors, sponsors, teachers, or life coaches. For some they will be rabbis, priests, imams, ministers or nuns. Mentors can be poets, artists, contemporary authors, historical figures, and writers who share their experiences in ways that inspire us and give us hope. With our journals, our teachers, our mentors, and kindred spirits alongside us, we can avoid living in the future and in the past. We can be present in the now, one moment at a time.

Journaling can also nurture the inherent creativity with which I believe each one of us is born. You may not yet *think* you are a creative person, or that journaling is a creative process. But as you experience nature and the power of poetry, and as you meditate upon quotes from wisdom writers and sacred texts as sources that may hold many metaphors for your own life, you may find the inspiration you need to discover the deepest vein of your own creative longings. These longings – sometimes buried deep in the past or just beneath the surface of a life spent digging well-meaning but shallow wells for many years – will often emerge to our greatest surprise.

Having said this, it will be important to remember that a journaling practice is best if it includes compassion toward the self. With some persistence, judgments we may have made about ourselves for years will continue to show up in our lives. Yet these judgments can be sifted like the daily work of an anthropologist. These difficult areas of our lives can be gently unearthed from the bedrock of faulty beliefs, and, over time, we can be set free beyond our wildest dreams.

Journaling is primarily a labor of self-love. It is loving yourself enough to want to engage in the deep mystery and truth of your own self, not only things of the past, but in the here and now. Don't we all want to find love and to continue on the true path that enables us to live our lives most authentically? Knowing and recovering ourselves takes commitment. This requires us to explore our basic wants and needs: love and work that is satisfying, whether that is raising a family, a career choice, or a part-time endeavor. We will also explore our wounds and mistakes, our joys and our gifts, and our relationships. We will need to dig deeply to find our past and present yearnings for clues, such as those we had when we were children or young adults, and what it is we dream about, even if we think we cannot attain it in the present. We may be invited to explore a relationship with the divine – either through a religious tradition or a nonreligious set of beliefs – which may serve to be the guidelines that help us to align our values with our desires. All of these discoveries will be pathways to our true self. Ultimately, living into our true self will be transformative, even while we embrace being fully human, and perhaps by making many mistakes along the way.

Questions for Journaling

1. Is there a symbol, metaphor, story, parable or image that you have found intriguing and helpful on your journey of life? Dig into it by naming it and expressing your thoughts around it in your journal. Describe how it connects to your soul.

2. Perhaps there are quotes from one or more writers you have read that inspire you. Journal about these quotes and see if some image appears in your imagination as you write. Then take some time to be with this image. Write any thoughts that resonate around this image and how it pertains to your life, such as a *desire* you might not have noticed before.

3. If questions 1 and 2 are not helpful, look through picture books or magazines and tear out images that attract you and journal about the qualities in the images that you are drawn to.

4. Do a collage on a theme in your life that seems to be speaking to you, such as a call to self-care, care of others, some aspect of your work, or something you've been wanting to change in your life. Then journal about the collage. What do the images and words in the collage suggest? What are the possibilities for your life?

Finding Your Voice

"When you share your story of struggle, you offer me companionship in mine, and that's the most powerful soul medicine I know ... writing from a deeply human place of vulnerability is an act of compassion, as well as self-therapy."
~ PARKER PALMER, ON THE BRINK OF EVERYTHING

Finding our voice in life is important. Our voice is an extension of the true self we are becoming. Hopefully our voice becomes more consistent – though stronger and more authentic – by the surprising discoveries we make about life, ourselves, and others. We all have work to do here, and our voices are needed. Not everyone will agree or approve of us, but we're learning that this is not as important as it used to be. As our lives unfold in and outside of our journals, we will know the places where we can no longer compromise, as well as the places where we need to grow.

As a writer who had journaled and written poetry for almost as long as my career as a technical writer and freelance journalist, I never considered myself a creative writer. I knew a part of me was creative, but I didn't believe that my voice would matter to anyone but myself. It took me many years to acknowledge that human interest stories, and the way they are told, for example, are creative nonfiction and often contain spiritual wisdom. Many of us may feel we are not truly writers or creatives because we are not published, or the artistic and creative things we do are "only" hobbies. Yet, we may want to set a goal to expand our gifts and share what we have experienced and the wisdom we have been given.

Author Parker Palmer says a writer needs to figure out if "their chief aim is to write or publish." Many people come to both of these goals at different stages and for different reasons in their lifetime. Yet Palmer warns in his book, *On the Brink of Everything*, that keeping one's *unhealthy* ego out of writing is important:

> *"I was writing to impress rather than express, always a bad idea.... My best writing originates not in expertise but in a place called 'beginner's mind.'"*

Similarly, when we engage in a journaling practice, we will want to engage ourselves with a beginner's mind. We'll want to accept that whatever comes out of our thoughts and feelings, our senses and intuition, and the part of ourselves that is seeking a spiritual path, will ultimately be of value. Open mindedness will help us become conscious and stay awake, and it will provide a place for our sensitive and spiritual natures to unfold – even the difficult, unruly, and messy parts of who we are.

It is also best to have our motivations for journal writing be clear. First and foremost, journaling is for ourselves. In journaling for ourselves, we get in touch with our strengths *and* weaknesses, our judgments *and* the grace to accept life, our messiness *and* inner beauty, our brokenness *and* wholeness. As Paintner suggests in the chapter's opening quote, all of this can lead to being transformed through a pilgrimage of journaling.

As we commit to our journals, these true and false selves may appear in many aspects of our life. Yet, how can we differentiate them? How can we become more truly who we are and are meant to be in our daily and moment-by-moment living, our listening, and our interacting with our world?

Our purpose for doing something isn't always clear. We may feel dimly nudged or clearly compelled in some way to enter into relationship with someone or something, but after we do, we may find ourselves in a hazy, foggy period trying to figure out the why. The purpose is sometimes hidden or not obvious. This can last days – or even years.

Several years ago, I felt repeatedly nudged to invite author Paula D'Arcy to give a writers' retreat for my spiritual community. I put it off for a while, returning to it many times over several months. It clearly seemed an energy came alive in me whenever I considered the possibility of inviting her. I had personal reasons why this appealed to me: I longed for a writing retreat that could be transformational in my creative and metaphysical life – something spiritually based, authentic, and yet creative without religious language. D'Arcy's writing had these qualities in two of her books I read at the time, *The Gift of the Redbird* and *Waking Up to This Day*. I also knew inviting her would

> "The sole tamer of the [negative] ego is love.... [Yet] the ego is a fundamentally positive energy with many positive qualities: aspiration, diligence, responsibility, self-respect, discipline, and integrity."
>
> ~ **Kabir Helminski,** Living Presence

36

benefit others. In the end, my spiritual community agreed to host this dear and talented woman who had been transformed by God's love through personal tragedy and a commitment to her own spiritual journey.

I had no idea what to expect at the writers' retreat, but I prayed it would be life changing. After I read aloud to the group as part of a writing exercise, the message in what I had written was slowly revealed: I was desperate for change – but I had lost my voice. Not the voice that wants to "fit in" in this world, but the voice that had been given to me mysteriously at birth, the voice that held my passion and my truth – and was dying to speak. Not just in my journals or in the articles I wrote, but also in the decisions I made and in my conversations with the people I loved. I'd been too busy and too afraid to truly listen. But that week, things shifted.

I thought about the irony of being a writer and yet losing one's voice. The truth is, each of us has an innate and unique voice – whether we write, journal, or not.

My life changed a lot after that retreat: within three months I left a job in which I was dying on the vine. I enrolled in spiritual growth courses and led an effort in my spiritual community to publish a book of meditations about deeply personal struggles and life-giving experiences, poetry, prayers, photography and art. As I wrote sometime later, I did have some clues, but not a clear picture about the ultimate purpose of all the changes: a freelancing business, great urges of creative expression, and a time of deep self-honesty and healing. Yet I knew in my heart it was *enough* to follow the longing to write creatively, to grow spiritually, and to surrender to that which fed my soul. Without compromising my values or neglecting my responsibilities, there were also plenty of opportunities to say "no thank you" and to make room for that which was truly life-giving. As I deepened my trust in Spirit's voice – and learned to trust the true voice in me – a more authentic life unfolded.

Questions for Journaling

1. How are you finding your voice? What do you engage in that is life-giving?

2. How would you describe your voice?

3. What do you do well? Is your voice connected to that? How?

4. If not, what can you do to find your voice?

Losing Faith, Gaining Trust

Our culture – and so many of us – are at the breaking point, stressed by personal, family, and work-related societal demands and realities. It is no wonder that we may have dismissed a more spiritual approach to our life. Perhaps it is because of a tendency to intellectualize and hold rigid opinions, or to follow a philosophical or political ideology that forsakes all else. Some of us have lost faith because of our society's social and educational institutions, or our struggles and misunderstandings with our families, or how we interpret our past. We may have lost faith in religious institutions and communities as we have watched them fight and fail to be the models of change, growth, and integrity that we long for them to be. Some of us have become exhausted and overwhelmed by the sheer complexity of postmodern life and all its demands, invitations, and its endless possibilities in this complex age of hi-tech and social media.

Moreover, we may have been conditioned by our families, our friendships, our chosen communities, and our culture not to value a greater spiritual awareness, whether through a particular religious philosophy or a set of nonreligious beliefs. Maybe because of our negative religious experiences or cynical thinking about religion, we have chosen not to seek the experience of spiritual enlightenment in our lives. Or our outlook on life has been shaped by our despair over political and economic systems that have led to continued war, poverty, oppression and division.

It's important to remember that to embrace the spiritual life, we do not have to suddenly abandon or judge who we have been, or the reasons for the important decisions we have made, or our essential beliefs, points of view, deepest feelings or otherwise. Instead, we can begin to *trust this*: no matter where we are, we can begin right where we are.

Tending to one's spiritual life is countercultural, even in some religious communities. It is so difficult when so much of life points to the surface of things – like conforming blindly rather than searching inwardly for answers. Seeking the authentic self and exploring whom we are called to become is either not honored, or not in the minds of most people. It seems to me we all have difficulty finding a way of life that allows spiritual *and* human love to flourish, being faithful to our responsibilities *and* finding that inner path of purpose that only we are meant to find. One reason could be is that we're so busy doing for others (including our work) but we are neglecting ourselves. Unfortunately, this is one of the deeply ingrained norms in our culture.

Consequently, self-care will initially feel selfish to many of us. Reprioritizing our time allotments with family, various causes, communities, volunteering, recovery work, overworking and so on, may become necessary for us to be able to sink into what is most deeply drawing the attention of our soul. Doing this may present another obstacle: if we do not risk others' disapproval, we may never know what that calling is. However, I'm convinced that discovering the divine and our truest self are two of the most amazing, grounding, and life-changing choices we will ever make.

Meditations

"This is never a painless experience, but once we have committed ourselves to the search for truth, to seeing ourselves as we really are, we must see without judging what we see."
~ *Kabir Helminski, Living Presence*

"The call of the pilgrim is to stay awake to our own patterns of life and death… When we feel the death impulse arising….we can turn toward it with compassion…"
~ *Christine Valters Paintner, The Soul of a Pilgrim*

"Just as a candle cannot burn without fire, [we] cannot live without a spiritual life."
~ *The Buddha*

Questions for Journaling

1. What meaningful experience have you had of late? Write about it until you've expressed everything you noticed about the experience and have said everything you want to say. Was it:

    *   a dream?

    *   an interaction or conversation with someone?

    *   a meaningful book?

    *   an amazing thing your child or someone said or did?

    *   a coincidence, moment of clarity, or deep peace?

    *   an intense feeling?

    *   a desire to do something you've been wanting, yet unable, to do?

2. What is Life saying to you now? Before writing each of your thoughts, answer this question by writing "*Right now, life is*

40

saying to me...." for each new thought. Keep writing until you run out of responses to this question.

3. Respond to a personal question of your own, a question that may open a pathway to where you might be headed, such as:

   - What creative pursuit do I dream or fantasize about?

   - What changes in my homelife or social life do I want to make?

   - What things, people, or activities do I need to let go of, to open some space for me to spend time with myself and to follow my dreams, invitations, or callings?

   - What new thing can I do every day to nurture my own spirit?

   - What program, teaching, course, or spiritual experience do I desire, or need to find?

4. What is your idea of a spiritual path? Can you find an image in a book, magazine, online blog or website that speaks to your sense of what a spiritual path may embody for you? Does this image give you a metaphor you can work with? Journal your thoughts, identifying the characteristics of your desired spiritual path.

5. Write as many personal questions as you wish. (Examples might be: Why do I feel so unhappy? What am I longing for? How can I get there?) Take time to journal your responses each day but remember the amount you write is not the goal. Rather, try to get to the bottom of what you feel, think, or sense about the heart of these questions. Later, reflect and meditate on which question(s) seem to be the most important at this time.

Exercise

Sit quietly now and take a few deep breaths... Connect with your inner self by placing your hand and gently rubbing it over your heart.... When you feel ready, repeat this mantra written by Joyce Rupp several times, *slowly*:

"I will be open to who I am and who I can become......"

CHAPTER 3

Journaling the Depths

Introduction

There are many opportunities in any given day to journal what we notice. Yet, we do not just journal – we live life – and then return to the pages to capture all that we are learning and all that is being given for our continued growth. Through the practice of journaling, we can explore, reframe and deeply savor our experiences, thus integrating them more fully in our lives. We listen for the still small voice as we explore our dreams, longings, and values. A journaling practice ultimately stretches us beyond our known limitations and capabilities. We become more vulnerable and honest. Using the journaling process as a spiritual tool, we come to be more in touch with our true self – the part of us that is willing to grow and be changed. This practice can aid in the transformation of our negative traits, or wounded ego, to a place where our true self, with the help of the healthy ego, can be recognized and lived into more fully. Our true self, always ready to be awakened, ultimately reflects the Universal Light in each of us.

This chapter focuses on some common themes that we all experience at one time or another. Each of the topics contain meditative quotes for reflection, questions for journaling, and exercises for the reader. On the surface, these themes appear mostly as struggles or difficult aspects of life. Yet, we can learn to trust that when we tend to them by journaling and reflecting upon our own words and experiences, our inner consciousness expands, thus readying us to be guided to the wisdom we are seeking in any given situation. Here are some common themes we can expect to be journaling about:

- Confronting Persistent Thoughts and Feelings
- Having Expectations and Dealing with Disappointment
- Acknowledging Discouragement
- Processing Conflict in Relationships
- Grieving Life's Changes and Losses
- Losing a Loved One to Death
- Longing to Be Free of Negative Emotions
- Figuring Out What You Need
- Comparing Yourself to Others
- When Your Life is Out of Balance
- Being True to Yourself

Confronting Persistent Thoughts and Feelings

Persistent or obsessive thoughts or feelings – often characterized by uneasiness, guilt, fear or an inability to stop thinking about them – are great material for journaling. At times we may find ourselves ruminating over our interactions with others, or thoughts about the past or future as though we are caught in a web. These thoughts, for example, can manifest as being overly reliant on how another person (or others in a family or community) thinks how we should live our lives. It is often the journaling process that will help us mine the depths of these thoughts, and to eventually know what action is needed on our part. The action we take may be to request something from another person, such as clarification of what was meant. Or, it may be a memory or voice (critical, demanding, etc.) that continues to appear in your thoughts that needs to be acknowledged. It is likely the journaling will bring you some insight, resolution, or relief once it appears on the page.

When you are journaling about such thoughts and feelings, do not hold back on what needs to be honestly expressed and admitted. For example, say you are deeply disappointed with someone. Do not immediately shift into writing that dismisses your disappointment. Instead, explore the disappointment fully. Write about the resentments you may feel in connection to the issue at hand, and how you've been let down. Were you having expectations? Admitting these things doesn't mean you have to act on your findings, at least not yet. You can fully experience the thoughts and emotional connections within yourself and then allow them to rest before taking action. This exercise takes us off autopilot from our reactions – whether we have a tendency to challenge the other person or stuff the entire experience – until the next time it happens, and we repeat the unhealthy cycle again.

Consider a time after meeting with someone you have known for a while, or are still getting to know. You may have things in common: you volunteer somewhere together, exercise, work together, or are involved in something your children share. Perhaps you come away with judgments masked as questions or concerns that may not yet be clear in your mind. Yet you feel an uneasiness about the relationship and you'd like to explore it, to get closer to the bottom of it where the root of the gnawing feelings or thoughts reside. At the end of this section, there are a number of questions and exercises you can do in your journal to find out what is going on with you.

True self-acceptance is a journey of a lifetime and may be no easy thing to attain. However, teachers are always around us through those we meet and interact with. As we honestly journal our experiences and our relationship with ourself, we begin to experience the incremental changes that self-acceptance in each situation brings. If we don't give up, we eventually come to a stable place of accepting ourselves – our faults, our failures and our wounds, as well as our strengths, our gifts and the Light within us. It is not so much a destination but a process that is filled with breakthroughs, unique moments, and food for the soul.

I recently went to a gathering of people that were discussing ways to be spiritually well. Someone shared that we needed to do a certain spiritual practice a certain number of times per week to achieve any progress in it, otherwise progress could not be attained. I remember bristling at this statement. After a few days of getting nowhere, I realized my resistance to it needed my attention. Perhaps I would benefit by putting more effort into the practice, so I journaled about that. My next step was to address the feelings of taking the individual's advice personally, such as hearing it as a mandate to conform to the group in order to "do it right" or truly belong. I wrote about it several times over the coming week and found peace in the fact that I was, perhaps, in a different place than the person who had shared this idea. I was making progress doing the practice once a week, which fit into my full schedule. I did not feel a need to judge them for thinking what was required in their life should also apply to others – for I have done this too, many times. By processing this in my journal and taking time to reflect, I was able to be with what I was discerning from the true self instead of reacting from the false self. Operating from the false self often comes from a place of fear and doing what others approve – or just the opposite – digging in our heels (the ego) and making snap judgments about others. For me, the issue was resolved.

In summary, whenever we cannot let something go that bothers us – such as persistent thoughts and feelings – we can use the journal to empty our thoughts, state our intentions, ask for insight, and ultimately find a path of wisdom through the *lesson* that is occurring in that moment of our lives.

Meditations

"I started trusting my intuition more, my sense of the rightness of something, even if it didn't seem like the logical thing to do."
~ Christine Valters Paintner, The Soul's Slow Ripening

"… the vast majority of us go to our graves without ever really knowing who we are. We unconsciously live someone else's life, or at least someone else's expectations for us. We are so unaccustomed to being our true self."
~ Peter Scazzero, Emotionally Healthy Spirituality Day by Day

"If we don't give up, we eventually come to a stable place of accepting ourselves – our faults, our failures and our wounds, as well as our strengths, our gifts and the Light within us. It is not so much a destination but a process that is filled with breakthroughs, unique moments, and food for the soul."
~ Jo-Ellen A. Darling

47

Questions for Journaling

1. Who or what situation, words, or attitudes exchanged in the past week or so have left you feeling uneasy, hurt, angry, guilty, afraid or bereft?

2. Spend some quiet time to name whatever someone said (or that you said or felt in response) that has hooked you into a feeling of guilt, uneasiness, confusion, fear or questioning. Take a walk before you begin if you need some space to clear your mind.

3. Perhaps you can recall and gently summarize the important points of the conversation that led up to the recent interaction – what the other did or said and what you did or said – or what they or you *didn't* say or do but may have been *implied*. Now is the time to say (in your journal) what you needed to say, what you want to know from them, and especially what you need to know about yourself.

4. Check your assumptions: *an assumption is a belief or claim that you take for granted without examining it.*

   • Are you making assumptions or a judgment about the other person?

   • What assumptions do you make about yourself (i.e., I could have done a better job in that moment, I should not have expressed my feelings, etc.). What does "doing a better job" look and feel like? Or, is what you did or said enough?

   • What if you are wrong about the other person's motivations?

   • What are your own intentions and expectations in this relationship?

5. In your journal, ask questions about the interactions you are writing about and *keep the focus on yourself.* In the end, you

cannot change anyone else, but you can change yourself. For example, how does it look when you see what occurred from an unaffected outsider's point of view?

6. Name any resistance you have to seeing this from a more objective place. Do you have a tendency to not give people the benefit of the doubts you have about them? Why do you think this is so?

7. Continue journaling until the well runs dry: your questions, your assumptions, your assertions, your beliefs, and your own hunches about your feelings, and reasons for your own reaction or perspective.

8. This may or may not be appropriate: do you need to make an apology for something you did or said? It's important to identify and rule this out if your guilt is valid and a sincere apology is needed. Sometimes there is no faster way to wipe the slate clean. How would you apologize? What would you say, or not need to say?

9. Do you need to go back and clarify something you said to someone? Or do you need clarification from someone else, such as: "What did you mean when you said ...?" This makes clear what you or they may have interpreted incorrectly, which can defuse your feelings or the situation.

10. What is the invitation here? Can you approach the relationship in a new way without pointing out all the things that are wrong with someone else (or yourself)? Or do you need to discuss the issue and then decide if you will keep or let go of the relationship, or perhaps at least, put boundaries in place?

Exercises

After you have identified and reflected on persistent or obsessive thoughts and/or feelings, create a ritual for letting go of them. This will help you create a symbolic act of actually letting go besides "thinking about letting go." Here are some suggestions:

a. Write a letter to the *thought or feeling* that you've identified, as if writing to a troubled friend. Thank them for showing up and giving you what you needed to know, but now it is time to let them go, as they no longer serve your purpose in life. Burn the letter or give it a proper burial (rip it in shreds and bury it in the garden).

b. A cairn is a small mound or stack of stones erected as a memorial or marker. Go to a natural setting where you can build a cairn, such as on a hiking trail, beach, or next to a river or stream. Take a black or colored marker with you and write what is being "let go" on one or more of the stones. Sit for a few moments after you create the cairn and speak to it gently, perhaps reading the letter you wrote in (a) above.

c. Create a God box, much like an old tissue box or other small box, plain or decorated, and keep it somewhere private. On a slip of paper, write a note to your Higher Power or the God of your understanding about the persistent thoughts and feelings that you desire to be released. Repeat this as often as necessary.

d. Create a collage with images and words from magazines or other media which speak to the issue at hand. What surprises do you notice in the collage that are new in regards to working it through?

Having Expectations and Dealing with Disappointment

Disappointment is an inevitable part of life. How we handle disappointment can make or break a life well lived. My brother refers to this as managing our expectations. Maybe you have heard the adage "An expectation is a resentment waiting to happen." Thinking your kids will go to daycare today, your son will take care of the lawn, or the mail will come today, are reasonable things to expect. We need to have some expectation as to how things work, otherwise we'd live in constant chaos and fear.

Yet, other people's choices in life often do not turn out the way we expected or wished they would. Many of us may never have been shown how to handle disappointments in a healthy way, or to even expect them as a normal and regular part of life. Many people and events in life will never go our way or as planned, no matter what we do or how hard we try. When I'm struggling with this, I like to remember John Lennon's quote:

"Life is what happens to you when you are busy making other plans."

I met someone once whose spouse wanted a divorce. He told me he felt that God wanted his wife to stay married to him. It seemed that he could not accept that he was no longer loved by this woman. I think many share his belief that God doesn't want divorce, or that God would want to see his wife continue to love her husband. Yet, I have learned that living in denial of other people's choices ultimately hurts us. This denial can take many forms: obsessions or addictions to alcohol, drugs, sex, pornography, shopping, travel, gambling, controlling others, people-pleasing, thinking that we know what is best for other people – and even addiction to religion. Healthy religion never leads to denial, but always to the truth. And sometimes the truth really hurts.

This denial can also lead us to a life of fantasy, where we believe everything is okay but we don't really deal with our feelings, thoughts, or relationship problems. Instead, we run away and hide from what life is trying to tell us, so we avoid reality. We don't realize or trust that working through the problems and "accepting life on life's terms" can be good for us. What is good to remember is that we *always* have a certain amount of choice: we either allow ourselves to experience the disappointment, work through it, then let it go and move on, or we do everything in our power to avoid the truth of what has happened: the truth that we are sad, hurt – and maybe even devastated. Our culture doesn't exactly accommodate authentic grieving about the losses we experience in life. Rather, we are encouraged to move on and get past them as quickly as possible.

But one thing is for sure: we cannot control how fast the soul will heal. It's better to release the timing and be faithful to the work of the soul, or "God's timing" as some know it to be. These disappointments can be the big, crushing kind such as the man's wife who left him, or the loss of a job or career, or when someone we love dies. Or they can be the lesser kinds of disappointments that also need our attention, like when a person's attitude changes toward us, or someone is unkind, or when friends change and we are no longer connected, for whatever reason. We can review our own interactions with them and see if we need to apologize, or if it seems that their responses are really about them, and not us – or a combination of these things.

This is the suffering in life that some say we don't need to do. Others say the suffering is necessary, because otherwise we are in denial and build coping mechanisms that ensure we don't let painful things happen to us again. In my experience, it gets easier when I allow the pain and disappointment to be real because I usually grow from that experience. I become stronger and wiser and usually more tender. I begin to realize that the things that don't work out the way I wanted them to, actually create space for new opportunities for my growth. I might even begin to really lean into a power greater than myself because I am basically acknowledging that I am powerless over other people and I don't have all the answers. The next time you feel disappointed, you might ask yourself: "How important is this?" If it's very important and you face it head-on, you will likely experience untold graces – perhaps more freedom and trust – which often come from the hard work of your acceptance of reality.

When we face reality, our egos take the hit and go through the necessary lessons in humility. These experiences often feel like humiliations, but they do not have to be the shameful kind. It is just another experience in life trying to tell us that we cannot coerce, manipulate or demand what we want from others, no matter how subtle our attempt to do this. Then we decide what to do next: we can let go of the person(s), pain or conflict, or accept the changes that have occurred and then move on – continuing the relationship in a new way, or disengaging from the relationship altogether.

Meditations

"Looking at the shattered surface of our common life can send us into despair. Seeing the wholeness beneath the shards can encourage us to keep reaching deep for something better – something that's already there, hidden in plain sight."
~ Parker Palmer, On the Brink of Everything

"What does it mean to be an inhabitant of the world's edge? To go out to wild threshold places, into the holy darkness, and embrace a fertile and wide expanse of possibility there beyond the safe constructs of culture and the expectations that slowly suffocate our creative hearts?"
~ Christine Valters Paintner, The Soul's Slow Ripening

"Your complicity with other people's images and expectations of you allows them to box you in completely."
~ John O'Donohue, Eternal Echoes

Questions for Journaling

1. Name a recent situation where you felt a significant level of disappointment. Don't leave out your negative feelings when writing about it; rather, put down all the gory details.

   a. Write about it again almost as a reporter would write a short news story, giving both the pros and cons of each side of the story.

   b. How invested were you in the outcome of the situation, i.e., to get your own way, that your expectations would be met, or that something that had been agreed upon would go as planned? Describe in detail.

2. Now name a situation when you disappointed someone else. Why was the person disappointed? What happened? Did you break a promise or need to change plans because of an important personal issue that came up? Or were you just too tired to go through with the plans? Be honest.

3. How good are you at allowing others to change their minds? How good are you at allowing yourself to change *your* mind? How do you arrive at decisions after disappointment?

4. How important to you is *keeping a commitment?*

   a. Do you try to keep them as best as possible?

   b. Do you apologize or explain when you have to break an agreed-upon plan or commitment? Or do you just disappear?

   c. Have you learned to discern what kinds of commitments you *cannot* keep?

5. Are you overly committed in your life? Do you expect everyone else to be the same way and when they back out, you carry resentments or feel you must now end the relationship in anger?

6. Can you decide not to engage in commitments where the other parties are not as committed?

7. How well do you forgive others? How well do you forgive yourself? Even when you are in the wrong, can you forgive yourself in gentleness and then find a way to make amends, risking whether someone else will accept your amends or not?

Exercises

1. Select one of the Meditations in this section and reflect upon its truth for you. Highlight words and phrases that speak to you or resonate with you. Finally, choose a single word, phrase, or sentence and describe how it connects to your true self.

2. If you have been greatly disappointed lately with someone who is important to you, and you said things you wished you had not, write a letter to the person explaining what you realize now in retrospect. Be tender toward yourself *and* them. Mail the letter if you wish, or save its contents for a conversation over the phone or in person.

3. If you are disappointed with yourself, use the dialog exercise discussed in Chapter 1.

   a. Explore how your true self and false self were participating in the situation that led up to the disappointment.

   b. When you finish, see if there are patterns which give insight into your relationships.

   c. Bring compassion to your false way of acting in the world. Listen to its voice, dialog with it, and express compassion and love to this part of yourself. What are the results of doing this?

Acknowledging Discouragement

Discouragement is a form of disappointment that blocks our courage to act. It can take all shapes and sizes, but it usually occurs when:

- We've experienced a time of staleness, lack of energy, loss of perspective, and disengagement with life on several levels that keeps us stuck.
- We feel we will continue to be disappointed (in a marriage, friendship, job, etc.), so we dig in and just stay stuck in the safe routines of our lives.
- Or it may be a deeply frustrated response to something we are trying to do or accomplish in our lives that is not going the way we want it to.

From my Journal on April 19, 2019 (Easter weekend)

"I continue to live, at times, with a feeling that life 'overtakes me,' the demands, possibilities, and choices all converge at my doorstep and it seems that I often think or feel that I'm forced to choose, even when I'm not ready. I'm learning to wait for these 'minor but important choices' to become right within me, and trust that I'm not being 'selfish' or living outside of God's will. I see that the Spirit's ways are not my ways, and yet my experiences in life reinvigorate me when I discover wisdom in those experiences. There is always a nugget in them, whether it is my own reaction, or something else.

"This morning I made a choice to not attend an event with my husband. I asked him how he would feel about that; I take into consideration his feelings as well as mine. I prefer to have the gift of silence on this day, to rest – and reflect – and tend to the fire burning in my own heart and soul. That fire is to continue growing in the wisdom of the divine's leading in my life. I'm learning wisdom is never for the sake of wisdom itself. It is for the sake of wise choices and fanning the fires of love so that my actions in life come from a grounded and loving place inside. In this instance, it is self-love from the practice of self-care, but also a deeper connection to Spirit – the one who gives 'a peace that surpasses all understanding.' This is both the self-love and love from Spirit that I need and desire. It helps me love others in the short and long run."

Life is not a straight line. It is circular and spiraling, with infinite depth, side roads of possibility and paths of wisdom. Life also takes us to deeply painful places at times. Yet, meeting these hardships and feeling discouraged can eventually lead us to joy and deep connection to our Higher Power and to ourselves.

Silence and solitude are not things our culture supports or that we might gravitate toward automatically. Yet times of silence and solitude can bring great healing when we are discouraged. We must find these opportunities by trial and error and by grace – or grace alone. In 2009 I attended a retreat titled "*An Invitation to Love.*" On that weekend, I found silence and solitude – both in the building as my fellow attendees and I kept our own silence – and also outdoors in nature. That invitation of love led me to experience these gifts in a more committed way as I enrolled in a program and spent one weekend a month for the next few years, giving myself time to experience the sacred. In those years and the years that followed, a larger picture of a global spiritual community was revealed to me: from monks living in monasteries and temples, to the many religious and spiritual communities alive in the world, to millions of individuals all over the globe practicing their own silence and solitude. I have found that silence and solitude ultimately support a contemplative and meditative life that can harvest an abundance of loving action in our world.

I am learning that my desire to do good in the world does not have to drive me to burnout, or being overwhelmed or unhappy in doing it. In my own tradition, Jesus came to give us life abundantly, not to drain our vitality for systems that require much, but ignore a person's right to self-care. I'm not saying we do not ever give of ourselves if we have to sacrifice something, or if it's inconvenient. I am saying that we step back and discern what is needed when it affects our health, our spiritual path, and our life balance. It's not always about what *we* want; rather I'm learning to trust that God will always give me what I need. Not everyone in our sacred communities, our nonprofit work, or in our life will like us or love us for living this way, but there will always be those to help us. It is Spirit's way of letting us know we are not alone.

Meditations

"Silence and solitude are not things our culture supports or that we might gravitate toward automatically. Yet times of silence and solitude can bring great healing when we are discouraged."
   ~ Jo-Ellen A. Darling

"Gradually something seems to close off within you and habit takes over so smoothly. Now it all happens automatically. You have achieved cohesion and stability in your life, but you have paid an awful price – the death of your longing and the loss of the future you long for."
   ~ John O'Donohue, Eternal Echoes

"Our thoughts and habits have a way of bringing us on well-worn paths of action and thinking. Taking another route on an inward pilgrimage means challenging some of the routines which keep us stuck."
   ~ Christine Valters Paintner, The Soul of a Pilgrim

Questions for Journaling

1. What do you crave? Look at how you spend your time to find clues. For example, are you addicted to feel-good movies and television? There is nothing inherently wrong with watching good and positive films, documentaries, and shows. But could you spend more of your time exploring how you want to make changes in your life and less time living on autopilot, entertainment, and watching the dreams that come true for others and not for yourself?

2. What gives you "life?" How does it feel in your body? What emotions do you experience when you are engaged with a life-giving activity?

   For example, when I worked on this book, there was something that happened in my body and soul. Hope filled my heart because journaling, writing and sharing about the struggles in my life – and my spiritual path through those struggles – brought me great joy.

3. What one thing can you change or do today that can connect you to those longings in your true self? Can you spend time journaling these questions, then share your thoughts with a trusted person? Can you make an action plan, even if you feel it's a waste of time?

Exercises

1. Be sure to do the Questions for Journaling above. If you feel led to outline a plan of steps to nurture something that you think will be life-giving, entrust it to your Higher Power. Create a ritual or ceremony around the initial steps that can possibly lead you out of your discouragement or being stuck.

You may not be able to see that far ahead, so just a few steps may be all that is needed. Go with what "gives you life" (check your gut and your intuition), even if it doesn't make a lot of sense for you to do it.

For example, when my desire to make a commitment to write creatively became hugely apparent to me after much reflective journaling, I found and joined a writers' group… That led to arranging a writers' workshop with the group's facilitator, and a week-long writers' retreat with author Paula D'Arcy. That led to writing my own poetry and reflections, and creating a book project for a community to share their sacred writings and artwork. That led to facilitating contemplative writing retreats. That led to the writing of this book…

2. Finish the sentence stem, "Today I will…." until there is nothing more to say. Read it every day for a week, journaling more on the responses (i.e., Today I will …. dream about putting myself through medical school, or …. apply for a job in a pediatrician's practice, etc.). Do some more journaling around each response that you wrote, especially the ones that spark your interest, ignite your joy, or make you "come alive."

Processing Conflict in Relationships

As uncomfortable as conflict can be, discord can show us what's important in our lives. There will be many occasions in life that can lead to conflict with others. This will happen in our families, places of work, with our friends, in our communities, and of course between the many segments of our society – some of which we may be a part. We might have expectations of how people are supposed to be, and when they're not, we react rather than *act*. We disagree on ways of doing things, or we want things our way.

There are also the personality traits and character flaws in all of us that are annoying and sometimes damaging to others, as well as theirs are to us. If we try to resolve issues through criticism, judgment, manipulation or retaliation, we can miss opportunities to find peace and serenity with those we care about and love. How we manage our differences will be key to spiritual growth: to understand others better, to process *through* our fear, hurt, rejection, disapproval, anger – all the feelings and misperceptions that can arise when conflict occurs.

We can also be conflicted within our own selves. We sometimes say and do things that leave us feeling split or out of alignment with our best nature. If we pay attention, stay open, and listen to ourselves and the still, small voice of the God of our understanding, we begin to experience peace in our relationships.

When in conflict, discerning the wisdom that brings true serenity may require patience on our part. Patience is not always easy, but we can practice it on ourselves in our journaling. If you have trouble being honest with others about your true feelings, the journal can hold all of that and give you courage to express what you need to express to others. You may even begin to feel a growing sense of self-compassion, which is one of the fruits of facing reality, of acknowledging the truth, and perhaps experiencing divine love.

In my own life, I've worked through many conflicts in my journal. Something I've discovered is that conflict wasn't always dealt with in a healthy way when I was growing up. I'm quite sure my parents' generation wasn't shown healthy conflict resolution either. Disagreements could not always be talked about, nor did I express mine in a respectful way as a teen and for many years into adulthood. At the time I came of age – around 1972 – society was filled with turbulence and violent expressions of conflicting needs and viewpoints from every corner of our society. As a result of the conflict in my inner life and that of my society, dealing with conflict was a real stumbling block for many years. But somewhere deep inside I knew, despite how I was behaving, that I had to find a way through the turmoil.

So, I allowed myself to take healthy breaks from people I did not or could not get along with. I tried to figure out my boundaries and how to implement them. Journaling was one way that provided a safe haven for me to express not only the negative, but to also see more clearly my own true desires to get along with other people, despite our differences.

Eventually, two things became clear. First, I began to forgive, accept, and get along with my family and others for who they were, as well as myself. Second, I discovered some of my gifts, as well as the deep longing for my own journey to wholeness. These shards of light that had been clouded, repressed, buried and abandoned in me when I was young – began to flicker – sometimes brightly.

It took a long time for the inner and outer conflict I experienced frequently between young adulthood and midlife to subside. In retrospect, humility was a great lesson that I needed to learn. Often my words were hurtful, sarcastic or rude, especially when I felt provoked. "I am just sticking up for myself," I thought. When I experienced others' reactions, I came to see I was also hurting myself, and only then did I become willing to surrender. I carried guilt in the surrendering, but I realized the guilt had to be let go as well. I did this by admitting to what I had done and said, and made amends. This new pattern, repeated over and over, gave me the grace, courage, and willingness to do the hard work of living into my true self.

I came to learn that I'm created in the image of the Ultimate Other, as a dear friend of mine refers to his higher power. I now realize that a "template of goodness" has been innately passed on to me, for I am a spiritual being as well as a human being. This means this goodness has been given to all others as well. I've been so wrong about other people so often throughout my life, before I actually, really knew this fact. I first had to do the work of discovering my own deepest, truest humanity – and the divine reflection in me – to understand and know this.

We enter this world pure and vulnerable, needing love and care. As children, our parents are our gods. In childhood and our teens, we begin to experience the brokenness of life and all the ways our true selves are oppressed: we must fit in, we must comply, we must obey. These things in themselves are not bad – but doing them at the cost of being who we are has longtime consequences. The good news is the human spirit is resilient and we can begin an authentic journey of self-discovery at any point – beginning right now.

Meditations

"When do we engage, and when do we step back? When do we move deeper into our relationships, to further engage a conflict, work through an issue, or deepen our activism around a cause? And when do we step back, take a time out, or move toward acceptance and letting go?"
~ *Doug Wysockey-Johnson, Relationship Paradoxes: Engaging and Letting Go*

"Could a humble person be one who considers all people as equals? Who isn't so concerned about what others say or think about him or her or about trying to impress others? An authentically humble person might be someone who is working on being true to Self."
~ *Kay Lindahl, The Sacred Art of Listening*

"When it is dark enough, you can see the stars."
~ *Ralph Waldo Emerson*

Questions & Exercises for Journaling

Try to do one question at a time before reading or doing the next question or exercise.

1. Take some time to write out or "complain about" the recent conflicts and/or disappointments in your life. Be brutally honest: express your anger, criticisms, frustrations, unhappiness and other feelings.

2. When do you feel emotionally "hung over?" What are your symptoms (i.e., loss of sleep, inability to let go or forgive the other, resentments, deep unhappiness, obsessive thinking, low self-regard, negative outlook on life, loss of hope, not showing up for activities, turning down invitations, etc.)?

3. Take some time before you read over what you have written. Is there a pattern in your journal that you recognize as disruptive, sabotaging, or even hurtful to yourself – or someone else?

4. If you can't name the issue or pattern, spend some time in your journal (a few days or a week). If it's still unclear, take it to a friend, licensed therapist or spiritual advisor. What do they see as you describe it to them? What have you noticed from sharing it with someone else?

5. What has been *your role* in these conflicts or disappointments (some examples follow)?

    • Being overly attached to an outcome, to have life be "a certain way"

    • Overly dependent on someone else to fulfill your need for "happiness"

    • Inability to make your own plans and choices without the approval of someone else

    • *Expecting* to be disappointed in a particular area of your life ("It never works out," "He/She won't support my wants and needs," etc.)

6. Name some things you can do today or in the days and weeks ahead to help you deal with the conflict or disappointment, such as: exercising, taking walks, writing more or engaging in some other creative pursuit, praying each morning or night with a lighted candle, seeking out community, reading a sacred text or spiritual book, joining an online spiritual community,

finding a religious service or non-religious gathering that nourishes you, joining or supporting others in a common cause, hanging with gentle friends, having some silence and quiet time a few days a week in your own home, spending time in nature, or committing to making a spiritual retreat. Follow this up with an action plan for the ones in this list that really attract you and that you trust would be good for you.

Note: If something seems like a stretch, such as you never initiate time with people, but always wait for others to call you, then maybe it's time to take a risk and call someone.

7. Is there some root in your childhood that may have set the pattern for your repeated responses to this recurring conflict or disappointment? Does the current conflict or disappointment remind you of anything in your past?

8. Do you need to apologize for something, to yourself and/or to someone else? Write a letter that describes specifically what you want to say. You can send it or remember its contents and speak these thoughts directly to the person involved.

9. Can you make living amends by thinking about treating yourself or someone else differently as a result of what you have discovered? Living amends is a change in your attitude and behavior that is in line with who you truly are and who you want to be. It is also taking a risk that their reaction isn't as important as *your* response – that your sense of justice, mercy, and desire to be better are the most important things.

10. How can you defuse your reactiveness to the person(s) or situations you find yourself in conflict with?
    *   Try prayer or meditation as often as you need to prepare your own heart and mind to *let go* when you are in their presence.

- Read excerpts from a spiritual book or religious text to find healing for your own thoughts, such as the Psalms of the Old Testament, the koans of Zen Buddhism, or *The Awakened Heart: Opening Yourself to the Love You Need* by Gerald G. May, M.D. Align yourself with the Spirit of peace before entering the situations that are tripping you up.

- Pray for others who create conflict for you. Hold compassion for those that hurt you. One way is to imagine them as adults who have had many life experiences of their own that were hurtful or negative, perhaps as children.

- Pray for yourself with compassionate awareness. Be gentle with yourself. Avoid self-judgment and find encouragement in the fact that you are staying openminded.

- Set boundaries for yourself. If the person you are dealing with is sarcastic, don't be sarcastic in return. Figure out what you want or need to keep your boundaries firm. One way is to detach with love, which is to not take things personally, but to still be able to view the other as a work in progress – just like we all are.

- Connect with your true self through dialog and journaling. Where does the true self stand in regards to this conflict? What do you truly want? This may also help you see why you may be contributing to the situation or conflict. What actions or *inactions* can you take?

Grieving Life's Changes and Losses

From the moment of birth, we change, grow, and experience losses. Grief, then, should be a normal part of life. However, if losses are not processed, the result can be an accumulation of grief over the years. When significant losses are not consciously grieved, they may cause us to continue to make decisions that do not serve our lives. These swept-aside, ungrieved losses can significantly delay or cause us to never truly find our joy, claim our gifts, or realize the callings that are possible for a full and meaningful life.

The Losses in Friendships

Relationship with others is one of the primary places where change occurs over our entire lives. In John O'Donohue's classic book, *Eternal Echoes*, he says the most common grief experienced in the life of all human beings is the loss and resulting absence of friends:

> *"There are whole regions of absence in every life. Losing a friend is the most frequent experience of absence. The departure of the friend leaves this space sore with loss... it is the longing for the departed friend that makes the absence acute."*

Maybe there's a metaphor for change and loss that we can consider here. Imagine the process of life as the ebbing and flowing of the tides, the waxing and waning of the moon, and the daily rhythm of the sun, from sunrise to sunset. In these repeated instances of nature abides an inherent renewal, as each rhythm is repeated. I think of ebbing as receding. What goes away, or what we lose, also makes room in our lives for the new: evening ends and morning brings a new day, the high tide recedes, revealing the beautiful shells and debris on the beach. Sometimes we must let go and release our energy in the direction of another person to make space for a new perspective, or for what or who is to follow.

In contrast, I think of flowing as a current of movement toward, or in concert with another. We fall into step or join with others, in ease and grace, or from a place of commitment or period of hardship, and then changes occur in and outside of these relationships. Some of those changes will lead one or both persons away, to periods of diminished engagement – when their physical presence no longer accompanies us – sometimes briefly, sometimes for a season, or sometimes for the rest of our lives.

As we pay close attention to these losses, we soon find others streaming into our lives as we make decisions to join in and follow newly discovered desires, friends, or purpose. We might make new choices and set new intentions for doing something important – perhaps a relationship or some endeavor, such as a career, volunteer work, or a creative pursuit that reflects our deepest joy.

Then, one day, the tide arrives with an old friend or acquaintance reappearing on the shore. We reconnect again, briefly or for a longer period. We acknowledge the lessons we were given as we hold our mirrors up to each other. We offer love or service, unless there is no more to actively give, except kindness, good wishes, and the olive branch of peace for the journey.

This happened in a relationship with a long-time friend who often talked about owls. I purchased two owl figures and sent her one of them as a symbol of our physical parting and the silence we held between us, at her request. We once actively shared our life experiences and the fruits of spiritual growth. We had been there for each other and I believe we both learned a great deal from each other's spiritual journey. Now we had taken flight into new phases of life without contact. For me, those owls were symbols of the spiritual journey we had shared.

Capitalist Culture

In our country's capitalist culture, individualism and self-reliance are valued and rewarded as the standard archetypes of how to be and succeed in life. Yet embracing these models without a spiritual connection can also reinforce social isolation and the avoidance of intimacy with others. We then unconsciously subscribe and depend on these cultural values – especially in our work and careers – for approval and agendas that have little to do with our own souls. It's not that capitalism is bad in itself. Like anything it can be used for good:

home ownership, getting an education, opportunities for recreation, and sharing what you have with others.

But oftentimes, we can live according to an agenda that is created without our conscious consent, and we forfeit any hope of making better decisions for ourselves and our loved ones. Instead, we become prone to seeing ourselves and others as "commodities" in the market-place of ideas and culture (i.e., human "capital"). For example, overtime pays well, but when you are pressured or forced to do overtime because the company refuses to hire enough workers, then your life balance is infringed upon at the expense of your health and your family. We may then convince ourselves that we have no choice rather than exploring legitimate options that may be available to us. Maybe we are called to take a stand in changing our work cultures to be more humane by allowing a shorter work week and parental leave for certain family situations.

As I've alluded to earlier, capitalist culture and mores exclude the values of personal vulnerability and the importance of soul. Another problem is that we often take these values into our churches, social organizations, and altruistic communities. I have often experienced capitalist values at work in spiritual communities, such as an emphasis on overcommitment and doing; the lack of offering people periods of rest and time to just be; opportunities for spiritual nurture; and valuing uniqueness and autonomy. The resulting wounding (such as conflicts due to differences of opinion, the drive for power and control, mistrust, gossip, etc.) can be more excruciating to experience than in other social groups because our expectations of what a spiritual community looks like is often much different than what was just described.

Prescribed Burns

The USDA Forest Service encourages the use of controlled burns – also known as *prescribed* burns – for forestry management. According to their website, it is a way to "achieve improved forest and rangeland health and helps reduce the threat of large fire events. Controlled burning can be managed or controlled *to reduce the intensity and magnitude of bigger wildfires by reducing the accumulation of flammable fuels (nutrients)...* [after the fire], the abundant supply of nutrients helps new seedlings, brush, and grasses to grow quickly and become established following a wildfire."

Consider the transforming power of the flammable material in our own lives: as we face into our hot issues, we may discover losses that sit beneath the surface of our lives and fuel them in unexpected and often unhealthy ways. The emerging nutrients we discover and life-giving soil we find, however, may help us re-envision our own lives as we acknowledge, embrace, and integrate the losses of our past. We not only grieve – we pay attention to the interior changes – to that which gives us life and moves us forward on the journey. Journaling holds a place for us to be more conscious and eventually at peace with our losses.

Other losses – such as the loss of a job or career path – can birth a new calling. Acknowledging the losses in our childhood or events from the past can foster healing and lead us to forgiveness – of self and others – and bring us to a new level of self-respect and self-love. Recovery from addiction can lead us to a life of true fellowship with others and personal growth, when perhaps for the first time we follow our dreams and give of ourselves in new ways. There is no limit to the types of potential losses that can be transformed into fruitful experiences.

In my friendship with the woman who loved owls, I was initially hurt when she no longer wanted contact. There were many areas of growth after our parting, however. Her request, I soon realized, was more about her needs than anything I had done wrong. This had great implications for how I interpreted other friendship changes. Letting go with love instead of resentment and hurt had freed me to give others more freedom without taking their actions so personally – and more freedom to explore my relationships in new ways. By acknowledging my own strength and wisdom, I could stop guarding my heart so much, second guessing my decisions in relationships, and expecting others to respond the way I thought they should. Instead, I began to accept myself and others much more for who they were – even when people came and went – knowing that true friendships would survive in the long-term. I no longer thought that I had control over this process. I did not need to jump through hoops to be a good friend. Instead, I could be myself: heart open and free!

Meditations

"It takes a long time to recognize how some key people on your life's journey exercise so much control over your mind, behavior and actions…. Real friendship is a powerful presence in helping you to see the prisons within which you live."
   ~ John O'Donohue, Eternal Echoes

"Above all, self-nurturing is about self-acceptance. When we recognize that self-care begins with ourselves, we no longer think of those around us as being totally responsible for our well-being."
   ~ Alan D. Wolfelt, Ph.D., Understanding Your Grief

"Journaling holds a place for us to be more conscious and eventually at peace with our losses."
   ~ Jo-Ellen A. Darling

Questions for Journaling

1. When you are grieving, do you allow yourself to cry? Some call it the gift of tears. Tears wash our souls. They are a release for our sadness. Tears are a way to mourn.

2. Start with today: what is currently stirring in you that needs your attention? Perhaps it is a memory, or a previous or current relationship. Write about the feelings and the interactions that

71

were (or are) most intense or significant. Try to remember truthfully what was said or done without exaggerating the story, even if it makes you wrong or appear unkind. Journal for as long as you need without moving on to the next questions.

3. Can you identify some of the specific losses that occurred as a result of the memory or relationship interaction that you described in step 2? Losses such as your hopes, dreams, and desires are as important as losing a loved one to death or separation.

4. Now in retrospect, what choices did you make (good or bad)? What knowledge or wisdom did you gain as a result of this experience?

5. What are you grateful for now? What do you see that you were unable to see before now?

6. How has Spirit played a role in your life through this time of loss, or now as you currently begin to let go? What can you see that you could not see before now?

Exercise

Upon waking some morning, read the following poem followed by a few minutes of silence. Read it again in silence or out loud, and spend a few more minutes in silence. When you feel ready, journal your thoughts about this poem, how it relates to you, and what threads are being revealed to you in this time of your life.

The Way It Is

There's a thread you follow. It goes among
things that change. But it doesn't change.
People wonder about what you are pursuing.
You have to explain about the thread.

But it is hard for others to see.
While you hold it you can't get lost.
Tragedies happen; people get hurt
or die; and you suffer and get old.
Nothing you do can stop time's unfolding.
You don't ever let go of the thread.

By William Stafford

Losing a Loved One to Death

"My journal was my friend, holding all that had happened."

Losing a loved one is a significant event. In our culture, millions of people are grieving every single day, but their grief is often an underworld of silent sorrow. The irony is that we are living longer and our relationships last longer, thus bonding us more deeply together. This can make losing an elderly spouse or parent, or an adult sibling, child, or friend, as painful and tragic as losing them earlier in life. To make matters worse for those who are grieving, everyday life on the surface often takes at least a couple of years before the fracture of a loved one's death begins to heal.

In November of 2018, my close friend Rose died unexpectedly. I missed her memorial luncheon because my 84-year-old father was hospitalized in another state at the same time, and died two weeks later. During his hospitalization, I was exhausted, devastated, and became sick a few days before his funeral. We had not expected his death just before Thanksgiving, and the experience of his medical complications from surgery a month earlier was traumatic. He was eventually diagnosed with acquired hemophilia, and yet none of the medical staff warned us that bleeding as a cause of death was even a possibility. Nor were we told, when the time came, that he was in fact going to die. When I asked the hospital's hematologist about his prognosis, the doctor told me he expected a "full recovery." But we knew he was in his last days, and we prepared to let him go. He died three days later.

When I returned to Pennsylvania after my father's funeral, I was clearly angry at the medical profession. I felt enraged by the pain he suffered, and how we had suffered as a family from the poor communication, in hindsight, that we had received from the hospital's medical staff. I identified the misplaced anger I felt toward a bank teller and a postal worker during the Christmas holiday season, who, from my perspective, weren't doing their jobs. My journal was my friend, holding all that had happened.

I wept as I journaled and played my father's favorite holiday music – music we both had loved. I wrote poems and letters to him, and expressed frustration in my journal with those who could not save him and did not appropriately care for our family at the time, such as offering him hospice or preparing us for his death. Through those tender holidays, my husband was tremendously supportive as I recalled my memories of Dad. Importantly, I shared my trauma with a trusted counselor. After I briefly attended a well-meaning grief group, I chose to hold off for the right one when it wasn't helping.

In the New Year, I began to be consoled spiritually by the God of my understanding and my own gradual attempts to take care of myself throughout that year. This time of self-care was partly expressed through the letters I wrote to the doctors and hospital administrators, expressing my disappointment to them so that I could sleep at night. I wanted them to know how families experience the negative effects of not nearly enough communication during these stressful events, the lack of straight forward answers, and the lack of hospital staff that failed to provide proper medication for his pain over an entire shift the day before he died. A year later melancholy resurfaced as the fall colors began to bloom around me. Fortunately, a friend facilitated a different grief group, which got me through those holidays and the one-year anniversary of his death.

Mourning Our Grief

As a writer, you learn early on that reading precedes writing. This is also true in the practice of journaling. There are many excellent books and authors who write about grief, but reading about grief and having nowhere to process it can be problematic. In his book *Understanding Your Grief*, Alan D. Wolfelt, Ph.D., explains one of grief's greatest misconceptions: that "grief and mourning are the same thing." He distinguishes between the two as follows:

> *"Grief is the constellation of internal thoughts and feelings we have when someone we love dies…* Mourning *is when you take the grief you have on the inside and express it outside of yourself."*

A wise therapist also told me, "The way you get through trauma is to process it." So it is with our sorrows, and maybe especially those we have not yet grieved. An accompanying journal is one way that provides the space and time for mourning our grief; it allows us to plan what we need to do to take care of ourselves during this important time, and to savor the growth and healing that follows. Martha Whitmore Hickman states in her beautiful book of daily meditations, *Healing After Loss*, that we are our own expert grievers and that each grief is unique with its own rhythms and schedule, and often prolonged and not where we think our healing from grief should be.

Bereavement groups[2], 12-step groups, individual therapy, talking with soul friends, spiritual directors, and spouses are ways to mourn and process grief with others. During the Covid-19 pandemic, I was amazed to learn that there are stars that have collapsed, but we can still see their light from earth. When I mentioned this to my husband Mike, he said "This could be a great metaphor for those we love who pass away… although they die, their light shines on." This conversation helped with my own grief during the 2020 pandemic as family

---

[2] Most hospitals and many churches run ongoing grief groups or programs. Check your local churches and hospital's community programs for details.

friends, close friends, and over a million other human beings across the globe were lost to the virus at that time. I will never look at the stars the same way again.

Writing poetry is another way to mourn our grief, giving voice to the pain of grief and receiving the healing that is offered to us through our own words. It is a mystical process, originating from the gifts we have been born with: the capacity to feel, to bond, and to love. The benefits and possibilities of creativity and journaling are discussed more thoroughly in Chapter 4.

Meditations

"As a culture we rarely acknowledge the value of being uncomfortable. We strongly discourage grieving people to stay with their sadness. Instead, we tell them to 'cheer up' or 'move on.' Rarely are they encouraged to explore what grief can teach them."
~ Christine Valters Paintner, The Soul of a Pilgrim

"An accompanying journal is one way that provides the space and time for mourning our grief; it allows us to plan what we need to do to take care of ourselves during this important time, and to savor the growth and healing that follows."
~ Jo-Ellen A. Darling

"To counterbalance your normal and necessary mourning, each and every day plan – in advance – something you enjoy. Reading, baking, going for a walk, having lunch with a friend, gardening, playing computer games – whatever brings you enjoyment."
~ Alan D. Wolfelt, Ph.D., Understanding Your Grief

Questions for Journaling

1. Write about your loved one's death for a 10 or 15-minute period or more (set an alarm). Make lists of important memories that

come to mind, positive or otherwise, with as little or as much detail that is needed.

2.   What is it you wish to carry forward from your loved one's life? Which of their character traits, or aspects of their legacy, inspire you? If there are none, go to the next step.

3.   Write about the *painful memories* whenever they come up. At some point, enough will be enough. Can you begin to let go gently or assertively when these memories reappear after you have given them sufficient attention? Do you need to speak to someone, such as a trained therapist, about these memories?

4.   How can spiritual practices, prayers, and your relationship with Spirit help you through this time of loss? Be specific.

5.   What insights have you gained about your relationship with the deceased that you could not see before now?

6.   What memories keep coming up in your life? Perhaps like an old recording, these conversations – or your own thoughts about them – continue to occupy the precious moments of your life without resolve. Rather than allow them to play like an unwanted intrusion, can you "acknowledge the value of being uncomfortable" with them, as Christine Valters Paintner writes in *The Soul of a Pilgrim*, by attending to them, dialoging with them, and learning from them?

7.   When you are grieving, allow yourself to cry. Tears are a release for your sadness. Tears are a way to *mourn*.

Exercises

1.   When you are in a feeling place of grief or celebration (re-membering a poignant moment, what the person meant to you, how the person loved you, etc.), write a poem, a meditative

77

reflection, or free verse about the sadness, trauma, healing or other aspect of your grief. *Do not edit as you write.*

    a.   When you're done, go back and smooth it out, adding words, punctuation, changing how lines are split (if it's a poem), etc.

    b.   On another day, print out the poem and read it a couple of times. See what new words come to you and jot them down, but don't try to make it perfect just now. Stay with your feelings.

    c.   In the coming days or a month from now, reread your poem, and make final changes as desired. Print and frame it where you will see it. Savor those words and read them often. Feel yourself heal.

2.   Making a memory collage using pictures from books and magazines, and adding your own photos and symbols, is another way to express your grief creatively. Is there another creative pursuit that can help you mourn a loved one?

3.   Is there a metaphor from nature or otherwise that brings you comfort in the loss of someone you love? Journal your thoughts and feelings.

Longing to Be Free of Negative Emotions

"Ultimately, it is a choice about whether we are going to love ourselves – or not."

As we all know, feelings can be scary! Our negative emotions – anger, jealousy, envy, self-recrimination, depression, hurt, despair, and hopelessness – have a great deal of power at times. Yet, we can make a decision to learn from them, be compassionate with ourselves when we experience them, ask for help if we need to, and learn to manage them with kindness and firmness. Let's face it: it's so much easier to feel joyous wonder, contentedness, gratitude, success, and serenity. While these are as important as our negative feelings, it is the negative feelings that are most often judged, ignored and ironically, undervalued.

A first step may be to understand the emotional issues beneath the negative feelings and the beliefs we have about ourselves and others that might be causing these intrusions. This requires a commitment to understand ourselves and to not repress these feelings when they arise. Practicing awareness will be key as we consciously allow the feelings to come up. We may well want to respond to others or ourselves only after giving ourselves time to process them. This can look like taking a break until we calm down, going for a walk alone or with a friend to talk things over, or spending several days or weeks journaling about them to gain every insight available to help us to understand ourselves and be more accountable to ourselves – and others, if need be.

If we are just beginning to deal honestly with our negative feelings and attitudes, it may require the help of a professional. Certainly, if you feel that you cannot control these negative feelings, especially those that are explosive or are disrupting your life and controlling you, you may want to give yourself permission to meet with a therapist. It is one way of taking responsibility, taking care of yourself, and being a friend to yourself. You don't have to do this alone.

Although this list is not complete, here are some other scenarios which could illicit strong emotions:

- When someone dies or leaves (sadness, abandonment, grief)
- When you feel victimized or threatened (fear, terror)
- When you feel extremely isolated or alone (loneliness, self-pity)

- When you are feeling an unwanted sexual attraction or preoccupation with someone (obsessed)
- When you are feeling down, or anger has turned in on yourself for many days or weeks with no end in sight (depressed, discouraged)
- When you are feeling lost in life (fearful, empty, searching)
- When you feel invisible and that you do not matter to anyone (unworthy, unappreciated)
- When you feel upset by someone's words or actions (hurt, rejected)
- When you feel over-responsible for others (overwhelmed, stuck, resentful)
- When you feel guilty for not being or doing what others want from you (guilt, shame)
- When you want to hurt yourself or someone else (rage, fear)
- When your personal issues and concerns about others consumes your life (worry, anxiety, poor boundaries)
- When you need help but are unable to ask for it (low self-esteem, shame)

A first step in working through negative emotions is to know that underneath many of these feelings are "human needs" that we may never have received from our early caregivers. It's not necessarily because they didn't want to provide them, but much more likely that they themselves may not have had them to give. When thinking of these caregivers, we can remember these sayings: "We cannot give what we do not have" and "We cannot know what we do not know." These words of wisdom will engender, at the very least, seeds of compassion for those who may have failed us.

Another step in becoming free of negative emotions is to allow self-understanding to soak deeply into our hearts, as we give ourselves permission to step back and to practice a loving self-response, perhaps before we are able to practice it on others. Initially we may not feel like we want to treat ourselves with love, but the more we practice self-understanding and self-compassion, the more likely we will begin to experience freedom to respond to ourselves with more gentleness. Eventually, after much patience and practice, it will become second nature to *welcome* the essential energy of our negative feelings – which can provide wisdom – versus ignoring, repressing and disparaging these feelings.

Finally, we will want to inventory our honest attitudes toward self and others to help us see the destructive patterns that keep us entrenched in faulty beliefs and behaviors. Doing this in our journal and with a 12-step sponsor, spiritual guide, psychologist, or kindred spirit will be extremely helpful. We don't need to face this monumental task alone.

Often, we look to people, things, and experiences to make us feel good. We watch movies, go shopping, take classes, and stay busy to get our minds off an ancient feeling of unworthiness stemming from past interpretations of what was happening to us at that time. Perhaps our parents divorced or abandoned us in some way; we were treated unfairly and disrespectfully in school, in our neighborhood or in youth organizations, by kids and adults alike; or we just didn't have parents, teachers, mentors or even religious training that could give us a roadmap for how to manage life. Maybe we were scapegoats and bullied in some way because we were jocks, nerds, freaks, or deemed fake because we weren't cool enough to fit in or belong. We all carry scars in this life.

Befriending Ourselves

One thing we can do in a journal is allow ourselves to experience the gentle process of befriending ourselves. What does this mean? First, it's recognizing our body and mind are connected to our emotions. I am certainly more prone to negative emotions when I don't do the work of taking an inventory of how I treat my body and train my mind. Instead of tearing ourselves up inside our heads, we turn to authors who share wisdom about life based on their experiences; we find groups, mentors and friends that can give us life support. We can start a group ourselves; if you want to journey with like-minded people, you'll be in luck. Instead of just tolerating a problem in our lives, we can begin to allow our true self to quietly speak the words of kindness, gentleness, and wisdom that *we* need to hear.

Befriending ourselves may also mean making lifestyle changes that alleviate the pressure and stress we or something else is placing on us. For example, one of my issues is erratic sleep patterns. I've had to make many changes in order to manage this recurring problem, which definitely impacts my emotional and spiritual balance. I've tried supplements and natural remedies, such as melatonin and tart cherry juice, which may help with sleeping through the night. I watch what I eat and drink, especially late in the day, such as caffeine, fat and sugar. There are also foods I cannot tolerate, such as fast food and white bread, and other foods that I cannot live without, such as getting enough protein and veggies. A lifestyle that includes exercise is essential for me – swimming laps, contra dancing, yoga, and walking. I don't do them all every day or even every week, but they help me to sleep so I commit to doing some of them regularly. I also try to rise in the morning and retire at night around the same time for most of the week. Otherwise, my sleep is interrupted, my daily routines are highly impacted, and I'm robbed of a vital sense of well-being.

Very importantly, I find that prayer and meditation help with the anxieties, stress and worries I feel in life. A prayer of gratitude before

I go to bed – however briefly – helps to release negative thoughts and feelings. However, when I cannot sleep and I must get up, I try to remember the millions of other souls who are awake and struggling during the night. I play sacred or gentle music as I remember all the monks (of all religions) who rise at all hours of the night to chant and pray for the betterment of this world. I light candles and journal my prayers and thoughts and then practice silent meditation for a period of time. I invite the God of my understanding to reveal his or her heart to me. I often find I am being held in ways during these interrupted nights that are not so apparent in the wakeful hours of daylight. Eventually I return to bed or start my day with an intention of gratitude.

Finally, I always try to remember that life happens imperfectly, and when issues come up that relate to self-image, I must do some extra work. Self-image is only an image of who we think we are. Yet, we may need to dig below the surface to find out who we really are, and where our true home is in this life. We need to find and accept that we are weak and limited human beings, and yet, that our weaknesses can also be our strengths, and that we indeed have, as author Joyce Rupp says, a "vast potential of goodness." Although we may have obvious and detrimental weaknesses, we can always be transformed in the areas of those weaknesses which, paradoxically, make us stronger.

It may seem overwhelming to think about getting some assistance to deal with a personal issue, and we may think we do not have the time or the money. Yet, by avoiding a support group, taking a class, committing to a program, or seeing a therapist, one defends against getting healthy all in the name of a busy life. Sometimes we will have to give something up in order to do what is truly needed. However, when we face our fears, decide to put ourselves first, and choose to believe that we are worth it and are an important part of our own lives (and not just essential in the lives of family members, our workplace, our boss, and other areas of responsibility we may hold), we may find a surprising gift in store. Ultimately, it is a choice about whether we are going to love ourselves – or not.

Meditations

"I surrender my need and desire to be in control of every event, circumstance, and person I will meet today."

~ *Peter Scazzero, Emotionally Healthy Spirituality Day by Day*

"Instead of just tolerating a problem in our lives, we can begin to allow our true self to quietly speak the words of kindness, gentleness, and wisdom that *we* need to hear."

~ *Jo-Ellen A. Darling*

"If we continue to run away from our own grief, anger, resistance, or even joy, then we will not be able to stay present when a friend needs us. The inner work we do, we also do on behalf of our community."

~ *Christine Valters Paintner, The Artist's Rule*

Questions for Journaling

1. How do I treat myself, especially if I am feeling needy, fragile, or contentious with others?

2. Read John O'Donohue's poem on page 86 titled "A Blessing." Respond to his words, phrases and lines that are healing for you. Notice if the words resonate somewhere in your body, such as a feeling of warmth – or if they trigger an emotion, such as a flicker of hope or sadness. Notice too, if your mind is resistant or open to any of his ideas. Journal your thoughts and review them before you retire tonight.

Exercises

1. Before you even commit to the process of healing some aspect of your emotional life, create a map of steps that you can take in a direction that feels right to you. Do not skip writing steps that feel totally unnatural to you, and do not sidestep the ones that seem impossible to you either. (Complete this step before going to the next one.)

2. Now review the list you made and pay attention to the options that feel more natural or resonate healing in your body, mind, and emotions. For example, if you think that doing three months of therapy would be really helpful, yet there's a financial problem, don't rule it out completely at this point in time. See if the therapist will work with you on a "sliding scale" before you decide to abandon it. Or, you may be drawn to taking a class where you do not have to expose yourself too much to others to learn more about an issue in your life. Or, you may decide to research what Spiritual Direction is all about. Google "spiritual direction" or "what is spiritual direction?"

3. Do the exercises in "Writing Prompts for Tending the Soul" in Appendix B to locate the hot issues that need to be focused on at this time in your life. Review all of your responses and focus on those which may suggest gaps in your *body-mind-emotion* program of self-care.

4. What steps will you do today to begin to tend to the areas of self-care that are *dying* for your attention?

A Blessing

May you listen to your longing to be free.

May the frames of your belonging be large enough for the dreams of your soul.

May you arise each day with a voice of blessing whispering in your heart that something good is going to happen to you.

May you find a harmony between your soul and your life.

May the mansion of your soul never become a haunted place.

May you know the eternal longing which lives at the heart of time.

May there be kindness in your gaze when you look within.

May you never place walls between the light and yourself.

May your angel free you from the prisons of guilt, fear, disappointment, and despair.

May you allow the wild beauty of the invisible world to gather you, mind you, and embrace you in belonging.

By John O'Donohue

Figuring Out What You Need

"The providence that weaves your days sees the greater horizon and knows what your life needs in order for you to come fully to birth as the person you are called to be."
~JOHN O'DONOHUE, ETERNAL ECHOES

We live in a complex age of information and amazing technology that keeps us connected to the world, our communities, and everyone we know. We are heavily influenced not only by advertising, entertainment, and the media, but by the people and communities we invite into our lives. If influences are not wisely chosen – such as who and what we read, watch, and listen to, and why we are attracted to them – we may find ourselves not living the life we need or want to live, but living a life based largely on what others say, value, and want us to do. Yet, we grow spiritually by becoming aware of our connection to our true self. This is where spiritual discernment and journaling will play critical roles in our lives.

I recall a period of extreme busyness that became detrimental to my wellbeing, and I soon realized a deep need to surrender the reigns of how I was living. This decision came right after a vacation. The time to reflect and be away made it a little easier to begin to question my current thinking and where my life was going. I was doing what seemed to be many good things: volunteering at my church, facilitating a writing group, serving a few friends in need, and caring for elderly parents. These commitments, along with keeping up with friends and communities, working on my marriage, and keeping up with my own routines for selfcare – exercise, eating right, spiritual nurture, grieving recent losses, and getting enough rest and sleep – had become too much for me. The truth is, I was feeling distraught.

I began to reassess my state of exhaustion, and also how I honestly felt about what I was committing myself to. I decided to cut back on volunteer activities, but I chose to spend more time with a dear elderly friend each week. I explored getting training in contemplative leadership, but when the class was cancelled, I decided to commit myself to the writing of this book, because frankly, it was life-giving. Since we were planning to sell our home and move, I committed to doing that over many months with my husband. I also attended a few retreats and made sure I had time for rest.

Perhaps you are in a similar place. Maybe your whole life isn't out of balance, but there might be a part of your life that needs some minor – or even radical – adjustments. Perhaps life doesn't sparkle like it once did. Changes have occurred in your friendships or your marriage, but you now realize that you had not really noticed them;

you did not have the energy to be aware of the changes while they were happening. Maybe you had a crisis come into your life with a force like a river, continuously flowing at a steady pace with no relief in sight. Life made it impossible to see what was happening or to even think about changing course – until now.

Maybe you are at a fork in that river now, realizing if you don't soon find a harbor in which to reflect upon your life – your commitments and your needs, desires, and longings – you may continue to go down a path of numbness, despair, and living on autopilot. If you continue down that perilous path, you may be tempted to find love in all the wrong places, or you will only replace the external things with other things: people and activities that eventually take you to the same spiritual, emotional, and life-draining landscapes. The influences in your life may have a hold on you so deeply, you can't even begin to feel or see what your own truth is, or you can't seem to find and nurture your authentic self, where the voice of truth can be heard and trusted.

At this critical juncture, it may be important to stop pushing yourself. You may need to take a break and give yourself time to heal. You don't have to give up everything, but you probably need to figure out what takes priority in your life. Everyone's circumstances are different. Only you can name where you must continue to give, as well as where you must, or are able to, let go.

Eugene Peterson makes a thought-provoking statement in his book, *The Contemplative Pastor,* saying: "I am busy because I am lazy." He goes on to say:

> *"I indolently let others decide what I will do instead of resolutely deciding for myself ... By lazily abdicating the essential work of deciding and directing, establishing values, and setting goals, other people do it for us."*

In my early thirties, I flew to California to visit a dear friend. While there, I found a book on her shelf, titled *What Do Women Want: Exploding the Myth of Dependency* by Luise Eichenbaum and Susie Orbach. Reading this book changed my life. At the time, I truly did not know what my needs or wants in life were, except that I wanted to find love again and heal from the pain I was living in. What I now know is that I was still in the process of forming a healthy ego. The things I envisioned for my life did not seem attainable to me, and I filled my life with things that weren't necessarily satisfying. Eichenbaum and Orbach's book was a seed planted that helped me see that I deserved to explore and find out what I really needed – and what I didn't want or need – essentially, to begin to discover my values and my truest self. Up to that point, I didn't have the tools to thrive into the great adventure of living into my own personhood. Taking a break and "stumbling" upon this book, I was given the gift of exploring a new path.

Maslow's "Hierarchy of Needs"

Healthy psychology tells us we have innate developmental stages and needs that, if attained in our lives, will help us to become the best

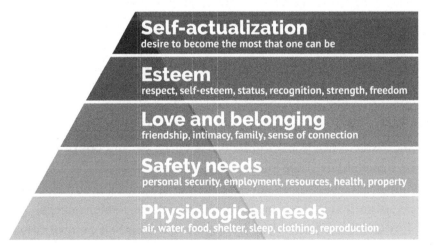

version of ourselves. A lack of their fulfillment can lead us to addictive behaviors, a lack of conscious awareness – and ultimately – unfulfilling and self-destructive lives. American psychologist Abraham Maslow is best known for creating a human "Hierarchy of Needs," depicted as a pyramid. Beginning at the bottom of the pyramid (birth) and moving upward through the stages of mature adulthood, he named these ascending needs in human life: Physiological needs, needs for Safety, needs for Love and Belonging, needs for Esteem, and the need "to become the most that one can be"(Self-Actualization)."

Essentially, we move from highly dependent infants to *potentially* highly-conscious adults, making choices that are good for us and the world. Sometimes these needs will be met out of order. Depending on our age, we may realize we have experienced some of these needs on the pyramid, and yet others will be greatly unfulfilled in us. Of course, it takes more than the study of psychology to experience this psychological growth in a successful way. If we didn't have certain needs met in childhood or young adulthood, we may need to go back and do the conscious work in those areas of our lives. If we never experienced positive growth in one or more of these areas of human needs, we will want to increase our awareness about them, as well as how the lack of their fulfillment has affected the quality of our lives. We may need to intentionally work at giving ourselves these crucial experiences for our own wholeness to ripen. Maslow suggests that attending to this hierarchy of needs is a lifetime effort.

United Kingdom psychology researcher Saul McLeod, MRes, Ph.D., explains that Maslow eventually changed his perception that all lower-level needs – assuming that some of those needs were met in childhood – such as Physiological, Safety, Love and Belonging, and Esteem needs – could be met later in life and out of the order he had initially listed them (i.e., biological growth). McLeod also found that Maslow had later added three additional needs: Cognitive needs and Aesthetic needs (listed above the Esteem needs), and Transcendence needs (listed above the need for Self-Actualization).

As we learn to figure out what we need, we can return to Maslow's Hierarchy of Needs as a reminder for what may be missing in our lives. In concert with our trust in a higher power, we can learn to choose well the persons, groups, and communities to accompany us in our growth. It will take dedicated work, but we will be well-rewarded.

Meditations

"There is no one – regardless of how beautiful, sure, competent, or powerful – who is not damaged internally in some way... behind the play of your image and the style you cut in the world, your wounds continue to call out for healing."

~ *John O'Donohue, Eternal Echoes*

"What we choose to give our attention to, we energize... The more conscious we can make this process, the less we will energize those things that conflict with our well-being and values."

~ *Kabir Helminski, Living Presence*

"Writing [journaling] allows my mask to fall away so my true face can appear and I can get a clearer look at things I need to be facing into."

~ *Parker Palmer, On the Brink*

Questions for Journaling

1. Looking at Maslow's Pyramid, which level(s) of human need do you currently feel are fulfilled or unfulfilled? Honestly journal your responses to these questions:

    a. **Physiological** – Are you taking care of yourself physically? Are you exercising, eating well and sleeping well? Do you have warm physical contact with others? Do you wear appropriate clothing that keeps your body sheltered and is good for your posture, for example? Is there anything you want or need to change in this area of the pyramid?

b. **Safety** – Do you live in a secure environment, free from violence and crime? Do you have enough work and income to live on? Are you safe at work or are you being harassed in some way? Do you have access to healthcare? Are there resources (money set aside or social services) that serve as a safety net in case something goes wrong? Is there anything you want or need to change in this area of the pyramid?

c. **Love & Belonging** – Do you have a sense of connection with family and friends? Are there other communities that keep you connected to others with similar interests and values? Is there someone in life that you can trust and confide in, especially when things become really difficult? Is there anything you want or need to change in this area of the pyramid?

d. **Self-Esteem** – Is your self-esteem and self-respect intact? Do you see yourself as a worthwhile person making a contribution at work, home, or elsewhere? Or do you feel that you or your work do not really matter? Are you strong enough and free enough in your personal decision-making to make the changes that can help you grow in these areas? If not, who can help? What do you want or need to change in this area of the pyramid?

e. **Self-Actualization** – Do you believe you can become the best version of yourself? Are you willing to work toward that and receive the graces, joys and blessings that come with putting yourself out there for the benefit of yourself, your loved ones, and others? Are you willing to leave certain things and people behind and embrace the unknown to follow your dreams? What do you want or need to change in this area of the pyramid?

2. What are some things you can do in the deficit areas you identified in step 1? Who can help you? If nothing seems to come to mind, speak to friends or associates about it. For example, if you are looking for a hobby or something fun to do in your life, ask people what they do for fun or for hobbies. Think about what you liked as a child or young adult and never had the chance to engage in. Think about things you've seen *others* do that you wish you could try. I remember going to a Broadway show in my twenties and feeling truly envious of the dancers who were performing in "*A Chorus Line.*" I never became a professional dancer, but 20 years later I was invited to a contra dance, a lively, fun and aerobic form of folk dancing that changed my life. I met many wonderful people through the dance community, including my husband. In retrospect, contra dancing has partially fulfilled in me the area of Love and Belonging on Maslow's pyramid.

3. What current area of your life, or specific situation in your life, needs your attention? How has it been showing up in your life? What area of Maslow's pyramid would you say it fits into?

4. What chronic feeling states, thinking patterns, and living patterns are *not* life-giving for you? Dialogue with your "life" to find out what it's asking of you at this time. Use your dominant and nondominant hands for writing your responses between what your life is saying to you, and your responses (thoughts and feelings) about what your life is saying to you.

5. Write a letter to yourself from your life, your true self, or from your Higher Power using your *nondominant* hand. Use your *dominant* hand to respond or ask questions. What does God, your true self, or your life wish for you?

Exercises

1. After a few days, review the material you have journaled from the Questions for Journaling.

    a. What key things have emerged? What do you need to do?

    b. What are the possibilities for healing your life?

    c. What has your Higher Power or the divine pointed to?

    d. Will you ignore that voice, or will you trust and follow it? Why?

2. Do something this month that is totally new to your life experience, and then journal about it:

    a. It could be something as simple as giving up caffeine or trying a new hobby.

    b. It could be to throw a small dinner party or to pray each day.

    c. It might be to join the gym or commit to walking to ease some of the stress in your life.

    d. Try attending a 12-step meeting or a spiritual gathering, online or in person.

    e. It could be saying yes to an invitation that you would normally or automatically say no to, such as attending a Meet-Up in a public place (take a friend with you and be safe!) or dating people that are not "your type."

Comparing Yourself to Others

"Discovering our own presence is the beginning of being free
of the compulsive and demanding ego ... free of the coercions
of the ego, we can become our authentic selves."

~ KABIR HELMINSKI, LIVING PRESENCE

We probably have been compared to our siblings, neighbors, classmates, coworkers, and peers at some point in our lives. Our culture is based on competition at every turn, and we seem to naturally compare ourselves to others to measure how we're doing. This is harmless in and of itself, if we can see others as equal souls doing the best they can. But if we don't see them that way, there can be a dark side to comparing ourselves with others.

When listening to another without fully understanding their circumstances, we might want to highlight a related story from our own lives that has a more positive outcome. We may have handled a similar situation with ease and grace, for example, whereas the other admitted to failing or struggling on some level. (I have done this more often than I care to admit.) Instead of always bringing the conversation back to ourselves, we can try deep listening. When we do this, our ego is overruled by the true self. If we tend to highlight ourselves rather than empathizing with others, we can lose touch with our own authenticity and chance to be a loving witness. Don't we sometimes refuse to put ourselves in another's shoes, and instead try to fix them?

Our motivation and desire for doing something well – or being our best – can come from a different place in us than the true self – such as a driving need to be admired, special, or important. The need for admiration is often unconscious and comes from a place of wounding, or perhaps not being loved for who we are. As we pursue a spiritual path, we can be discerning of our motivations. Perhaps we will find comparing ourself to others and attention-seeking to be huge stumbling blocks to the authentic self.

However, it's important to pay attention to feelings of jealousy and envy and the thoughts that accompany them. If we dismiss them as if they're no big deal, they will surely come up again. It's better to address these thoughts and feelings in our journals as they occur. We don't need to be ashamed of these thoughts and feelings. We only need to pay attention when they arrive so we can discover the gifts beneath them!

Rather, think of the feelings and thoughts around jealousy and envy as energy having a particular manifestation: it makes you and others "less than" and builds a wall from behind which we can justify our criticisms. If we truly want peace in our lives, our healthy, authentic self will experience the essence of others as equals. There is nothing competitive about being authentic – unless you make it so. Celebrating others' gifts helps us with humility. Only then can we appreciate our own gifts without a false sense of self.

Embracing and having compassion for the parts of ourselves that are wounded by jealousy and envy is a necessary process. Our journaling can help us process this wound, which if ignored, can lead to repeated resentments. Nipping these thoughts in the bud – by changing or challenging our thoughts in those moments – is the first step. Otherwise, being jealous and envious surely keeps us at a distance from others and from our own best self.

When I catch myself comparing myself to another, I can turn toward the Spirit of love. This turning can become second nature, but there are moments – and even days or weeks, depending on what is happening in my life – when I forget. If I am expressing deep gratitude for my own life, however, I will typically have less inclination to compare myself to another. Because I have an ongoing conversation with my Higher Power about who I am, where I am, and what I am supposed to be doing in my life, grace eventually shows up – even when something doesn't turn out the way I wanted it to. I trust that my contributions in life do make a difference, and I am able to surrender to the idea that a higher authority is working in my life for purposes unknown to me. One of the signs often revealed to me when things are completely out of my control is that the Spirit is abundantly blessing *others*. Paradoxically, their blessing becomes my blessing. In those times I am often overcome with an awareness that I am indeed trying to be teachable, to stay on track, and that "all is well."

Replacing comparative thinking with my gratitude for what my life looks like – exactly as it is in this very moment – is a way I can connect with the God of my understanding. When I mess up, I try to pray and ask for help or forgiveness. When I do something well, I pray for humility and try to give deep thanks, whether I feel gratitude or not. Even though my life is not perfect (it never is, according to the ego, and it never will be, according to the sages), having gratitude is the best defense to fend off a destructive way of thinking about others and myself. It's also a sure way to connect spiritually and energetically to community, and to realize, ultimately, that I am one among many, and we are all in this dance together.

Meditations

"We can take a step back from the world of attraction, comparison, dependence on externals, remember this vitality within us, and connect with it. Perhaps then we can be liberated from our compulsions and can learn to act through spirit, rather than through our limited egos."
    ~ *Kabir Helminski, Living Presence*

"Too frequently our inner journeys have no depth. We move forward feverishly into new situations and experiences which neither nourish nor challenge us, because we have left our deeper selves behind."
    ~ *John O'Donohue, Eternal Echoes*

"Humility can be a spiritual doorway that leads to generosity toward self and others."

  ~ Jo-Ellen A. Darling

Questions for Journaling

1. Did you grow up with a sibling or a friend who received much attention and whose shadow you have always lived in? Do you have other memories of being compared to someone else? What were the circumstances? Spend some time journaling about the feelings you had when this happened. How do the thoughts and feelings still come up in the present for you? What situations particularly trigger feelings of envy or feeling *less than*?

2. Oftentimes, shame is an underlying wound of being compared to someone else. If this happened as a child or young adult, can you have a conversation with your inner child or your younger age adult from years past (or your current self) that may reveal memories where the shame is continuing to live? Use the dialoging exercise in Chapter 1 under "Journaling is a Process."

3. Is there currently a group of people or someone that you admire, but you think or feel you can never measure up to? Name them and journal all of your thoughts about why you feel this way. Do not edit what comes out on the page, other-wise, you will not be able to challenge or honestly explore your thoughts about this. Let it roll!

4. Can you write a poem, haiku, or other reflection that speaks to the shame or the essence of what you are feeling right now? (See "Nature's Poetry: Haiku and Senryū" in Chapter 4 for writing these forms of poetry.) Here are some Haiku and Senreyū verses I wrote in my journal when I was wrestling with shame:

Shame I
Shame sticks thick like tar
Yet hides unmercifully
Under feathers white

Shame II
If I could speak to shame
I wouldn't say "Go away" –
I'd love it to death!

5. Read Derek Walcott's poem below the **Exercises**:

    a. Reflect on its meaning to you.

    b. Can you picture yourself coming to the place the author describes?

    c. What parts of you are able to grasp his words?

    d. Have you ever had the experience of "coming home to yourself" after the breakup of a relationship? What was most powerful in that experience?

Exercises

1. The next time you are in the presence of someone you know who triggers your jealousy or envy, pay attention to your internal responses to them. Are there any other feelings present besides jealousy and envy? Recall your thoughts while you were in their presence and be as specific as you can. Be honest!

2. If you can, bless the other person in some way: whether by writing a blessing in your journal for them; sending them a note; having a conversation and listening well to them; or offering them verbal encouragement. Later, journal about this. How do you feel and what do you think about that encounter?

3. When you know you will be in a group of people where you often feel less than – or feel that you don't belong in some way – pray before you meet. Identify the fears and insecurities and let yourself feel the fear – then ask your Higher Power to go with you. Courage is often described as "fear that has said its prayers."

4. Connecting with your Higher Power in any situation is always appropriate. Learn to ask for help in the moments when you are spiritually "off" or you feel ungenerous. Above all, pray for humility, for humility can be a doorway to generosity.

Love after Love

The time will come
when, with elation,
you will greet yourself arriving
at your own door, in your own mirror,
and each will smile at the other's welcome,

And say, sit here, eat.
You will love again the stranger who was your self.
Give wine. Give bread. Give back your heart
to itself, to the stranger who has loved you

all your life, whom you ignored
for another, who knows you by heart.
Take down the love letters from the bookshelf,
the photographs, the desperate notes,
peel your image from the mirror.
Sit, feast on your life.

By Derek Walcott

When Your Life is Out of Balance

*"It is such a travesty – of possibility and freedom –
to think we have no choice."*

~ JOHN O'DONOHUE, ETERNAL ECHOES

We often find ourselves out of balance between two worlds. It's a given that sometimes life will demand more of our time in the external world, such as when we are working and going to school, working and raising children, or caregiving elderly parents. Or perhaps we are working hard to accomplish a major vocational or career goal that we find meaningful and valuable for our future plans. At other times, we may be much more focused on our interior lives, such as when we are trying to find our legs to begin a new life after devastating pain, loss, or disappointment. In finding our balance, we may need to set aside time and energy to review and reflect upon where we are, and where we truly want to be.

Writer Joyce Rupp uses the metaphor of a swinging door to illustrate how we traverse these two worlds that can lead us to be out of balance much of the time. She writes:

*"Our culture of extreme extroversion and work-orientation
causes us to swing the door outward and lures our focus toward
the outside world much longer than is good for our spiritual
well-being."*

Finding balance in life is a way to know what is important – what we need to keep as well as what can be released. What we *don't* need is just as important as discovering what we *do* need. To help us discover this, we may need to examine how we spend our time. Doing this exercise – in concert with journaling – creates a record of our thoughts and feelings around finding balance, something we can return to again and again for further insight.

In reviewing our time, we look at both our inner and outer worlds, deciding if what we are doing in each of these spheres is truly life-giving – or at least, nourishing in *some* important aspect. Each one of us is tasked to know what gives us life and what brings us balance. It is true, much will depend on our attitude: even our responsibilities – when we feel overburdened and trapped – can be lovingly reflected upon for minor, nuanced changes that can improve the quality of our lives.

Except for the past decade or so, I have lived most of my life out-of-balance from doing, and not enough time for being. Yet, there's also a strong part of me that loves to do. I relish writing lists and completing tasks. I enjoy having goals and the process of meeting those goals, step-by-step. I am grateful that I have meals to prepare and gardens to water. I enjoy recreation with my husband and the activities of self-care – yoga, swimming, eating right, meditating, journaling, and spending time in nature. I make time for my relationships with family, friends, and communities. In some ways, *doing* is a way of *being* that fits me well.

When deciding how we want or feel called to live our lives, it is unlikely it will be 50 percent of our time in each of these two areas of inward vs. outward living (or living purely as an introvert or an extrovert) – for that is not the real point of this exercise. What feels balanced to you will not be right for someone else and will often depend on the time of life a person is living in. For example, in my forties and early fifties I was active – doing and accomplishing – about 90 percent of the time. I spent only 10 percent of my time – or even less – in solitude and reflection. A decade later I'm spending much more time in reflection and activities that require quiet and solitude.

Nine years before I retired, an opportunity arose to explore a way of being in silence and solitude. For nearly four years, I spent a weekend each month (except for summers) at a retreat center with a community of contemplatives. It was an amazing time which began a deeper process of healing in my life and connecting with the divine. More recently I've learned that living too much of the time in silence and solitude – which is different for everyone – isn't good for me either. It is truly an individual balancing act for each one of us. If we make a commitment to take time for reflection, we will find the right mix.

This process, however, isn't typically black and white. In fact, there will likely be many shades of gray and overlap. There are times of letting go and surrender that coincide with taking new risks and engagement. There are unexpected thresholds to cross – invitations that bid us to new ways of doing and being. These invitations may lead us to liminal spaces – or times of waiting and transition as we continue to tease out the strands of doing and being in our lives that truly nurture our souls. We may want to journal our way through each of these experiences of searching and sifting through our lives. This can help us make choices that are good for us and may benefit others, too. We may also want to speak to others during these times of discernment.

I recall a time when I began to attend a similar but different community than the one I was part of for many years. After attending the new community a few times, I felt a deeper connection to God, to myself, and to the people. On the other hand, I continued with my old community. The stark difference between them eventually became crystal clear: the new community was more life-giving, whereas the former community no longer fed my soul.

It was time to change course, yet I recognized it would be a big shift for me with some risk involved. Letting go of one might mean letting go of friends while not yet knowing anyone in the other fellowship. It might mean explaining to my friends in one group why I was moving over, and not being sure of their continued friendship. Although I could still engage in both, I knew I wanted a different focus in my life. I waited until the time was ripe and gave myself more fully to where I had been drawn, to what had helped and nurtured me the most, and to what had given me the most serenity and authentic engagement. Today I have no regrets about that decision, and my friendships in the old community remain strong.

The Paradox

Naturally, many of our activities in the outer world support our desire to journey within. A book study, meditation group, yoga practice, online community, or attending lectures or sacred services – while on the outside are ways to engage with the outer world – can be ways that will strengthen and feed us interiorly. Sometimes our commitments to others, such as caregiving a friend or family member, also strengthens our desire for the sacred in life – it can show us what is truly meaningful. The power of discovering what works for each of us occurs precisely by allowing ourselves to take intentional steps to experience these invitations, opportunities, or nudges. Without taking the step to try them, we can remain stuck in our heads and continue to be out of balance with our lives. However, choosing to participate in the dance of figuring out what we need in life brings us closer to the center of our spiritual path and our true self. Journaling and savoring these experiences will help us see more clearly what is true and right for each of us.

Meditations

"Opening ourselves, our motivations, and the whole complex situation to the divine Light helps us understand whether it is time for waiting or whether we are avoiding the journey we need to take."
~ *Nancy L. Bieber, Decision Making & Spiritual Discernment*

"Remember that what is fruitful and life-giving is what nourishes us for the great work we each need to do... The more nourished we are, the more we seek out what feels nourishing. The more depleted we are, the less able we are to make wise choices on behalf of our own deepest care."

~ *Christine Valters Paintner, The Soul of a Pilgrim*

"… The outer lines of a clear choice or life-path should also remain porous in order to allow *our other unchosen lives* to continue to bless us."

~ *John O'Donohue, Eternal Echoes*

Questions for Journaling

1. Do these questions after you've taken an inventory of your time under the **Exercises** that follow.

   a. When you finish, highlight areas where you are out of balance in your commitments and in your down-time/ leisure time. In other words, where do you need to be more of the time and less of the time?

   b. Identify where you spend too much time in the external world, meeting the demands or requirements of others. Journal your thoughts and feelings about these areas of commitment. Where are you overcommitted and where can you cut back?

   c. Identify where you spend too little time in the internal world, such as not enough time just being with yourself, or too much time focusing on other people's problems or issues. Can you find time in your schedule to make space for soul time? Journal your thoughts and feelings around these questions.

2. What are the things in your inventory that might be good for you, even though you may feel uncomfortable doing them initially, such as a weekly walk or book study with friends, physical exercise, or spending time apart from your family on a more regular basis for refreshment and reenergizing your spirit?

a. What is truly life-giving to you, in other words, anything that brings joy, inner clarity, hope, spiritual awareness, a sense of balance, serenity, creativity or fun? What things under **Doing Time** nurture your inner being? Journal your thoughts and feelings about these.

b. Can you find time each week (or month) to engage in what you identified above in "a", no matter what it is? It could be some form of artwork, hobby, time with others, time alone, meditation, being in nature, something fun, etc. This will be different for each person, so don't go with the "I should" unless it sparks a moment of desire or connection when you think and write about it. Some part of you will sense if it is right or not.

c. If there's an area that you're not sure you're out of balance with, do a pros and cons list of how you are spending time there. How does the activity fulfill some aspect of who you are, or how doesn't it? Then prioritize each side of the list, beginning with #1, numbering the pros and cons that are most and least important or valuable to you.

d. What are your dreams for the future, even if you don't have the resources of time or money to edge toward them now?

e. Make a collage about one of your dreams. Can you identify one small step that you can take toward this dream or desire? You might do some further reading or exploring about your dream, using your imagination to brainstorm the possibilities of where you might be able to make a connection now.

Note: One of the things I did after attending Paula D'Arcy's writing retreat – which opened my soul to both the need for deeper healing and a commitment to creativity in my life – was to begin facilitating writing and journaling retreats. Although I was not ready to write this book – a long held desire back then – sharing a creative and spiritual space with others helped me move toward my dream.

    f. Journal all these questions thoroughly over the next several days or weeks. Then, make a few decisions about your current time allocations. Try not to modify too many things at once. Make a change or two and give it a month to see how it works.

3. Reflect upon one or more of the Meditation quotes above. What are these saying about the choices you are making currently in your life, or the changes you want to make? How do these authors' words grab your attention? How do they make you feel?

Exercises

Note: Blank versions of the three example tables (Table A, Table B, and Table C) shown on the next pages are provided in Appendix D.

1. Using Table 1, make an inventory of things you do on a *daily* basis:

    a. In the first column, enter the number of hours you are awake and asleep each day.

    b. List all the daily activities in your life and the approximate number of hours/minutes you spend on them (see *Table 1* below).

    c. Enter your results in the **Subtotal Time** row.

2. Using Table 2, make an inventory of things you do on a *weekly* basis.

    a. Fill in the hours/minutes that you engage in those activities (see *Table 2* below).

b. Enter your results in the **Subtotal Time** rows from Table 1 and Table 2. Add these two subtotal rows together and enter your results in the **Total Doing** row. Subtract the **Total Doing** hours/minutes from the number of **hours you are awake** reach column.

3. Using Table 3, make an inventory of how you spend being alone with yourself on a *weekly* basis.

a. List all the daily ways you spend in quiet activities or in silence, and the approximate hours/minutes you spend on them (see *Table 3* below).

b. In the **Total Being** row, add the hours/minutes in each weekday column.

c. Enter your **Total Doing** time in the next row from Table 2.

d. Add the **Total Being** and **Total Doing** in each column and record them in the **Subtotal Time** row.

e. Subtract the **Subtotal** hours from the number of hours you are awake each day and record in the bottom row.

f. If you come up with a deficit, such as **-2.0 hours**, in any of the columns in *Table 3*, you may have overestimated the time you actually spend doing something. Go back and revise some of the activities to make them equal to the number of hours you are awake (17 hours in this example).

TABLE 1: "Doing Time" Activity Table – Daily

(TABLE 1) Based on 17-hr. day (or 7 hours of sleep)	SUN.	MON.	TUES.	WED.	THUR.	FRI.	SAT.	KEEP, CHANGE OR LET GO
Meals	3 HR	2 HR	3 HR	3 HR	3 HR	1 HR		
Daily Hygiene/ Dressing	.5 HR	1 HR	.5 HR	1 HR	.5 HR	1 HR	.5 HR	
Commuting (RT)		1.5 HR	1.5 HR	1.5 HR	1.5 HR	1.5 HR		
Working or Volunteering		4 HR	4 HR	4 HR	4 HR	4 HR		
Family Time	2 HR	2 HR	2 HR	2 HR	2 HR	2 HR	2 HR	
Read/TV/ Internet	2.5 HR		2.5 HR		2.5 HR			
Exercise/Health	1 HR	1 HR	1 HR	1 HR	1 HR	1 HR	1 HR	
Other								
SUBTOTAL TIME (Table 1)	9 HR	11.5 HR	14.5 HR	12.5 HR	14.5 HR	10.5 HR	3.5 HR	

TABLE 2: "Doing Time" Activity Table — Weekly

(TABLE 2)	SUN.	MON.	TUES.	WED.	THUR.	FRI.	SAT.	KEEP, CHANGE OR LET GO
Laundry/House		1 HR		1 HR		1 HR	2 HR	
Bills/Finances		1 HR					1 HR	
Shopping/ Errands		2 HR		2 HR				
Date Night(s)/ Social Time						3 HR	4 HR	
Hobbies							2 HR	
Volunteering								
Friendships	.5 HR		.5 HR	.5 HR	.5 HR	.5 HR		
Recreation	2 HR						2 HR	
Group Activities	1 HR							
Subtotal Time (From Table 2)	3.5 HR	4 HR	.5 HR	3.5 HR	.5 HR	4.5 HR	11 HR	
Subtotal Time (From Table 1)	9 HR	11.5 HR	14.5 HR	12.5 HR	14.5 HR	10.5 HR	3.5 HR	
TOTAL DOING	12.5 HR	15.5 HR	15 HR	16 HR	15 HR	15 HR	14.5 HR	
Less Hours Awake = Free Time Left for BEING TIME	4.5 HR	1.5 HR	2 HR	1 HR	2 HR	2 HR	2.5 HR	

TABLE 3: "Being Time" Activity Table – Daily/Weekly

(TABLE 3)	SUN.	MON.	TUES.	WED.	THUR.	FRI.	SAT.	KEEP, CHANGE OR LET GO
Reflection Time/ Journaling	1 HR	1 HR	1 HR	1 HR	1 HR	1 HR	1 HR	
Relaxing/ Napping	.5 HR		.5 HR		.5 HR		.5 HR	
Spiritual Practices	1 HR							
Time in Nature			1 HR					
Other								
Other								
Other								
TOTAL BEING (Table 3)	2.5 HR	1 HR	2.5 HR	1 HR	1.5 HR	1 HR	1.5 HR	
TOTAL DOING (From Table 2)	12.5 HR	15.5 HR	15 HR	16 HR	15 HR	15 HR	14.5 HR	
SUBTOTAL – Add Total Being & Total Doing Time	15 HR	16.5 HR	17.5 HR	17 HR	16.5 HR	16 HR	16 HR	
Less Hours Awake = Personal Time Left in the Day	2 HR	.5 HR	0 HR	0 HR	.5 HR	1 HR	1 HR	

Being True to Yourself

Some of the most powerful words my spouse has spoken over the years are: "You're allowed to be who you are." His words not only validate his acceptance of me, but reveal his acknowledgement that we are two very different people and we will often not respond to life in the same way. Remembering his words helps me when I'm struggling to make a choice or take a stand that I know will not go over well with him or others. As we discussed in Chapter 1, seeking the authentic self and exploring whom we are called to become is not necessarily honored by most people. Allowing ourselves to truly live from the true self is even harder.

Shakespeare's famous line "To thine own self be true" is a beautiful principle to live by. Many of us may need to search in the deep pockets of our souls to give ourselves permission to live authentically. Others will go in a completely self-centered direction, and it will be an excuse for selfishness and a lack of empathy toward others. However, since life is not black and white, we will all need to negotiate these lines and explore what these words mean to each of us.

In the dictionary, *narcissism* is defined as "excessive preoccupation with or admiration of oneself." More specifically in psychology, it is a personality disorder "characterized by an exaggerated sense of self-importance, need for admiration, and lack of empathy." Though only a small number of the population have narcissistic personality disorder, most of us express narcissistic tendencies over time. For instance, it's a natural stage with children until puberty but then becomes problematic afterwards, according to the famed psychologist, Sigmund Freud. The truth is, we can make all kinds of selfish, self-centered, and unloving choices that will lead us (and sometimes others) down a miserable path. So, even the words "To thine own self be true" must be handled with care. Since these famous words have meant different things in every generation, it's important to find what they mean to each one of us individually.

Early in my adulthood, I had no concept of what it meant to be true to myself. As I worked through my confusion and self-identity, however, I began to see that beneath much of my misperceptions were thoughts, words, feelings, and actions that were false – in some way – in how I lived. It gradually became clear that there was another, deeper self inside, a person whose ideas, written words, feelings and actions were much more connected to my soul. I trusted this because these experiences felt whole and produced peace in my soul. They did not bring shame or more confusion and they enabled me to respect myself, *as well as* others.

We all know in our gut – eventually if not immediately – when something is wrong. We are often conditioned to let these signals pass, however, without examining or acting on them. We may shrug them off, be afraid of them and justify them, and we don't see the erosion done to our own souls. In the early years of my first marriage, we had an anniversary coming up and yet I chose to be away visiting friends. I honestly had not even considered how this would affect my spouse or our marriage. I'm sure I would have been wounded if the tables were turned. Although he was a kind and good person, I had married him with great ambivalence and for all the wrong reasons. However, instead of breaking it off, I began to focus on my own life and my responses to him. Eventually the time to let go arrived. This experience was one of my greatest lessons in life.

Living from the True Self

"The True Self always has something good to say. The False Self babbles on, largely about itself."

~ RICHARD ROHR, IMMORTAL DIAMOND

As we begin to practice paying attention and being true to ourself – via the healthy ego and our searching souls – we will find a new energy from which to live. This energy is like a flame inside us that burns ever brighter, yet shows us how to navigate the path of both light *and* darkness. As we choose less and less to take the road of darkness – defined here as living perpetually in negative thoughts and emotions and evading opportunities for growth and change for the better – our choices will move more and more toward the light. We will begin to discover a self in us that is beyond what we know today – or knew yesterday.

Being true to yourself can often begin by making choices that will benefit yourself without considering its impact on others, such as the practice of self-care. It takes courage to care for a neglected self. I believe living from the true self, however, eventually leads to the added dimension of a deeper spiritual connection to others and the divine energy. There are many people we can name that live (or have lived) for others, and yet have lived from the true self. This is because their concern for other people is greater than their smaller concerns for themselves – such as their personal comfort or self-image. A person living from a fully-realized true self will be spiritually evolved, able to give up personal comfort, and even happiness (think of all the parents in this world who do this for their children). Instead, they will experience great joy in making decisions based on something higher than their own self-interest. Take for instance, Martin Luther King, Mahatma Gandhi, and Mother Theresa. Though these are extraordinary examples, I am sure this world is filled with people who are able to live at varying degrees of these transcendent spiritual qualities. But how does one attain it?

Accessing our true self requires a starting point. That point will always be in the present moment. If the present moment seems too difficult to imagine a new beginning, we may need to go back to something prior – an event, a feeling, or a powerful connection in the past when we knew in our hearts that we were living from an authentic place. So our beginning can then be from that previous point, as we transport the associated memory into the present moment through an energized recall.

About 10 years ago, I attended a birthday party given to honor a woman who had been cherished as one of the elders in our fellowship. I felt truly honored and much gratitude to have been invited to such a celebration. The experience of meeting many more of the women in her life at that gathering was also uplifting. As I reflected on this experience and recorded these thoughts and feelings in my journal over the next few days, I became aware of a slow-growing thought inside that suggested I did not really belong with these women, and that I did not deserve to be invited. This was clearly not how the honoree or others had seen me, nor how I felt when I was there. Yet this thought was hanging around like a bothersome gnat. I remember experiencing an actual erosion of my soul during that 24-hour period that I could not seem to shake.

Eventually, I got in touch with my deeper, stronger self and I resolved to confront these intrusive thoughts. I went to a private place and dialoged out loud with them, forbidding them to take root in my soul. I countered the words with the truth – that I did belong, was valued by several of the guests, including the woman being honored, and was welcome among them. I clearly remember the effect was immediate and the negative energy was diffused. This dialog with the energy of my thoughts – which created feelings of low self-esteem, unworthiness, and dysphoria – could also have been dialoged in my journal using my dominant and nondominant hands, as discussed in Chapter 1.

I realized that we have to stand up to these types of debilitating thoughts and call them out for what they are: poisonous weeds in the garden of our soul. As I reflected on this experience in the days that followed, I saw that commitment to my spiritual growth, plus a deepening connection to the divine and to many of the women at that celebration, was the fuel that supported my decision to stand up to these thoughts that had been around far too long. The experience became one of the touchstones that I would return to whenever I became too hung up on self-disparaging thoughts or memories from the past.

More amazing was that my true self – in that moment – had overgrown the small self, the part of me that was either willing to put up with these lies, or not yet strong enough to root them out. Yet the stronger bonding between the Spirit and self had been made through an act of loving trust. Acting in that moment gave rise to many more experiences of a growing self-acceptance and self-compassion through intentional acts of deep listening and awareness.

Finally, being true to yourself doesn't mean you never get angry, cry, or complain. In fact, thoughts and feelings can come from the true self as much as from the false self, but they are often different experiences. Feelings from the true self feel as if you are coming home to yourself. For example, I believe that when you are weeping deeply, it is your true self who weeps.

The true self embraces the feelings honestly, but doesn't judge them. Instead, she holds them like an infant in her arms, full of love and trust in her own soul and an openness to what they are trying to tell her. She realizes that even under the hurt and resentment, there is a caring heart. The resentment is the injustice she finds in certain situations around her. Her anger may point to the heartbreak that someone else is causing her, and yet she will eventually find the sadness underneath, and the forgiveness in her heart. Her protectiveness of her loved ones, including herself, is her main concern. But she is also capable of great compassion toward the one doing wrong. The true self is the heart of who we are, and when we find it, we will never be the same again.

Meditations

"Your soul always remains faithful to your longing to become who you really are. The vanished self from an earlier time of life remains within you, waiting to be released and integrated."

  ~ *John O'Donohue, Eternal Echoes*

"The longest journey seems to be the letting go of the expectations, the assumptions, the woundedness; all the ways we seek just what we are looking for rather than what is waiting to be revealed."

  ~ *Christine Valters Paintner, The Soul's Slow Ripening*

"More amazing was that my true self – in that moment – had overgrown the small self, the part of me that was either willing to put up with these lies, or not yet strong enough to root them out."

  ~ *Jo-Ellen A. Darling*

Questions for Journaling

1. What areas of growth do you see in terms of a growing sense of your true self? How have you begun to embrace the false self, and at the same time giving it less power in your life?

2. What clues do you have about what is waiting to be revealed in your life?

3. Do you need a new outlook on life? What specifically does it need less of? More of?

4. What part of yourself did you leave behind in an earlier life that you might need to rediscover?

5. How can you regularly practice self-forgiveness and self-compassion? Be concrete.

Exercises

1. Notice over the next week how you have been *true to yourself.*
   When did you know it? Is it when you spoke up and wondered where the words had come from? Was it a spontaneous
   comment or loving gesture you made toward someone, or
   yourself? Make these journal entries each day. There may only
   be one or two things on the list, but pay attention to them. At
   the end of the week, celebrate the harvest of wisdom that you
   have gained from this reflective journaling.

2. Also notice how you have been *untrue to yourself.* How did you
   know it? By letting feelings of unease, guilt, or regret pass by,
   unexamined? By agreeing to one more thing you do not want
   or have time to do? Perhaps you did not stand up for yourself
   when others were critical and/or disparaging toward you.
   Journal what you find in these thoughts and feelings, and most
   of all, be gentle with yourself.

CHAPTER 4

Creativity and Journaling

Journaling and the Creative Process

"The deepest call to a creative life comes from within your own interiority."

~ JOHN O'DONOHUE, ETERNAL ECHOES

S elf-knowledge is one of the fruits that comes from a commitment to the creative process. We've been getting to know ourselves better and what does and doesn't bring us joy and peace,
purpose and direction – the living streams that feed the deeper wells
of our lives. We might recognize these joys as a fleeting moment, or
a deep and abiding sense of being grounded, or an unexpected yet
much-needed challenge that awakens and enlivens us. We have begun
to pay attention to these treasures in our lives.

Life is creative, and creativity is *life-giving*. There are many sources of creativity and our task is to identify those that nourish us the most. If we're connecting at least partly to a spiritual path which enables us to make choices to live our lives in concert with the true self, then we can take the next step of identifying the creative pursuits that truly feed our souls. Even if we don't already know – or are not clearly heading toward – our life's purpose, creativity can be one of the pathways to the true self.

There are many ways to creatively bring depth to our lives. Arranging our living spaces so that energy flows (rather than blocks) is a joyful and creative process known as *Feng Shui*. This choice can affect our daily lives in a profound way. Choosing color and texture for decorating, and clothing that feels right is a creative choice as well. What makes our choice satisfying is how it makes us feel. We can ask ourselves: is there a deep connection between me and my environment? Or, does this object or living space currently reflect some aspect of my inner landscape, thus reflecting the qualities I value, such as beauty, organization, less clutter, colors that lift the soul, unique artistic décor, sustainability or fair trade?

When a creatively spiritual process for living takes hold in our lives, staying stuck is no longer an option. Once you find what inspires you – what feeds you, what brings needed balance into your life as well as what challenges you to grow – you may have to find a different way to live in the world.

Making Time for Creative Pursuits

Over the years, I belonged to organizations that required much effort from its members to keep all the programs, fundraisers, and events going. Often, there were more opportunities for service than people were willing or able to participate in. Sometimes it seemed to be an unwinnable battle. But people can't be made to participate, no matter how hard we try; there must be freedom in their choosing. We can only give so much, and it is unfair to expect others or ourselves to carry more than they or we can handle. It seemed the more I did, the more I was asked to do. Eventually, I began to see that my own life was being neglected.

At first, I disengaged entirely, and sought other, more "balanced" organizations to serve. However, under the surface of my desire to flee was the difficulty I had with saying "no" when my time or energy was requested. I was afraid I would be criticized, no longer accepted – or worse – I would have to endure the voices of my own feelings of guilt. As Joyce Rupp explains in her book, *Open the Door:*

> *"The decisions we make can disappoint others.... We may find ourselves having to guard our solitude... Self-doubt, guilt about moving on, questions about the timing and fear of an inability to close the door often arise."*

Yet I've learned that only I can allow myself to fall victim to this way of feeling and thinking. For many years, my projections stemmed from my childhood. As the oldest who had more responsibilities perhaps than my siblings, I saw how well it pleased my parents. But now as an adult, I am free to say no, to not feel guilty about tending to my own life, and what I feel the Spirit and my deepest self has called me to do. Finding a life path is an individual process, and it's up to you and me to figure this out. When I realized I was neglecting my own life in these organizations, the question for me became: could I remain and practice my boundaries while continuing the discernment process about whether to stay long-term or not? The final phase that helped me to change my relationship with one of these worthy organizations was to find the courage to be a member without always doing what I was asked to do.

Getting honest about my fear of saying "no" as often as I needed to – and keeping that boundary firm – was immensely freeing. After much journaling, I shared my decision at length with others. I saw that it was a new level of self-responsibility in me that, in earlier years,

I was unwilling to accept. My need for people's approval – and my need to be accepted – were much stronger than following my life path. This is what makes life difficult: the hard choices are never easy. Rather, they often point to a path we may fear, as Nancy L. Bieber explains in her book, *Decision Making & Spiritual Discernment:*

> *"Even a little fearfulness can keep us from moving ahead in our decision making. If we're apprehensive about something, we often avoid it... Fear limits our choices. When we're guided by fear, we can't hear the Spirit's whispers; consequently, we fail to perceive the steps we need to follow to take the best path. [Yet]... there is a part of us that would love to trust a wisdom greater than our own."*

Even during crises – when we need to put others first – we *must* continue to nourish ourselves or we will lose our own "sense of life," as John O'Donohue states in a later quote. To free up our time and make a deeper commitment to ourselves and our gifts for creative pursuits will be life-enhancing. Time for creative pursuits must be protected, and only *we* can be responsible for making and guarding that time. It is not always easy, but if we allow the spirit of creativity to be something in ourselves that we can honor, just as we honor the time we make for the needs of others, a deepened connection to our own lives and purpose can bring us real joy and growth.

Meditations

"Much of what passes for creativity is clever know-how... When creativity dries up, the analysts turn on themselves and begin to empty out the inner world; this has contributed to the terrible loss of soul in our culture."
~ *John O'Donohue, Eternal Echoes*

"Soul loves the journey itself."
~ *David Whyte, The Heart Aroused*

"I saw that it was a new level of self-responsibility in me that, in earlier years, I was unwilling to accept. My need for people's approval – and my need to be accepted – were much stronger than following my life path."
~ *Jo-Ellen A. Darling*

Questions for Journaling

1. What have you been saying "yes" to that you no longer want to do? Pay attention to your feelings and sensations in your body. How do you feel – and what body sensations do you feel when you say yes, but you really want to say no?

2. On the flip side, are you saying no to something you really want to say yes to? Pay attention to your feelings and body sensations when your choice does not align with your desire. How do you feel when you say no, but you really want to say yes?

3. Begin to gently journal about this thing you have said yes or no to that is now conflicting with your true self.

   a. What are some of the reasons you agreed to this? Do those reasons still stand?

   b. Will this thing be life-giving, or will it be life-depleting? Or is the timing off (i.e., not yet)?

   c. Can you tell the difference between not wanting to do something, but also knowing in your heart you still *need* to do it? Is there a way to continue with your commitment in a life-giving way?

    d. If not, how do you want to let go? Write a scenario as to how you see it happening and how you would communicate that to someone. Be honest.

4.   Depending on what you want to let go of, can you give it a period of days or weeks before you decide to let go? For example, if it's a job you want to leave, can you take your time and explore your options, deciding or planning what you want to pursue next, before you give notice?

5.   Which important relationships will be affected by your choice? Would your partner/spouse want you to talk this over with them?

6.   Are you ready to experience a new level of *responsible freedom* that you have not experienced before? What are your thoughts about how this might play out? What might you have to give up in order to live more consistently from your true self?

Exercises

1.   Think of a time in your life when you let go of a commitment in a way that burned a bridge. Do you have a pattern of letting go this way, for whatever reason? For example, if you are hurt, angry, or disappointed, can you step aside from these emotions (after you work through them) and picture a different part of yourself explaining why you need to change course?

2.   Before you take the step, it may be wise to talk this over with trusted friends who may provide some perspective that you may have missed. Is there someone or others you can talk to?

3.   Read the quotations in this section and then take time to meditate on them. Read them a few times, silently and out loud. Which words or phrases stand out for you? Journal your thoughts and feelings about them.

Creative Writing

"These times of intense emotion, despair, and ambiguity often lead to deep veins of creative energy, like tapping an underground spring."

If we are faithful to our journaling practice, we may begin to find ourselves doing the creative writing that springs from the practice of being present to our own life. Other forms of creative writing – or the desire to do them – may find their way into our journals, as well: free verse and poetry, short stories, parables, meditations and reflections, children's stories, memoir, or ideas for magazine and journal articles. Depending on your desire to try new things, attending to the creative urge may crystalize ideas for longer forms of creative works in hobbies such as woodworking, sewing, cooking, building, painting, teaching, welding, dance, sculpture, pottery, crafts, books, plays, videos, documentaries, or movies. There is no end to creative possibilities: there is an infinite well of opportunity that is available to everyone. Yet, harvesting the fruits of the creative impulse largely depends on harnessing your life's focus. Resisting distractions and fanning the flames of your desire and the vocation of your heart's longing will bring joy. This joy can cultivate a deeper desire to commit to the time and energy of a creative practice.

Maybe you are feeling scattered and floundering in your creative thoughts and desires or feeling much too out-of-balance to find a creative thread to hold onto. Yet, when my life is out of balance, I do not stop reflective journaling. Rather, I journal to *keep* a balance, to learn from my experience of going out of balance, and to see and integrate the incredible wisdom that both life and Spirit reveal to me in these times of uncertainty. Some of my most fruitful creative times occur during periods of imbalance – such as when I'm in confusion, deep emotions, or spiritual pain. Creative desires often emerge when I'm growing to a new place, asking important questions, discerning a choice to be made, or going deep within my own soul, or the soul of the Divine. These times of intense emotion, despair, and ambiguity often lead to deep veins of creative energy, like tapping an underground spring. We can then begin to find the courage to share our creative works with others through hobby-based interest groups, self-publishing, or submissions to publications, whether poems or book queries, or to enter these works of art in collections, competitions, or formal or informal exhibitions. When we do this, we are honoring our work and sharing it with others.

Journaling Our Inner Poet

Sometimes we may feel inspired to write poetry in our journals. It's essential to just go with it. I never thought about writing poetry as a way to connect spiritually or nourish my own creativity until I attended author Paula D'Arcy's writers' retreat. During the retreat, D'Arcy led us through various spontaneous writing techniques and exercises, such as using writing prompts (also known as sentence stems), converting prose to poetic forms, answering questions about life, and using a line from a book or poem as a launching pad to write our own reflection or poem. I got in touch with much personal pain at that retreat, and the day after it ended, I wrote several powerful and healing poems. These poems gave me a creative voice that would continue to flourish and be a powerful agent in my own healing.

As I wrote those poems, I listened to the deep emotion in my body and the voice of my own soul. I let the words flow without editing or interrupting them. As I wrote, I invariably felt powerful moments of healing. I found myself in touch with a deeper self, a truth-telling voice that had long lived deep down inside. It was as if I was meeting the stages of my soul as each poem rose to the surface: an explorer child, a teenager in rebellion, an adult searching for love and meaning. Through this process, I connected with a loving Presence. Compassion deepened, and tears flowed.

Within a few years, my retirement approached. I became aware that in listening for the deep truths in my heart, a desire to write and share about the mysteries – life and death, God and the sacred, creativity and wellbeing – was gaining momentum. But what form would it take? I held this dream for two more years. Within four months of retiring, it became clear that it would be a book of reflections, questions, and meditations about the spiritual and human journey: the seeking heart, the discovery of the divine love, and how journaling had revealed and nurtured a spiritual path – something I had done faithfully for more than 30 years. I can only tell you this: when I followed a desire or invitation to go deeper in my life, surprising things always happened.

Meditations

"All your thoughts, feelings, and actions arise from a secret source within you, which desires life. This is where your "sense of life" is rooted."

~ John O'Donohue, Eternal Echoes

"There is no end to creative possibilities: there is an infinite well of opportunity that is available to everyone. Yet, harvesting the fruits of the creative impulse largely depends on harnessing your life's focus."

~ Jo-Ellen A. Darling

"[Thomas] Merton goes on to say the contradictions in our lives are the engines of creativity. It's true. If we got everything right or everything wrong, there'd be none of the divine discontent or the sense of possibility that animates our growth. What we get wrong makes us reach for something better. What we get right reassures us that the "better" is sometimes within our reach."

~ Parker Palmer, On the Brink of Everything

Questions for Journaling

1. What creative art or activity engages a part of you that you do not otherwise experience? What excites or enlivens you? Is it something that primarily engages your hands, or your whole body? Is it music, hiking, photography, or making pottery?

2. What gifts does this creative activity bring to you?

3. Is it difficult to make time for this art or activity in your life? Why? What sabotaging thoughts do you have that prevent you from making the time? Identify at least three of them.

4. How can you engage in your favorite creative activity more frequently?

5. If you have not yet experienced a creative activity that feeds your soul, journal your *desire* and then watch for that creative pursuit (and opportunities to try it out) be revealed in the days or weeks ahead.

6. Is there some creative thing you can do today, such as to find a space in your home to prepare for your commitment of a "creative pursuit," much like setting up a nursery when expecting a child?

Exercise

Look at the adult education classes offered in your community, or search online for college classes that you can audit, as well other workshops, retreats or gatherings that focus on a particular creative art or some aspect of the creative process. Make a commitment to experience this, even if there is doubt or resistance. If nothing else, it will be an exercise in exploring all you need in life to find what truly beckons you. As the adage goes: *nothing changes if nothing changes.*

Journaling in Response to Life's Questions

For about five years, I attended a monthly writers' group facilitated by my friend and author, Sherry Blackman. Before sharing our individual creative writing projects we had worked on since we last met, we wrote in response to Sherry's questions and writing prompts. This was tremendously fun and also revealing. Timed writing tends to capture what the "editor in your head" might otherwise dismiss. For example, thoughts or ideas that make us feel vulnerable are likely to appear. In one of our exercises, we wrote for just a few minutes without stopping to answer the following question:

"What do you no longer have?"

Searching the notebook I used in our group meetings, I found what I wrote:

- I am no longer in a difficult marriage, living a life of broken dreams and broken promises.

- I no longer have a lonely life void of the understanding of a higher power who is only about rules and rituals.

- I no longer have the huge hole in my heart that an awesome Spirit now fills with love, guidance, and possibilities.

- I no longer have contact with some of my old friends, which makes me sad but also keenly aware of their beauty and the role their friendships played at various points in my life – in retrospect these friends helped me through some very difficult times, and also deeply touched my heart.

- I no longer have a tense relationship with my Mom – thank God! – today we are great friends!!

If I answered that question today, there would likely be a totally different response. If I responded to that question many years prior to doing that exercise, perhaps I would have listed the many losses in my life if I was in the throes of grief. Yet in the moment I wrote my response, I saw how many losses had been transformed into new experiences and perspectives. Keeping a list of questions in your creative toolbox is a good way to provide instant access to your creative energies whenever you need inspiration for doing any creative activity – or when you feel stuck in your life.

Likewise, keeping a list of quotes for our meditation time can bring us into a spiritual flow on any given day. Remembering back to early sobriety, I lacked a vision of a higher power with whom I could engage on a daily basis. Part of what I needed was to find creative ways to connect with the God of my limited understanding. Some of my most powerful allies during this time were daily meditation books. These daily meditations – which often included how the mystery of God works in our lives – began to anchor me in my own life in a way I could not have been grounded without them. I'm deeply grateful for the wisdom reflections on spirituality and the themes of joyful, creative living shared by these authors.

Using Prompts to See Where We Are

One of the quickest ways to connect with the treasure of the unconscious mind is to respond to prompts or "sentence stems." We do this by starting with part of a sentence or a line from a poem or book, then writing without stopping or editing the content that flows onto the page. Embracing the attitude of the beginner's mind, we allow our spiritual tuning forks – a metaphor for your ability to pick up energy – to be a conduit for these hidden thoughts, feelings, sensations, memories, and creative ideas which can then flow into our conscious awareness.

I once used the first line in David Whyte's poem titled "*Self Portrait*" to see what was lurking beneath a recent grief that was not yet fully conscious. For each line on my page, I began with Whyte's line: *"I want to know ..."* What came out was a litany of questions and doubts I had about faith, life and death, the next life, and how my deceased loved ones were doing. It helped to see that these thoughts and ideas were normal, and it gave me permission to be where I was in the grief process.

Choose a writing prompt or question from a book you are reading, something you heard in a recent conversation, a line from a favorite poem, or a phrase or idea from a meditation book or some other source. You will know instinctively which sentence stem, question or prompt you should use because your internal tuning forks will prompt you to begin writing. A list of sentence stems and questions for journaling is provided in Appendix B.

Nature's Poetry: Haiku and Senryū

"Ultimately, where haiku come from is a mystery."
~ CLARK STRAND, SEEDS FROM A BIRCH TREE

A flock of blackbirds
sits high in Florida trees
just sunning themselves

A bamboo forest –
the living among the dead –
who are we to say?

Haiku and Senryū are forms of Japanese poetry. Writing these poems can be a segue into the creative process. You could say that haiku and senryū (pronounced high-coo and sen-*ryoo*) are minimalist forms of poetry, since they traditionally consist of three lines with 5, 7, and 5 syllables for each line, respectively. Their amazing power lies in the writer's intention to express the present moment in very few words. My love of haiku and senryū stems from how they bring depth to my practice of journaling as a spiritual path. Clark Strand captures this in his excellent book, *Seeds from a Birch Tree* (emphasis mine):

> *"Haiku is both a very outward and a profoundly contemplative inner kind of art. We realize that in looking* OUT, *we are also looking* IN.*"*

Although many personal experiences, situations, and people in our lives will inspire our journaling, haiku raises our level of attention through the practice of being totally present to the moment. While being present to nature – to which our lives are intricately connected – writing haiku and journaling become siblings as we practice, over and over again, the search for the treasure in the moments of our lives. Both journal writing and haiku are practices that inspire us to be more still, silent, and consciously attentive – more often. Once a haiku or journal entry is written, its verse or reflective language can be a placemark for that single moment of our lives – to be remembered, savored, and enjoyed. Each day we can be present to this process of presence, insight, and an appreciation for what is.

Haiku and senryū not only bring us deeply into the present moment, they are effective for stirring the creative juices. Traditional haiku is focused on some aspect or detail in nature. As we sit, watch, and wait, our eyes are opened to the natural world through imagery, like looking through high-powered binoculars, or when we are deep in mindfulness meditation. Senryū is similar, but also different. Like haiku, it is written in three lines of 5-7-5 syllables, but its intent is to include some aspect of human nature:

> *My pain is the child*
> *my freedom is her parent:*
> *let's unlock the door*

Sometimes senryū verse combines elements from the natural world *and* human nature:

> *Glistening snowstorm*
> *covering trees in silence*
> *trees deep in prayer*

Many haiku have turned up in my own journal pages and continue to preserve important memories, as well as to inspire my writing. Try writing haiku or senryū during or after times of journaling, reading, meditating, or being outdoors. Try your hand at senryū during or after times of trauma or intense emotional experiences. You will be amazed how writing haiku and senryū will begin to form a poetic sensibility within you, even if you've never written a line of poetry in your life!

Meditations

"Haiku is the one poetic form in all of world literature that concerns itself primarily with nature, the one form of poetry that makes nature a spiritual path."
~ CLARK STRAND, SEEDS FROM A BIRCH TREE

> *The royal palm trees*
> *great princes of the tropics –*
> *sway in a campground*

> Strange sounds and screeches
> in the Fakahatchee Strand...
> ghosts of wilderness

> *Buried under snow*
> *taking their rest before spring:*
> *dormant seeds still dream*

Little brown shorebird
struts near my foot, trusting me
not to bother her

*White-winged egrets float
over the pond and vanish
into tall grasses*

A runaway crab
lives in someone else's shell
and hides in seaweed

*A red-winged blackbird
sways on a stalk of wild grass
in the old lakebed*

Megalithic park
where brilliant leaves are falling
'round the ancient stones

*Welcome the sadness
befriend your grief of dear ones –
the love never ends*

An Everglades owl
wakes me in the dead of night –
a ghost from the past

*Cooing mourning dove
interrupts the campground noise
like med-i-ta-tion*

Questions for Journaling

1. How does the process of writing haiku feel to you?

2. What themes do you see in the haiku that you have written so far?

3. Try writing a few senryū as well, drawing from the well of your life experiences.

4. Which Japanese form of poetry do you prefer, haiku or senryū? How does each one tap into your creativity? When are you more likely to use one over the other?

Exercises for Fostering Creativity

1. Visit a favorite local or regional landscape for a day. Bring your lunch, journal, paints, sketchbook, camera, favorite book, or other creative tool. Enjoy the fruits of the day.

2. Read or reread a favorite author, watch an inspiring film or documentary, or review the life or works of a favorite artist or inspirational figure to invigorate your creative spirit.

3. Plan a half-day or full-day journey somewhere local, such as a lake, an old cemetery, or a park. Journal your way through your experiences by writing your insights, thoughts, questions, and everything else worth noting. What is being mirrored to you in the landscape?

4. Attend a silent retreat at a local retreat house for a day. Many retreat houses will allow you to visit and charge nominal fees for lunch or use of the property. Many of these facilities have art rooms, libraries, chapels, lovely grounds, walking paths and other unique features such as a labyrinth, where you can spend time in silence to allow your creative spirit to regenerate.

5. Travel locally or beyond with an intention beyond "vacationing." Let your intention set your agenda – such as "to reacquaint myself with myself," or "to reacquaint my connection with God," or "to stir my creative spirit in service of my own healing or the world's."

6. Reimagine your creative life by journaling how you'd like it to be and what particular elements would need to be present. Name any of your bottom lines in terms of these, such as "I must have a separate room or space in the home to work in," or "on Mondays I will spend two hours in my studio." List any goals that come to mind as to how to start and continue the process of establishing a creative practice.

7. Journal any impactful experiences on a daily basis, no matter how seemingly insignificant. An argument with your spouse, a negative feeling that won't quit, a surprise encounter, or a conversation with a child – all can move us to creative expression.

8. Write a letter to your inner self. What part of you needs tending? Is it an aspect of yourself, such as the wounded self, the vulnerable child of God, the professional in you that needs support, or some other part? When responding to questions or prompts, use your *nondominant* hand.

9. Write one or more questions to yourself that need to be asked. Journal your responses to these questions without editing the words as you write. Refer to the list of questions in Appendix B.

10. Go to a bookstore (or search online) to find a couple of daily meditation books that attract you. These can be found in the Self Help and Religion sections of most book carriers.

Grief as a Force for Creativity

"As I wrote, I invariably felt powerful moments of healing. I found myself in touch with a deeper self, a truth-telling voice that had long lived deep down inside."

After reading *Healing After Loss* by Martha Whitmore Hickman, I was immediately uplifted by her metaphor of a caterpillar, shaking off its dust (representing a time of grief) so it could fly. It had been a few weeks since I felt I was able to fly in the creative spirit. Having lost my father a few months before, these words reminded me that the hope of inner transformation through the process of grief could be a powerful ally in my writing life. Her butterfly meditation touched me that day, and the creative juices began to stir.

My grief was blessed by the writing of this poem. Its expression gave me great comfort as I worked through the trauma and loss of my father.

A Journey Through Winter

I am listening to winter,[3]
from the broken branches in my heart
to his December birthday that was not
to the holidays we spent apart –
to the roar of wind that took him away ...

I am listening to winter,
from the darkness of grief's long, painful night
to the sorrow and anger in me, burning bright
to the smile I miss, so full of light –
to the bare branch of silence his memory now brings ...

I am listening to winter,
for the hope of peace on a sterling snow

---

[3] Jo-Ellen A. Darling, Copyright © 2019. This line is inspired by the poem "Listening to Winter" by Macrina Wiederkehr in The Circle of Life, © 2005 by Joyce Rupp and Macrina Wiederkehr. Used by permission of Ave Maria Press. All rights reserved.

to the taste of tears in a sunset's glow
to heaven's winter I not yet know –
to the budded branch of his Eternal Spring …

By reading Hickman's daily meditations on grief, I began to grasp the complexity of grief that she writes about after the loss of her daughter. One of her discoveries was that in spite of death, the relationship with her daughter continued, only in a different way or form. I responded in my journal:

"Could my relationship with Dad be a new beginning, as much a part of the natural world as the supernatural world – maybe we are in the early stages of a new way of being father and daughter."

Rather than giving into confusion and despair during times of questioning, I can welcome the disparities, the confusion, and even the moments of despair by embracing them as part of one reality – and trusting that if I wait with awareness, everything is revealed in its time.

Grieving Your Life

Though we may not feel it when we're living in the shadows of grief, divine mystery and creativity are both accessible to us. It seems to be a mystery as to what leads us to the next thought, memory, or impression. How are these things revealed to us? Some would say the divine Spirit reveals them.

More than once in my life, I've experienced the powerful force of grief moving me to a place of threshold. During a two-year period in the last decade, past wounds and other adult losses had gathered like dark clouds beneath the surface of my life. Difficult memories swirled through one year to the next as I reflected upon and journaled them. Yet, Life with a capital "L" was undoubtedly inviting me to push through. I considered going back to therapy, but after meeting with a few therapists, it was clear I had the strength and skills to work with my Higher Power to guide me. Because of a longstanding connection to the Spirit, I knew more would be revealed.

In one of my journal entries during this time, these words were woven together like a tapestry:

> *Pain splits me open*
> *I freefall to the abyss…*
> *landing in the light*

This poem was paired with a powerful painting titled "Divine Hands" by artist Christine Labrum for a book of reflections that I co-edited in 2016.[4]

---

[4] "Divine Hands," Copyright © Christine Labrum, 2014. www.creatingspacetolisten.com

In another poem, these verses reflected the nature of the wounding I needed to grieve, and the force with which it needed to be expressed:

The gift and the wound –
two strands of one tapestry –
gallop like horses

I wrote these pieces soon after the riveting five-day writers' retreat with Paula D'Arcy in 2012, which I have mentioned before. To me, she was a well-loved writer, speaker, and Amma figure all in one. My expectations were high – for transformation as well as for friendship – but I did not expect the level of pain that was unleashed during the week-long retreat. The truth was, I wanted to be my shiny best self around her, but my inner, newly-budding true self – beneath some heavy pain at the time – eventually knew the real reason I was there: I had much grief work to do. Anyone who knows D'Arcy's writings knows about her own acquaintance with tragedy and grief from a drunk-driving accident that claimed her husband's and daughter's lives, leaving her to raise the child, then in her womb, alone. What better writer and person could I have been led to – or to begin this work with?

As Richard Rohr, Franciscan priest and author explains in one of his daily meditations:

"Human consciousness does not emerge at any depth except through struggling with our shadow. It is in facing our own contradictions that we grow. It is in the struggle with the shadow self, with failure, or with wounding that we break into higher levels of consciousness."

After the workshop, I committed to doing spiritual direction, for it seemed to be an invitation of Spirit that was helping me to grow.

I began to take my writing and my inner work to a new level, spending time with my grief and journaling it as often as time allowed. It has been an amazing journey of remembrance, self-forgiveness, and healing. I believe my Higher Power set the whole thing up, bringing an exquisite teacher and writer who led me, to a significant degree, to where I am today.

Meditations

"To live with a sense of balance, creativity, and integrity, so much depends on how and what we choose."
~ *John O'Donohue, Eternal Echoes*

"As we move through the work of healing, our deeper dignity, identity and purpose begin to shine through the shattering."
~ *Brie Stoner, Oneing: An Alternative Orthodoxy*

"Rather than giving into confusion and despair during times of questioning, I can welcome the disparities, the confusion, and even the moments of despair by embracing them as part of one reality – and trusting that everything is revealed in its time."
~ *Jo-Ellen A. Darling*

Questions for Journaling

1. Journal about an experience of grief that changed your life. Besides the sadness and difficulties, do not forget to include the good that may have come from the experience.

2. In reviewing your journal entry from step 1, find your own words that touch you deeply. It may be a phrase, a sentence or two, or a paragraph. Rewrite it in the form of a poem. Print it out and hang it where you live or work to remind you of the message from deep within that you want to remember.

3. Are you grieving now? Can you express this in some other kind of creative work besides writing? Perhaps something that requires being more hands-on – such as sewing, drawing, gardening, photography, or pottery?

4. What other creative things do you *enjoy* doing? Try doing one of them during a time of grief.

5. When you are grieving, do you allow yourself to cry? Some call it "the gift of tears." Tears wash our souls. They are a release for our sadness. Tears are a way to mourn.

Exercises

Note: After doing these exercises, journal your "take-aways" from the experience of doing them, and/or the impact of what you created, learned, etc.

1. Read a novel or nonfiction book that tells a story you think would interest you, such as an autobiography about someone's journey through grief.

2. Make a collage using magazine pictures, photos, and memorabilia you collected on a trip, etc.

3. Draw or paint your grief on posterboard.

4. Take a class in pottery, jewelry making, cooking, floral arrangement, etc. Check out your local adult education classes for ideas.

5. Read books that help you with your creative life, such as one of my favorites: *The Artist's Way: A Spiritual Path to Higher Creativity* by Julia Cameron. There are several book lists online about creativity, such as this one:

    https://www.lifehack.org/articles/productivity/top-25-books-unleash-your-creative-potential.html

6. Have a date night (or "day" date) with yourself. Eat out. Go to a museum. Attend a performance or visit a historical place that represents one of your favorite eras, such as the Colonial Era, the Big Band Era, the 1960s, etc.

Nurturing Our Creativity in Nature

Spending time in nature is essential for anyone following a spiritual path. All of us can experience healing when outdoors, particularly when we are intentional about it. This can be in the form of walking in a favorite local park, taking a scenic drive in the countryside, or an afternoon hike in the mountains. It can be a day of sitting on a seashore and connecting with the wildlife, forest bathing in the woods, rock climbing in the desert, or sailing, paddling, or boating on a lake. Sometimes we will want even longer periods of outdoor respite: camping in the state or national parks, hiking the Appalachian Trail, or traveling overseas to walk the Camino de Santiago in Spain.

If we are not able to participate in nature because of physical limitations, or we just aren't into nature per se, there are other avenues that can lend themselves to an experience of nature that we might not expect. We can ask to be taken outside or at least near a window where we can enjoy the trees or birds through a window.

Sitting outdoors with some time to spare, whether at home or on a weekend retreat, or in a quiet corner of that local park during a lunch hour, can bring us deeply in touch with the healing spirit of nature. As we tune into the quiet and indulge our senses in the visual, auditory, and sensual warmth of the sun and breezes on our skin, we are invited to let go of our doing and experience our being in a way we cannot when we are busy working, doing errands, taking care of our families, being social, and enjoying our hobbies.

These times of silence and solitude provide a way for us to connect with all living things, to our own selves, and to the God or spiritual values of our understanding. Connecting spiritually to all created things, we naturally begin to know that we are essential beings and indeed part of the grand scheme of the natural world. In Ken Burns' PBS Special, *The National Parks,* former Park Service Director George Hartzog uttered these words in the final episode of the series:

> *"When you stand silently in the presence of the great sequoias [trees], you can't help but recognize that you are a part of something that is way beyond whatever you envisioned that this world might be. You can't stand there all alone without understanding that there's a power in the world that is far greater than anything you've ever experienced… and that you're connected to that power, just as that sequoia is connected to that power… it permeates all of us. And when you understand that, it improves your relationship with your fellow man because you realize that he has the same capacity, he has the same access … he is your brother."*

Visiting Favorite Landscapes

As I walked one morning on a park trail near the Florida Everglades, I was reintroduced to the resurrection palm described on a placard near a huge live oak, one of my favorite southern trees. The resurrection palm is a vine that grows on the long-reaching limbs of the live oak. During the dry season and periods when there isn't much rain, the vine's tiny leaves become brown and look as though the plant has died. But it has not. It is simply in a dormant state. When it rains, the vine bursts into green once again – thus its name.

Spending time in nature provides many metaphors and similes which can inform each of our lives. The resurrection palm provides a paradox: it shows me that although life can languish onward without much nourishment and still survive, it will not thrive. Yet even these times of dormancy are necessary for my growth.

The seasons of my inner landscape may or may not cycle simultaneously with the natural seasons, but I find going inward in the midst of winter to be most powerful. The cold fresh air, snow, brightness of the stars, and the untamable wind provide a natural inclination to escape the harsh climate and, at times, fuels an unrelenting desire to find warm weather. But once I decide that going inward to the home fires in my own soul is warmth enough, winter truly becomes a womb that facilitates numerous subtle awakenings. The paradox of a deep spiritual time of birth occurring in the dead of winter also coincides with the Christian season of Lent – a time of fasting and prayer – which I also find soul-nourishing.

Imbolc, also known as (Saint) Brigid's Day, is a Gaelic traditional festival starting on Feb. 1, marking the beginning of spring according to the Ancient Celtic world. In early January one year, I planted an amaryllis bulb in a pot at the south-facing window of my dining room. An expectancy grew inside of me as I watched the stalk begin to grow immediately after being potted in a small amount of peat moss. By the time Imbolc arrived, large, beautiful red buds were sprouting and then bursting into gorgeous trumpets as my soul literally leapt with joy.

Participating in this ancient feast day allows one's imagination and intuition to shift and capture the nuanced and more subtle stages of spring happening in the throes of winter. These subtle changes might be a few warmer days, crocuses in the garden, or finding flocks of snow geese in a nearby farmer's field as they migrate north. As these subtle signs of spring begin to emerge and winter also begins to recede, it is time to enter into a new season of change, namely one that allows us to receive the wild beauty of new life emerging after a long period of dormancy.

Nature is like a well in this sense: it can provide endless nourishment, no matter the meteorological season or the season of our life. Our days are precious and the time we have to live them is often taken for granted. Drawing the necessary water from our chosen wells – even during periods of dormancy – can help us truly live with purpose and generativity.

As mentioned earlier in this chapter, there are other ways to indulge in the outdoors if we are not the hiking type, or if we do not consider ourselves lovers of nature. Birdwatching is one way to indulge in the outdoors. Picnics – alone with a book and journal – can often ease our soul and help us find our way. Nature is generative by its own nature – it can teach us so much beyond what is literally seen with the eyes. Visiting our favorite landscapes in each of the four seasons is another way to synch the cycles of the natural world to our own lives. This deepens a metaphorical awareness that our lives belong and are intrinsic to the principles of the Universe: our birth, continuous change, the full and fallow seasons of our lives, and our eventual dying and return to the earth … followed by the invisible, mystical realm beyond death.

I frequently walk in a favorite park that was created by an endowment left by a local woman and her family. Many groups of trees are placed beautifully along the walking trails of this park. I love to see them in all the seasons: bare, yet stately in winter; an abundance of flowering and pastel beauty in spring; lush greens in summer as each species bears the contours of its limbs and the unique shape of its leaves; and the sometimes softer, sometimes exploding colors in autumn.

On a fall day in 2018, I recorded thousands of Canadian geese flying directly over Louise W. Moore County Park with my cell phone. Scores of Canadian geese, in their huge and sometimes wandering formations, continued overhead for more than an hour. I had never witnessed such a gathering of geese migrating at one time. I captured the video a few weeks before my father died, and I viewed it often.

After his death, I felt that a message had been revealed to me: on the sad day we lost him, perhaps he had actually joined the thousands of souls who leave the earth every single day. The images of the geese overhead lifted my spirits to know that he too, had entered into the natural cycle of a different way of being. I did not know specifically where the geese were headed that day, nor did I know where in the universe my father had gone, or where his soul had landed, or where heaven was. Yet, I trusted deeply that something larger than the human mind and human spirit had taken him to a resting place for his soul, a place where he would embark on yet another kind of journey, a place that I would also experience someday, and perhaps where I would see him again.

Journaling Reflections from Nature

For some, a faith or connection to a higher power already possessed will be widened and deepened while we're in nature. For others, the life force pulsing through nature itself will provide the healing of our minds and hearts, engender balance in our bodies, and spawn hope for the future. Nature may therefore provide us with clues to our own life by reflecting images and metaphors that reveal universal truths that help us to integrate our own experiences of life, and our relationship to all living things. These experiences, great and small, can be tremendous sources of inspiration for creativity and journaling.

Early in my contemplative writing practice, I visited another local park and recorded my thoughts soon after watching a group of geese walking the precipice above the dam, which resulted in this reflection:

The Monocacy Geese

"Four Canadian geese stand at the helm of a waterfall in Monocacy Park where I often go to be, to pray, and to reflect. I am sitting on their level in a stone pavilion, off to the side. The senior goose walks along the slanted, slippery grade to the edge of the falls, about 12 feet high. She announces her intention in loud bouts of honking and easily flies over the falls and into the white frothing stream below. Soon after, two of her sister geese follow … but a third holds back.

This lone lady bird walks tentatively along the slanted upper precipice, as if not sure she should follow her sisters. Looking around, she eventually begins to honk, anxiety and courage like two strong wings rising inside of her. Upon reaching the waterfall's edge, she steps back. In the next moment she moves again to its border and stretches out her long neck, yet only to pull back again. I watch her for four or five more minutes with amazement. By now the other three geese are downstream and out of sight.

I continue to watch as she struggles to let go. Several times she moves back and forth along the slippery concrete slab and gushing water. Then, as my own mind drifts quietly, she spreads her wings and sails downward over the falls, landing in the rapids, bobbing downstream between a few boulders, eventually out of sight.

I wondered: Where will the stream take her?"

At the time I wrote "*The Monocacy Geese,*" I was in a period of some tension as I sought to find new direction in my life. There were many choices before me: a chance to be a board member of a school I dearly loved; enrolling in a certificate program at the local seminary to continue the path of deepening my relationship with a higher power; finding new ways to serve others; and discovering a committed writing path where I might offer my gifts in an entirely new direction.

In retrospect, rereading the *Monocacy Geese* allegory reveals something new. As I watched the ambivalent goose finally summon the courage to fly over the dam – as I hoped she would eventually – I now see that I eventually gave myself permission to follow the guidance that was coming to me regarding my own writing. Working on a book project mentioned earlier, I was able to publish several of my poems and reflections and to initiate a community format for others to do the same. This later inspired me to facilitate writing retreats and workshops locally, which deepened my own creative and spiritual process, and gave others an opportunity to write for their own spiritual growth.

Fanning the Creative Spark

While the true self embodies the creative spark, the well of creativity inside us sustains it. The more we free ourselves to use our creative energy, the more we realize this inner fire or flame is truly inextinguishable. We are all born with it and it is our responsibility to find it and fan it. In David Whyte's *The Heart Aroused: Poetry and the Preservation of the Soul in Corporate America*, he shares a poem titled "Out on the Ocean," written after a harrowing experience while kayaking in a storm. He says the last lines of his poem "came as a shock":

Always this energy smolders inside,
when it remains unlit,
the body fills with dense smoke.

In the same book, he reflects on those lines:

"We cannot neglect our interior fire without damaging ourselves in the process. A certain vitality smolders inside us irrespective of whether it has an outlet or not. When it remains unlit the body fills with dense smoke. I think we all live with the hope that we can put off our creative imperatives until a later time and not be any the worse for it. But refusing to give room to the fire, our bodies fill with an acrid smoke, as if we had covered the flame and starved it of oxygen. The interior of the body becomes numbed and choked with particulate matter. The toxic components of the smoke are resentment, blame, complaint, self-justification, and martyrdom."

Reflecting on Whyte's words, I have found journaling as one of the means to continue fanning the fire of my creativity. Journal writing is a creative *and* spiritual process. As I write about my life experiences without editing them, the richness of life reveals itself: sometimes I celebrate the joys of the high ground – things done well and the serendipity and rejoicing that is often present – while at other times I confess the unpleasant yet deeply-felt honesty from life's valleys and trenches. Whyte's comments suggest that even a terrifying experience can feed the creative urge and stave off the negative traits of ego from creeping back into our lives. The initially unpleasant reality of our need to change and grow may shore up a humility and strength that can engage our compassion for self and others. The simple joys and high points will give us energy and courage to believe in our creative work and in ourselves.

Finding our creative outlets is important. Journaling our own lives can inspire us to discover those outlets as we dive deep to find the truest expressions of our unique joys and struggles. When we are intentional about finding the creative pursuits in our lives, doors and windows may open, opportunities and people may show up, and the process of discerning our lives can lead us to more alignment with our deepest desires and perhaps a budding trust in a Loving Force that is guiding us.

Meditations

"Imagine what you consider beautiful and see if you can include death and decay. Autumn is the ultimate witness to the beauty found in death. Leaves explode with vibrant color just before their great release back to the earth."

~ *Christine Valters Paintner, The Artist's Rule*

"The challenge of winter is how to go within without feeling locked in. Winter has much to teach us about the inner journey. It suggests

a time of resting and deepening, a time to gather the resources needed in other seasons. Winter has a lovely way of calling us home to what is essential."
~ *Joyce Rupp & Macrina Wiederkehr, The Circle of Life*

"It is no surprise that in our loss of connection with Nature, we have forgotten how to pray. We even believe that we do not need to pray."
~ *John O'Donohue, Eternal Echoes*

Questions for Journaling

1. Which one of the above quotations attracts you? Journal a response to it as to how it speaks to your own life.

2. Explore how or why you do or do not pray. Is it possible that you do pray, but you may not have thought of it that way?

3. What is blocking you or holding you back from having an ongoing creative experience? When you think about allowing a creative process into your life, which thoughts and feelings emerge? Be honest.

4. Is there a creative pursuit you have been putting off – for good or no reason? Journal a plan that lets you begin the process of simply honoring *your desire* for creativity. Include notes on your calendar to make time to nurture this desire within you.

5. Are you an introvert or extrovert? Either way, do you give yourself space regarding difficult or troublesome issues that arise from day to day, week to week? Can nature be a source of peace for you, and can spending time in nature – whether going for a run, walking, fishing, birdwatching, kayaking, or reading at a picnic table – be your way of praying?

6. When you think about death and dying, what are your fears? Explore them by asking them questions, such as: "Fear, why are you afraid to die?" Journal your responses.

7. After reading the reflection of the *Monocacy Geese* earlier, "is it possible to allow anxiety to simply exist, without fighting or denying it, so it will partner with courage and help you fly?"

8. Can you relate to the last lines of David Whyte's poem? Is there a terrifying or exhilarating experience in your own life that gave you "shocking wisdom?" What was it? Try writing a poem about your experience.

Out on the Ocean

In these waves
I am caught on shoulders
lifting the sky,

each crest
breaks sharply
and suddenly rises,

in each steep wall
my arms work in the strong movement
of other arms,

the immense energy
each wave throws up with hand outstretched
grabs the paddle,

the blades flash
lifting veils of spray as the bow rears
terrified, then falls.

With five miles to go
of open ocean
the eyes pierce the horizon

the kayak pulls round
like a pony held by unseen reins
shying out of the ocean
and the spark behind fear,
recognized as life,
leaps into flame.

Always this energy smoulders inside,
when it remains unlit,
the body fills with dense smoke.

By David Whyte

Exercises

1. If you are not inclined to spend time alone outdoors or in silence, perhaps watch a sunrise or sunset from your home or from another place where these can be experienced (at the beach, in a parked car somewhere with a beautiful view, etc.).

2. Write about this experience. How did you feel? What did you think about? Did it bring peace or turmoil? Can you see how you are part of nature, that you are a part of a whole that encompasses your own life? Which part of this experience can you make more permanent in your way of seeing and being in your own life?

3. Can you bring something from nature into your home? Try planting an amaryllis bulb in an indoor pot in winter. Find a chrysalis in your yard or a nearby park in autumn, and wait for

the butterfly to emerge in spring. Note in your journal what you see happening in these tiny windows into nature. How does the process of a plant growing or a butterfly emerging connect you to your own sense of self and life?

4. If you spend time in nature this week, pay attention to how nature is revealing something important to you about your own life. Then journal about it.

Meditating on Our Journal Entries

There may be many reasons for journaling. One is to have a ritual that provides us with grounding and stability. Another is to create a place to confide our thoughts and feelings, our hopes and joys, our struggles, fears, and disappointments. Maybe we journal to have a time to dream, confess without judgment, and contemplate all things. Yet another aspect of journaling is to show us our growth and the lessons we're learning in any number of these areas in our lives.

Discovering the seeds of promise and hope in our lives is one of the great treasures of keeping a journal. Reviewing our journals regularly keeps us connected to our purpose and spiritual growth. It reminds us how we have made progress by showing our responses to what was important to us not so long ago. Like a river, life continues to flow sometimes quickly, bringing new happenings and experiences each day. We can easily forget the significance of our previous experiences, so we read our journal entries from time-to-time.

As we're faithful to our journals over days, weeks, months and years, our journals will reveal a more sustaining path. Sometimes, reading entire sections or an entire journal containing several months of our lives will be like watching a beautiful film about the person that we were and are, in all our deeply human and spiritual ways. We can also go back to a special time when we experienced an abundance of love, or an important lesson was given. We will be surprised by our growth: the darkness we made it through; the pain that we felt, expressed, and left behind; and the love that we found in unexpected places. Savoring these experiences and the insights we've gleaned from them builds a deepened faith in the meaningful journey of our life.

In the early years of our practice, journaling provides touchstones[5] that help us remember our growth and the resulting maturity. Remembering them helps us through difficult relationships and experiences as we continue to work through the past and present, seeking to discover who we truly are. The first half of our life is the time we forge an identity through work, discover our hobbies and interests, and find love in our lives. It is a time of developing the healthy ego, focusing on our talents, strengthening our positive personality traits, and finding time to do the things we love to do. Or, we may experience this cycle in the second half of our life if we missed these things in our earlier years.

As the second half of life approaches, we may begin to feel our unresolved grief. Perhaps we gave up on our dreams early on, out of necessity or choice. We may need to grieve the resulting losses we have been holding under wraps. We might begin to see, with clarity, the pervasiveness of the false self or "overcompensating self" that we thought was who we were. Now, we may want to go beyond even the positive qualities of our healthy ego – the part of us that excelled and made good choices. We may want to thank these parts of ourselves for a job well done as we outgrow and relax or release some of the roles we have done faithfully – such as parenting, managing others, or devoting ourselves to a job or career. These roles have impacted us greatly, forming our character, developing our gifts, and for many, preparing our readiness for a new life. One of the sure signs of our entry into the second half of life is the evidence of *new longings* we have in our hearts for something more, something deeper – the longing for a new beginning.

---

5 See Chapter 1 for more on anchors and touchstones.

As we make better and better decisions throughout every stage, we'll be led inevitably to the treasure of our true self. This awareness can make room for renewed experiences of joy, authenticity, and inner knowing. As we leave our fears behind and begin to face aging and our mortality, living from the true self helps us better understand the benefits of surrendering to these inevitable thresholds that claim us all.

During the pandemic, I was preparing to move. I decided to purge my earlier journals and keep only those of the last dozen years. Before I released them, I decided I would read through one of the journals dating back to the early 1990s. As I began to read, I could not put it down until I finished reading the entire journal – about a three-month period during my early sobriety – a difficult time. I saw how much I struggled to find peace and to value myself. I also saw how the Spirit met my need in so many ways. I came away with sadness, the kind you have when watching someone in a movie who is trying hard in life to change, and to find meaning and hope. Yet I also felt genuine compassion toward the young woman who took on that struggle at the age of 31. It was not an easy task. But in the years that followed, I made new friends and had many joyful experiences. Meeting my husband Mike – also on a spiritual path – was a dream come true. Even though I continued to make many mistakes right up to the present, continuing my spiritual journey through the practice of journaling has never failed to shed light and motivate me to keep moving forward in my life. Gratefully, my life has been enriched.

Meditations

"Sadly, many of us…. feel guilty expressing raw feelings such as sadness and anger. The problem is that when we deny our pain, losses, and feelings year after year, we transform slowly into empty shells with smiley faces painted on them. But when we begin to allow ourselves to feel a wider range of emotions (including sadness, depression, fear and anger), a profound change takes place in our relationship with God."

~ Peter Scazzero, Emotionally Healthy Spirituality Day by Day

"I promise you that the discovery of your True Self will feel like a thousand pounds of weight have fallen from your back. You will no longer have to build, protect, or promote any idealized self image. Living in the True Self is quite simply a much happier existence, even though we never live there a full twenty-four hours a day. But you henceforth have it as a place to always go back to. You have finally discovered the alternative to your False Self."

~ Richard Rohr, Immortal Diamond

"Spiritual transformation requires time in the same way that physical gestation does. We do not grow ourselves in a day any more than a child in the womb develops in less than an allotted period of maturation."

~ Joyce Rupp, Open the Door

Questions for Journaling

1. Go back and read a section of your journal in the recent past, or a year ago, or around some important, painful, or memorable time that you feel drawn to revisit.

   a. What are the dominant feelings or thoughts that you came away with?

   b. Did you have self-compassion as you read through your pages? Journal your thoughts about this.

   c. Did you have compassion for others, or see them in a different light? How?

2. Did you recognize a higher power, grace, or another spiritual energy at work in your life *as you were reading*? Describe this in your current journal:

   a. How does this spiritual energy make you feel now?

   b. Are you surprised, or have you known this for a while – or all along?

   c. How has your interaction with the divine changed since then? Are you more or less trusting? Even so, is your desire now to connect with the Spirit *more or less*?

Exercises

In David Whyte's poem, "*Self Portrait*," he uses the phrase "I want to know" over and over again to ask the reader some tough questions about whether certain things matter to them as much as they matter to him. In reading the poem, one cannot help but ponder these important questions.

Use Whyte's phrase as a writing prompt to draw out your own thoughts. Repeat the line over and over for each idea or thought that comes to mind. If you put a timer on this exercise, it may help you avoid the temptation to edit your responses. Pay attention to the voice coming through that is authentic and willing to reveal the things which you may not be consciously aware, and that really do matter to you.

Journaling Our Responses to the Books We Read

I love nonfiction books. After getting a college degree in English Literature, I soon became more interested in philosophy, self-help, religion, and spirituality. Although great writers such as Ernest Hemingway, Jane Austin, Fyodor Dostoevsky, William Shakespeare, Victor Hugo, and Flannery O'Connor certainly shaped my worldview and impacted my life in ways I probably am still not even aware, nonfiction has long held my interest and deeply influenced my overall life direction and spiritual formation. The point is, I found subjects that awakened my passion and that I intrinsically knew I needed to absorb for the changes and growth I yearned for in my life.

Besides biography, autobiography, and memoir, I am mostly drawn to writers – both religious and nonreligious, but all who are writing about the *spiritual* – especially those who have found a contemplative approach to life. Writers and poets such as Thich Nat Hahn, Kabir Helminski, Parker Palmer, Christine Valters Paintner, and Mary Oliver, among many others, are completely countercultural. While offering their reflections mostly around the loss of soul in a culture that more often ignores it, they offer little or no judgment about the culture we live in. Instead, these writers offer hope and encouragement to their readers to find an authentic spiritual path, which also means finding our authentic or true self. The writers just mentioned focus on peace, love, creativity, imagination, compassion and understanding based on the universal spiritual truths of their traditions (Buddhism, Sufism, Quakerism, and Contemplative Christianity). Each has not only found a spiritual path through the wilderness of contemporary culture, they have come to embrace the world, themselves, and their gifts in a way that has made them beacons of light to many. Just as many who are engaged in our broken politics have found a way to transcend the political labels of liberal and conservative, many spiritual seekers are finding paths that transcend theology and doctrine in favor of the necessary ways one can live newly discovered, life-giving spiritual truths in their daily lives. These contemporary authors have moved from a more traditional focus on religious belief and tradition to a spirituality that emphasizes daily practices which help us live from our most authentic self – or as some would say – our God-given self.

We can benefit tremendously from mentors and sojourners who are hungry and dedicated to new ways of thinking and being, those who have found a similar spiritual freedom that we are seeking for ourselves. Many who have been spiritually formed by theology and doctrine are now finding new freedom and growth in their faith that theology and doctrine have been unable to communicate and inspire over centuries of repetition – partly because of their tradition's *institutional resistance to change.*

I've come to understand in recent years how the divine often brings to light spiritual and/or religious truths that the churches are either fighting against (such as LGBTQ rights) or ignoring from their own complicity (such as institutional racism). One such example is the Black Lives Matter movement that reached a pinnacle during the Covid-19 pandemic in 2020. Movements like this one – comprised of individuals who study history, learn how to effect change, and then act with courage for the common good – often raise attention to the issues of which many of us are either willfully blind or passively asleep. Joblessness, poverty, systemic oppression, and the continued discrimination of persons who are black and brown, are just some of the problems which all of us share responsibility for, in one way or another. Although these are worthy topics to write about (you will hopefully be including your own responses to them in your journal), my desire for this book has been to focus on the spirituality of our journaling and the spirituality of whatever it is we choose to do with our time and energy. This obviously can include our activism in the important issues of our time.

"The unexamined life is not worth living," Socrates declared in the 3rd century, B.C. When we do the work of reflection and journaling and engage in books that open new windows into the soul, we are more likely to respond from a place of authenticity. The result is that we nurture that unique voice that is in every single one of us.

Since I was a young woman, I've been led to many writings that have inspired me to become spiritually and emotionally healthier in my life. Some of these books were about love, and some of them pointed to love. Many were not religious, yet in retrospect, spoke more authentically about love than some religious texts I've read over the years. It was this strain of love that I saw in the "spiritual writings" of the self-help movement that led me to seek my Higher Power, even among those voices that were not following the God of my tradition. Each one of us is endowed with a compass for truth, or a true north. But because I believe my Higher Power speaks through many people, I believe we often need the companionship of healthy spiritual guides to find and develop our spiritual path. A spiritual path can be journaling our life experiences while at the same time reading the amazing journeys taken by others – and seeing the divine power in the midst of it all.

The essential quality of creativity needed for journaling as a spiritual path should not be downplayed. At times, we will be resistant, blocked, or procrastinate doing the creative work we are invited, or were once longing, to do. In these moments, we can write about the procrastination or what is hindering our commitment to explore the creative process. We each need to find a way to acknowledge our own creativity – not with competition and comparing – but with inspiration and love as the fuel that guides us to our own stars. We don't have to be a writer or an artist if we are passionate about running a business or helping others directly. What we're aiming to do is to support our journaling and our spiritual awareness by engaging our creativity. Ultimately, we want to find a creative process that moves us to good, better, break-through, transcendence and for some – the Divine. This is an existential purpose we can discover and live by, with intention and joy.

Meditating and Journaling on Quotations that Inspire Us

"Our writing practice might garner some wisdom from this ancient way of wandering. What if we tried to direct things less and yield more to the flow of the current of creativity at work in our lives? What if we became less concerned with product and more so with process?"
~ Christine Valters Paintner, Writing as a Spiritual Practice

"Self-emptying is not for the sake of an abiding emptiness, but for the sake of what the emptying *creates*."
~ Brie Stoner, Oneing: An Alternative Orthodoxy

"The temptation of our day is to equate 'love' and 'conformity' – passive subservience to the mass-mind or to the organization."
~ Thomas Merton, New Seeds of Contemplation

Questions for Journaling

1. Who are your go-to authors and favorite spiritual texts? What do these authors and their writings make of the creative spirit?

2. As you read a favorite author, add quotations to your journal that really hit home. Journal about the words or phrases that ring true. What are they inspiring in you?

3. As you experience your own conscious growth, what is the difference between analysis and spiritual reflection? Are both required?

4. What else is required to prevent you from living constantly "in your head?"

5. How do spiritual and creative pursuits fit into your life?

    a. If you are heavy on the creative side, how can you weave one spiritual practice into your life that can nurture your creativity in a new way?

    b. If you are heavy on the spiritual side, how can you weave a creative pursuit into your life that can nurture your spirituality?

Blocks and Segues to the Creative Process – Exercise

1. On a large blank landscape-oriented page, draw a stick figure of yourself and several different sized blocks or rectangles around you until the stick figure is surrounded. Name the thoughts, questions or images that may be blocking you from your commitment to give yourself time for creative expression. If you run out of blocks, create more until you exhaust all the possibilities. (See the example on the next page.)

2. Create another shape, such as a circle or a cloud, and place them outside of the blocks. In each one, list the *creative desires* of your heart, *activities* that might be invitations to the creative process, or *things that nurture* your creativity. The range of possibilities is endless – it does not need to be something to do with writing. In fact, do not limit the creative ideas on your list to the creative arts.

3. For example, if the desire is to remodel or rearrange a room in your dwelling place, list that. Other ideas could include making bread, cooking a new meal, or starting a new knitting,

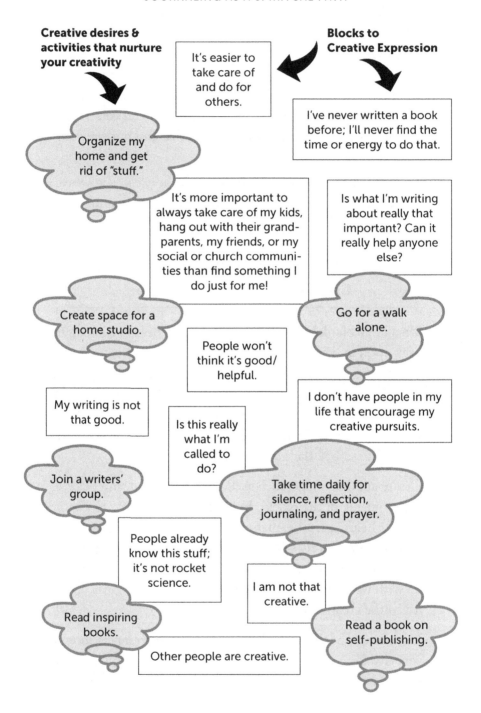

sewing or woodworking project; creating a new organization that helps people, building a tree house for your kids, taking an early morning walk at least once a week, or setting aside a day a month for quiet. It could also include responding creatively, such as sending someone a handwritten note instead of a text or an email. Whatever it is, add it to one of the clouds. Create as many shapes as are required to hold all the possibilities you come up with.

4. Review this for several days. Highlight the things you wrote that touch you in some way, even if you do not understand why. Meditate on these daily, write your internal responses in your journal, and select one or two shapes that contain those ideas that strongly speak to you now.

5. What changes are needed for you to integrate one or more of these desires for creative expression in your life?

Exercises for Creativity

1. Find something significant in your journal that you've totally forgotten about. Describe it and write about this discovery and what it means to you now.

2. Review the past seven days of your journal. Name anything that feels like a moment, process, or experience of creativity. It could have been a different way of responding to something, or something you did, like a hobby, preparing meals, or organizing your surroundings. What is it exactly that made it feel creative?

3. Create a special journal for the books you read, classes or workshops that you take for nourishing your creative or spiritual life, or vacations or pilgrimages that you go on. Use symbols, drawings, words or photographs; or do a collage of these experiences.

4. If you spend time in nature this week, pay attention to how nature may reveal something important to you about your own life. Journal about it.

5. What does your resistance to a creative commitment look like? Take about 5 minutes to think about or find an image of your resistance. Notice the first thing that comes to mind (or that you come across if searching for an image), no matter how silly it may seem. Write it down and journal about it and any other images that come to mind.

6. Read the two poems I offer below and on the next page.

    a. When you feel inspired, do you let it slip away and pass you by? Instead, jot down what made you feel inspired, even if you are not prepared to journal about it or act on that feeling now. Later, acknowledge what triggered it, and then knead it like clay into something that you might like to see happen in your life. It may be as simple as going to an arts and crafts store to look at picture frames or to get ideas for making your personal spaces more meaningful to you.

    b. Write a poem about the season you are in. Does it connect to your Higher Power or not? What spiritual qualities are you witnessing or experiencing directly? What is nature teaching you in this season?

A Poem and a Prayer

When the Dogwood Blooms

A living memory of my nuptials,
the rose-pink dogwood blooms –
as does the weeping cherry tree out back
and the forsythia along the fence –

my unexpected bridesmaids
waiting at the altar of love.

As I watch the Dogwood's poppy-pink
blossoms laugh through my morning window,
and the wind undergirds their beauty
against a gray sky waiting to rain,
I feel myself wanting more, so
I move to the sill for a fresher view
of my life in these rosy florets.

I savor moments like these –
to see my own life as frail and yet whole,
lasting only weeks in the Eternal frame,
living in pinkish splendor.

For days, I am busy or asleep
until again I behold these roseate beauties ...
Opened now like butterflies
they spread their wings,
lay bare their souls, ready to be no more
in this earthly form.

Then, one lonely day,
when I no longer look,
these tender blooms
drift quietly to the ground,
where they now sleep
in the rhododendron beds.

By Jo-Ellen A. Darling

Snow Prayer

Maybe God created the snowfall
to quiet our soul
to soften our mind
to show us what gentleness really means:
a surrender to what is right before us.

Maybe God created the snowfall
to blanket us in her love
to teach us to pray in the silence –
as do the trees, arms lifted high
in the glistening snowstorm:
trees deep in prayer.

Maybe God created the snowfall
to convey the inward seasons
to help us sit still, to watch in wonder
as the swirling, changing winds of life
bury our dreams in snowdrifts …
only to arrive again
in the melting snows of spring.

By Jo-Ellen A. Darling

CHAPTER 5

Journaling as a
Spiritual Practice

Spiritual Discernment

"To discern literally means to separate or sift out... This sifting
happens in a variety of ways — by understanding ourselves and how
we are wired, by being willing to look at decisions in light of a
broader picture, and by drawing on the wisdom of God,
however we name that power greater than ourselves."
~ DOUG WYSOCKEY-JOHNSON,
RELATIONSHIP PARADOXES: ENGAGING AND LETTING GO

The Free Dictionary's definition of discernment is "the act or process of exhibiting keen insight and judgment." The practice of spiritual discernment opens the way to continuous spiritual awakening. As we open ourselves to seeing from a wisdom perspective, we sit with the options before us. We may want to know how to proceed with a job or relationship. We may be contemplating important questions, such as the best course of action for our healthcare or other responsibilities. It may be that we want to know how to approach a neighbor, a family member, or our adult children for discussion about an issue we are having. We take into consideration the whole spectrum of our desires, values, and intentions, our personal needs, and the nudges we receive from Spirit. We do our homework and weigh the pros and cons. We reflect, pray, and meditate to receive the insight and wisdom we need, including how our decisions may impact other people. Some of us may have discussions with our sponsors, spiritual directors, therapists, spouses or a clearing committee to help us make our final decisions while we wait for clarity.

Spiritual discernment is a process which works best when in touch with not only ourselves, but also a spiritual or universal energy at work in our lives. We may have this energy operating in our life, but we may not call it a higher power yet. As we become more aware of our wholeness within a connection to this greater energy, we become more spiritually aware of the wisdom being revealed to us. This recognition brings forth a new dimension of "knowing" as we make the necessary decisions to make changes in our lives – both large and small – to live a life full of possibility beyond our current comprehension.

As human beings we each have a name, and that name represents our individuality. Though we are unique from all others, we still share our common humanity. Relationships begin with using our names and acknowledging each other's unique personhood. Likewise, there are many names we can use to identify a higher power in our lives. Some of these I have already used in this book. If you feel comfortable with this, I suggest you choose a name from the list in the Exercises below or some other term you have found that resonates with you. However-er, if it's not that important to you, or a name doesn't resonate with you now, you can wait for a name to come to *you*. If this is the case, then relish the waiting, as it might be the essential journey right now. When that name arrives, it will be a gift.

If you feel ready to choose a name for the divine now, it may be beneficial to use one which best fits where you are in your spiritual journey. For example, if you have been wounded by religion or by a punitive, unjust, overly strict or hypocritical image of God, you may wish to use a name that represents more of what you are seeking in the God of your understanding. It could be Love, Gentle Spirit, Inner Light, Transcendent One, Great Grandfather, Grandmother, or Inner Peace. Using a name that represents a spiritual quality – or the name of a person in your life who emanated that spiritual qual-ity – will help you to identify with it. This also has the benefit of acknowledging something or someone higher at work in your life without the harmful associations from the past.

As we name a higher power, it may become more personal. We may sense that we belong to a higher purpose than what we have previously experienced. We can begin to let go and share our burdens with a "benevolent other." We begin to trust that we are not alone.

Meditations

"For the Celtic monks, 'peregrinatio' [was] the call to wander for the love of God... This wandering was an invitation into letting go of our own agendas and discovering where God was leading... The impulse for the journey was always love."

~ *Christine Valters Paintner, The Soul of a Pilgrim*

" ... it [is] clear that the way you approach something (or someone) deeply affects everything that follows – it determines what you see. I saw that the heart's willingness to move with life, to allow circumstances and experiences to become the path, is a great variable.... I could see how many experiences and people I had missed... even when standing right before them for years."

~ *Paula D'Arcy, Waking Up to This Day*

"The human needs God as the garden needs spring."

~ *Kabir Helminski*

Questions for Journaling

1. Are you drawn to a name for the divine that embodies a spiritual quality that you are attracted to? Gently journal your thoughts and feelings about this. Try not to edit your thoughts. Keep writing until you are sure you are done.

2. Reread what you have written. As you read, highlight or underline the words and phrases that appear on your pages. Afterward, meditate on each highlighted word or phrase. What truth(s) stand out to you as you hold these ideas or concepts in meditation?

3. Read the Meditations above.

    a. Are your own agendas stopping you from experiencing growth in your life? Is love on your radar these days? If so – or not – how do you feel about where you are? What can you let go of?

    b. How do you approach others? Are you aware of the mystery of each person? Can you let go and "allow circumstances and experiences to become the path," as Paula D'Arcy suggests?

    c. What does Kabir Helminski's quote mean to you? Is it a burden, or does it suggest something else? Do you need to give "God" another name?

Exercises

1. In the days and weeks ahead, choose a name for your Higher
    Power. Or wait for a name to come to you, if none of these
    resonate.

Beloved	Creator God
Divine Presence	Brahma
Love	Great Spirit
Living Presence	Creator of Light
Source of All Being	God Within
Holy One/Holy Spirit	Universe
Allah	Transcendent One
The Universe	Inner Presence/Inner Teacher
Cosmic Christ	True Parent
God/Goddess	Wisdom
Living God	Sophia
Inner Light	Inner Peace
Unfailing Love	Amma/Abba
Light and Truth	(Great) Grandfather
Lord	(Great) Grandmother
Supreme Being	Mystical One
Higher Power	Courageous One
Mother Nature	Mother/Father
Spirit	Friend
Jesus	Gentle Spirit
Mohammed	Papa
Buddha	

2. You may want to write the chosen name on a sticky note and
    place it in one or two places where you live – a bathroom or
    bedroom mirror, a door that leads inside or outside, or in your
    car. If you are into artmaking, you can paint, color or create

something more beautiful to hang in your home that displays the chosen name.

3. With a small pad and pen, take a walk outside and notice anything that reminds you of what the divine may look or feel like to you. Don't discount anything because it may seem silly. For example, if you are attracted to the small paw prints of a raccoon in the path, let yourself be with that visually, or take a picture to gaze at later. How does this relate to your Higher Power?

4. Enjoy the process of discovering what is true for you, and journal the treasures that you are finding. Do the qualities of what you discover also reflect those of your Higher Power? If so, how?

Embracing Our Wholeness

"When we choose to traverse the invisible boundary of the known self and enter the unknown, we are saying: Yes, I want to grow, to become wiser, to be strengthened, to be less burdened by what weighs me down and keeps me from being my authentic self. I am willing to pay the price for this growth."

~ JOYCE RUPP, OPEN THE DOOR

Discovering an authentic spirituality is our birthright, along with many other aspects of our psycho-spiritual development, such as our creativity, our ability to think and reason, and to truly discover love, work, and our purpose in this life. If we remain unaware of these rich possibilities, we can, understandably, fall into hopelessness, cynicism, or become deeply stuck. Many of us have not yet been able to fully experience the joy of living – one of the hallmarks of finding a spiritual path. It is also difficult to endure the hard lessons we must struggle through that build our resilience if we are making choices simply aimed to please others or to preserve the status quo. We cannot experience our wholeness when we live this way. We must go deeper.

Even amidst the chaos and many voices clamoring for our attention in this world, each of us has an opportunity to discover our own spiritual path. Barriers to a spiritual path may include resistance to a deeper awareness of the spiritual because we are too busy. We may be so turned off by religion or spiritual subjects that we miss out on our own potential for spiritual experiences. Perhaps we are avoiding the pain of our past because it is just too big to deal with. It is easier – at least for a while – to live our lives on the surface, to go along with the crowd, the culture, or perhaps even the good communities we're part of. Yet we may not want to rock the boat, or dare to be too different. But when we neglect our spiritual self, parts of us remain in the dark, lacking the self-knowledge, meaning, and purpose that we need and want. Yet discovering these things holds a paradox: going deeper often requires descending into the darkness, the unknown terrain of our lives.

Finding our true self will help us to integrate all that we treasure and value in life. At the same time, we begin to let go of living by what we no longer value. This process begins to clarify the meaning and purpose of our lives and the particular pursuits we are called to do. Though not the same things, meaning, purpose and calling overlap and provide a spiritual framework for our lives.

Though we might have been led to believe that "real" spiritual paths are religious, one does not have to be religious to find a spiritual path. If we embrace the idea of living a more spiritual life, we may discover our deepest values – and our own goodness – to a large degree. Whether we follow, stay, or reject a particular faith tradition is not the point. Rather, a spiritual journey begins and continues by taking a first step toward knowing one's self, and another step in trusting something or someone larger at work in our life.

Since we are all connected, the possibilities of finding our essential spirituality can have an amazing impact on our lives. When we value life itself, we find the beauty in the world and in each other. We may experience a joyful openness as we begin to see our own and each other's gifts and what they have to offer the

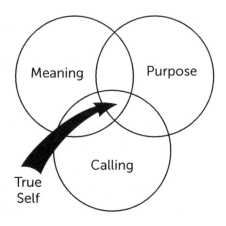

wider community. Guiding others to find the clues to their own beauty within is a high calling. When we ignore or dismiss a person's need for validation, comfort, or to express their struggle, we risk missed opportunities to show them compassion as they seek to find their way in the world. Likewise, when we give these things to ourselves, we may rise to our full potential and literally change the world.

Openness to Spiritual Growth is Essential

*"I've come to believe that the two greatest spiritual disciplines
are letting go and being open."*

~ LUANN SGRECCI O'CONNELL, SPIRITUAL DIRECTOR

Openness to spiritual growth requires a measure of humility – *realizing that we do not have all the answers.* This can be especially true even for those who have been on a spiritual path for a very long time. It is easy for us to begin to think we have something all figured out. We begin to really know this as we hit the walls of our own ego (false self), and experience the pain of our unwillingness to admit that we might be wrong or misled in our thinking. We can open ourselves to the possibility that we have much more to learn about ourselves, others, and the world. This openness can be extended to our views of science, politics, and intercultural and global experiences.

Many say that God's nature is reflected in the material world. Others believe we are embodied spirit, that all of creation is imprinted with the divine DNA by design. Some call it an energy; others call it panentheism. Life isn't just what you can see, smell, hear, taste or feel. Although our five senses are beautiful gifts, it is a higher power or higher consciousness that frees us from seeing at this limited level. A higher power points the way through our engagement with it. This intrinsic ability to connect with the Great Spirit has been given to everyone.

Each of us will grow at different rates. All spiritual paths will share certain qualities while, at the same time, reflect unique aspects of the journey we shall call our own. If we say yes – and yes and yes again – to the opportunity of spiritual growth, we are assured to grow throughout our lives. If we persevere in our search – for a power greater than ourselves, a wisdom deeper than our own, and a universal force of beauty and goodness beyond our current understanding – we'll be led to the experiences of deepened love, compassion, and a divine connection. I have found that when I'm open to receive my highest good, and recognize that good also in others and in the natural world, I am more deeply grounded in my spiritual path.

Discovering the spiritual underpinnings in our own life is essential to becoming transformed human beings. Finding the treasure within us – our goodness, our freedom, our responsible use of free will, our openness to others unlike ourselves or those we'd rather avoid, and our spiritual strength and capacity to grow and change and become all we are meant to be – this can sustain us to the end of our lives.

In my experience, Spirit delivers guidance if I am awake, attentive, open or intentionally seeking wisdom – even when I'm empty, depressed, and feeling resistant to change. And yet, as many of us now know, guidance often comes even without asking.

Someone asked me in 1986, "What is stopping you from having a friendship with God?" I was stunned – a *friendship* with God? It was the million-dollar question. My heart had trouble connecting with religion at the time, and my life was in shambles. But in hearing that question, I suddenly had hope. It seemed the question itself had cleared the path of any obstacle to the notion of living a meaningful life, and connecting with the deep goodness in this world. In truth, I longed to have meaning and purpose in my life, and it seemed it was offered then, so I accepted the invitation. I had no idea how it would turn out, but I picked up a pen and a pad of paper and began to journal – profusely. I also began to seek out others – by reading books and talking to those who were searching too. This friendship with Spirit continued by getting to know myself, and to form a friendship with myself. I didn't have to do anything but trust the Spirit's leading. I noticed how something came alive in me when this happened.

Before this shift occurred, I struggled with alcohol abuse, rejection, aimlessness, and a feeling of malaise that I couldn't shake. Even during this time of turmoil, my soul somehow knew that focusing on *things* like buying a nice car, owning a home, or going on an amazing vacation, would not satisfy my longing. Instead, my heart had broken open and received a new energy that was, until then, unavailable to me. In the moment of its arrival, this infused energy – this spiritual Presence – offered me its loving comfort and an invitation to a spiritual journey that would lead to an unimagined transformation of self.

Over the years, I had many dreams about this spiritual Presence that both revealed its nature and my connection to it. My most memorable dream is from the early 1990s. I was sailing alone on an enormous ship in the middle of the ocean, an image that would terrify most people. Yet, I was completely relaxed and without fear, enjoying the warmth of the sun and breeze on my skin. I soon became aware of a keen sense of being cared for by Someone beneath the deck. I also realized this Someone was steering the boat, that my life was totally and literally in someone else's hands. I could not see them from where I sat, but I knew in the deepest sense of the word, that they were there, holding me in love. My overall feeling in the dream was that "all was well." While processing the dream in my journal, I intuited its essential message: a deep trust had grown between us at an unconscious level. When I woke, I was more deeply conscious of this great gift of connection. Contact with a higher power had become personal. I sensed that God was not only present in my life, but significantly at that time, I was now in God's life. Receiving and waking to this deeply-felt dream was a treasure.

As I contemplate this dream today, I'm aware of another essential message that I would not have understood then, a meaning much more far-reaching in scope. But now, based on my years of prayer, meditation and the deepened layers of understanding and knowing – all fruits of tending to the spiritual life – the dream likely also represents my first significantly heartfelt connection to my true self. This person "beneath the deck" was, in essence, the authentic self who had existed in the unconscious all these years. The false self, who had lived "above the deck" in the world and always in control, was now an integrated whole – the person I was ultimately meant to become. The dream embodied this connection through my feelings of bliss, the experience of knowing this insight beyond the mind, and the intrinsic hope that was generated. To this day, discovering this treasure – of finding and connecting with my true self – accurately reflects an important idea spoken by a famous saint: "My deepest self is God."

Meditations

"Your False Self is your necessary warm-up act, the ego part of you that establishes your separate identity, especially in the first half of life. Basically it is your incomplete self trying to pass for your whole

self. We fall in love with the part so much that we deny the Whole."
~ *Richard Rohr, Immortal Diamond*

"A spiritual journey begins and continues by taking a first step toward knowing one's self, and another step in trusting something or someone larger at work in our life."
~ *Jo-Ellen A. Darling*

"Do we really expect to produce new life without pain? When does anything that is beautiful not require risk of failure, or the unknown?"
~ *Brie Stoner, Oneing: An Alternative Orthodoxy*

Exercises

1. Do you remember any nightdreams you have had in the past that may have pointed to something deeply spiritual in your life? If so, recall the dream and journal your thoughts, feelings, insights, etc. What wisdom could this dream of the past hold for you now?

2. Draw a map of your life that indicates significant experiences, beginning with your childhood up to the present.

3. Or, if you have already done a lot of work reflecting on your past, consider a more recent period of your life, such as the past 5 or 10 years, or even less time than that. The goal is to remember and name the experiences that are marking the way for you as you gain a sense of direction, or where you may be headed in your life.

    a. Use a large sheet of plain paper or cardboard. Draw a tree in the center of it and label it: Tree of Life. Then draw a door on the tree trunk.

    b. On the outer edge of the paper, draw a path that spirals eventually to the tree. At the beginning of the path, write

"My Birth" and the date. Name the significant events of your life, the good or positive events as well as the painful or negative ones. You can continue to think of your life over several days or weeks, or you may choose to do this in a single day or weekend.

c. When you think you are done with the map, respond to the questions for journaling below. As you go through the questions, you can add to your map the significant life experiences you initially missed or forgot.

Questions for Journaling

NOTE: The purpose of the following questions is not to begin living in the past. Rather, it is to see your journey from a place of wholeness. Let the observer in you – the objective one – see yourself with compassion as you have traversed the landscape of your life. If you are having trouble with this, it may help to see a trusted friend, therapist or other professional to work through difficult experiences and events.

1. Write a response to one or all of the Meditation quotes by the authors above and at the top of this chapter. You may want to give time in between your responses for each of these quotes, or do one a day to give space between your thoughts.

2. Go back and read your responses to one or more of the quotes. What are you learning about yourself? Finish this sentence stem and rewrite it several times until you exhaust all that comes to mind: "What I'm learning about myself is
    _____ "

3. Is humility difficult for you? Is the need to "always be right" a pattern? Is criticizing others a constant temptation? Write about a difficult encounter with someone. What are you learning about humility?

4. When you get up in the morning, light a candle and visualize the seed of wholeness within you. Draw it on your map or on another sheet of paper, if you'd like, and respond to these questions:

   a. Journal anything that comes to mind about this seed: what color or shape is it? Is the seed saying anything to you, or is it silent? Is there a word or phrase that comes to mind about the seed? Is there anything you want to say to this seed in response? Dialog with the seed using your *dominant* writing hand and your *nondominant hand*. See Chapter 1 for guidelines.

   b. You may want to find a seed in your yard, in a park, or where you walk. Plant it in a cup with soil to give you a living symbol that represents the seed in you. Watch it grow. From time to time, write what you notice about the life that is emerging. What else do you notice?

5. What "moments of choice" came to you in your life that, while looking back, were right for you?

   a What other choices were not right for you at the time, but turned out to be a critical link in the journey of your life?

   b. Can you see a choice that led to good in your life?

   c. Can you see any positive outcomes from a choice that initially had a negative impact on your life?

6. Who or what is truly life-giving to you?

   a. Something life-giving can be anything that lifts your spirits, brings you a sense of hope or joy, a sense of purpose, gratitude, deep contentment, or clarity about your true self or other aspect of your life. Journal as much as you can about the people, events, or things you identified.

7. Dialog with the shame or wounds in your life.

   a. Begin with your *dominant* hand to let the wound ask a question or make a comment.

   b. Then use your *nondominant* hand to respond to the words from the shame or wound. Dialog as long as there are responses to the comments or questions being asked.

8. Draw several geometric shapes on a landscape-oriented piece of paper; label them to represent the broken pieces of your life.

   a. These can be shame, anger, sadness, grief, alienation, loneliness, addiction, the past, etc.

   b. When finished naming them, draw a solid line across the page beneath these labels. Beneath the line, name the aspects of a growing wholeness in you (or its possibility). This aspect of your wholeness can be related to the broken pieces or not. Let your spirit enter into the possibility of new life coming from these difficult aspects of your history. Name the possibilities!

9. Look at the map of your spiritual journey as often as you'd like.

   a. What do you notice (or what stands out) about your life's progression up to now?

   b. Can you have compassion for yourself as you struggled through phases of your past where your choices were unwise?

   c. Are there connections along the path that you hadn't seen before?

10. Is there something you can do today to open the door at the Tree of Life (Exercise 3(a))?

   a. Is there some event or experience recently that hints to this? It could be simply reading this book and beginning to journal as a spiritual path for the first time, or it could be connecting with a therapist, friend, spiritual guide, prayer partner, spiritual group, or 12-step sponsor. Ask for wisdom and wait for an answer.

b. Revisit these questions until you sense they have given you all that you need to know for now.

Journaling as Meditation & Prayer

"Having a contemplative philosophy is perhaps particularly important for us today because we live in a culture which is not contemplative in its fundamental ethos. In the cultural environment in which we live, an emphasis on productivity and achievement is rarely accompanied by a corresponding emphasis on the wisdom of remaining grounded in the meaning and value of our lives prior to and beyond all that we produce and achieve."

~ JAMES FINLEY, THE CONTEMPLATIVE HEART

Although we can use journaling as a form of reflection in which we engage the mind, we can also take it a step further. Journaling is a form of meditation when we also involve our heart and our spiritual and creative capacities.

I practice two basic types of meditation. The first is to reflect on thoughts, words and ideas to a point where a higher truth becomes evident. This often happens after I read a passage from a meditation book or sacred text. I sit with the words or phrases and gently massage them with my responses in writing or I repeat them quietly, over and over. I pay attention to the words, phrases and feelings I have. The higher truth gained through this type of meditation can bring a deeply felt energy in the body – the result of powerful clarity or heightened awareness. Ultimately, a spark is ignited to take some action to bring something good forward in my life, or in the lives of others.

184

The second form of meditation is where I enter a deep silence and empty myself of all words and thoughts. I don't focus on having an awakening of heart or mind while practicing this type of meditation. Rather, I've trained my mind to make space for silence and to let go of random or obsessive thoughts – good, bad, and indifferent. The purpose of emptying the thoughts is to clear the mental pathways. Later in the day, something may come from that time of releasing my thoughts, so I turn to my journal to reflect on what is stirring within me. I typically do either one of these types of meditation in silence, individually, or in an online group. I use both of these forms of meditation interchangeably in any given day. I have come to value both practices as staples in maintaining my spiritual grounding.

Just as any person's practice of meditation can become stale, restless, and barren, so too can the practice of journaling. At times we may fall into patterns of being unfocused and feeling disconnected from ourselves for days. Our journaling can also fall into the self-centeredness of navel-gazing – paying too much attention and becoming overly attached to our superficial selves, being overconfident in seeing things our own way in relation to any person or issue, or our refusal to allow the light to enter into the conversation going on in our heads. When stuck in these patterns, it is possible to miss the new inspiration or the thing that is trying to get our attention – maybe it's wisdom or a challenge that we are avoiding.

If we have backslidden or relapsed on the spiritual path, we can return to self-care and nurturing our own life. Maybe we need to reengage with others through gatherings and fellowship, inspiring reading, and loving service to those in need. This will look different in everyone's life. We will need to reexamine our desires and hopes for using our gifts, whether we are in the first or second half of our lives. As discussed in Chapter 4, we can review our commitment to creativity, which can play a major role in stoking the fires within so that we are less prone to our souls drying up for long periods. Whatever we find, we don't give in to panic or become discouraged because even a prolonged period of dryness, disappointment, or wandering can be the beginning of renewal in our lives. At this juncture, when the ashes of our lives seem to outweigh the new growth that is trying to break through, it is wise to take a day for ourselves, to go to a quiet place just to be, and to ask ourselves the important questions.

Meditations

"There remains a deep longing in every person for self-discovery. No one can remain continually unmoved by the surprising things that rise to the surface of one's life."

~ *John O'Donohue, Eternal Echoes*

"We can only be freed by what lies ahead if we leave behind our baggage."

~ *Christine Valters Paintner, The Soul of a Pilgrim*

"Only when we accept our present condition can we set aside fear and discover the love and compassion that are our highest human endowments."

~ *Philip Simmons, Learning to Fall*

Questions for Journaling

1. Where are you now being called?

2. What or whom are you being called to release, and to what or whom are you being called to embrace?

3. Where in your mind and your heart, "and indeed your whole being" as Merton suggests in an earlier quote, will you thrive and do the most good at this time?

4. Spend some real time considering the questions above. Stay with the pain, joy, doubt, invitation, uncertainty, or confusion, and then find someone to share it with.

5. Journal your hopes and dreams often.

Exercises

1. Try 20-30 minutes of meditation in your home, in nature, or sitting on a bench in a favorite place outdoors. Approach it with an open mind to receive whatever impressions your Higher Power has for you. Journal your experience afterward.

2. Prayer can be many things, including speaking, writing, reading, painting, drawing, gardening, singing, or walking. How do you pray? If you are new to prayer, try one of these and notice your thoughts during the activity you choose. If you're experienced with prayer, what is your favorite way to pray? Why? Have you tried another way to pray lately?

3. Silence is also a form of prayer and meditation. It can either be focused on "emptying your thoughts," or allowing thoughts in response to a situation, a sacred reading, or a poem. Try these types of prayer, and journal afterward about your experience with them.

4. Check out the following spiritual practices this week, and choose one that attracts you. Make a plan to try it either in a group online, in a personal group locally, or on your own.

   a. **Mindfulness Walk or Walking Meditation**. Visit https://www.mindful.org/daily-mindful-walking-practice/ for instructions and more information.

   b. **Walking a Labyrinth**. Visit https://www.peacelabyrinth. org/how-to-walk-the-labyrinth for instructions and more information.

c. **Silent Retreats**. For more information and a variety of retreat centers for making a silent retreat, including tips for your first silent retreat, and silent retreat destinations in the U.S., visit https://siddhayatan.org/7-serene-silent-retreat-destinations

d. **Centering Prayer**. For instructions and more information, visit https://www.lindsayboyer.com/centering-prayer

e. **Wisdom School**: Meditation, Chant, Divine Exchange, visit https://wisdomwaypoints.org

Nature Is Our Teacher

"If a person keeps growing, his or her various false selves usually die in exposure to greater light."

~ RICHARD ROHR, IMMORTAL DIAMOND

From birth until death, our lives go through continuous seasons and cycles. This is not something we necessarily learn consciously, but if we're in the habit of examining our own lives and feeding our souls with good spiritual nurture, it is a truth that is hard to miss. Our awareness and acceptance of the life and death cycle sometimes comes through difficult or tragic events and experiences that bring us to our knees. Perhaps it's the surprising joys and blessings we receive and wholeheartedly embrace, such as becoming a parent, or finding a loving and committed partner. Maybe it's coming to the realization that a career choice – or choice of voluntary service – is really a vocation after all.

Consider the adage, "This too shall pass." It is a common phrase that is often used when we experience difficulty. But life requires us to acknowledge that even the joyful times that we experience will one day change. Sometimes the big difficulties and joys occur while we're young; sometimes they happen much later in life. I have a brother who unexpectedly became a loving parent for the first time in his forties, and a sister who met the love of her life in her fifties. These experiences both surprised and blessed them. Yet, I also think of the men, women and children who had no spouse, mother, father or other family member returning home on September 11, 2001, when United Flight 93 crashed, the Pentagon was bombed, and the Twin Towers fell in New York City. No matter the circumstances – sorrowful or joyous – these times will inevitably change us and become humus for our further growth.

> Even after death, trees abound with other forms of life. Bacteria are decomposing the plant tissues. Termites, woodboring beetles and carpenter ants are feeding within. These are eaten by woodpeckers, lizards, toads and shrews. The web of life will in time reduce this tree to a rich brown area of humus on the forest floor – waiting to be used by other living things.
>
> **Placard on the Royal Palm Hammock Nature Trail at Collier-Seminole State Park, Florida**

The longer we practice our journaling, the more likely it can and will shift us toward a more spiritual focus: the stuff of our lives will be mulched into a living garden of experience. Gains and losses in all areas of life will be the soil of our experiences, and these will inform our next steps – our decision making. The years of decisions will carve our lives into distinct seasons: work and love that is satisfying and/ or turbulent; losing or finding our way and eventually waking up; and perhaps a decision to embark on a more intentional season of growth. Growth may come in spurts or may seem to peter out altogether. These dead ends may feel discouraging or depressing. Yet, if we continue the search, we will find our way again – and again and again. Even times of unproductivity and unrealized dreams can be the fuel for our continued growth: what we lost or gave up will open the space for something new.

Nature – like our lives – is a continuum of change. When we look closely, we can see that it teaches not only the life and death cycles, but also adaptability – how we can prepare for some of the inevitable transitions as we sense the seasonal changes in our own lives. Nature reveals the existential consequences of not taking care of ourselves or the environment, but also the unpredictability of natural and personal disasters. Our role in caring for our world and supporting and helping each other as we meet and deal with life's personal challenges connects us intimately to the wholeness of nature.

In a similar way, nature reflects aspects of the divine or cosmic energy. Like nature, this energy is a constant in the background and foreground of our lives, whether we acknowledge it or not. This vast domain of the divine is like the ocean: we need only to go to it with openness to experience it. My sense is that Spirit never becomes unavailable, stops facilitating our growth, and never gives up on us. We can be awakened at any moment. Our journals will ground us in the present, holding the many threads, lessons, insights, and experiences that have made us who we are today.

For many years I met with a psychotherapist who was a wise and loving woman, and who helped me a great deal. Eventually I was ready to separate from that relationship. The process of letting go was indeed a process – our sessions became further and further apart until I finally stepped away. Even though I was not conscious of it at the time, my persistent feelings of resistance to continue our path together was a sign that I was ready to make the transition. I believe I was letting go because understanding my past – and depending on her perspective – could only take me so far. I needed to continue the journey of healing for sure, but I needed to eventually release her and go inward to find both the wise woman and the divine within, who would now guide my life. When we finally ended our sessions, I took the fruits of our relationship with me: relying more on God, trusting myself more, and the wisdom, love, and warmth I experienced from her. I eventually saw that if I gave my life the same commitment that I had given to the therapeutic process, I'd continue to grow and mature.

As I allowed myself to feel the fear and sadness, and trust more deeply that I had been well prepared, I began to trust more deeply that my Higher Power was guiding me through all the changes of remarriage, a new job, and a new home. At age 50, I mourned my days of being single and the changes that occurred in my body and in my friendships. I told someone I was ready to engage in spiritual direction, could she recommend someone to me? I entered a new season of life, feeling vulnerable but well prepared as I journaled my way through these experiences.

Four years later, my spiritual path took a turn that would deepen and facilitate my growth tremendously. I accepted the invitation to go deeper with my Higher Power by spending a weekend each month at a retreat house. I was introduced to many kindred spirits along the way and, ultimately, the beginnings of a tremendous peace through solitude and silence that I had not experienced before.

What I also learned during this time was to avoid attaching myself to the approval or disapproval of others, or whether I was liked or not. As free as this may sound, it was sometimes a lonely experience. Sometimes we are judged or misunderstood. At other times, people want to fix us and our problems. (How often I have done these things to others in my life!) When I feel this loneliness, I spend time in nature. I walk in a favorite park where the trees are my friends. At other times, I sit near a stream to hear water lapping on the rocks. I sense the breeze and sun on my skin, connecting me to the Source of all being. Sometimes I kayak along the shoreline of a lake, stopping to just listen or watch the raptors flying overhead. Almost always, simply being in nature can restore me to a place of true belonging.

Meditations

"Within all great things (including change and loss) is the invisible movement of a *great* love."
   ~ Paula D'Arcy, Founder of Red Bird Foundation

"Creation itself – not ritual or spaces constructed by human hands – was [St.] Francis' primary cathedral."
   ~ Richard Rohr's Daily Meditation, Center for Action
   and Contemplation

"The longer we practice our journaling, the more likely it can and will shift us toward a more spiritual focus: the stuff of our lives will be mulched into a living garden of experience. Gains and losses in all areas of life will be the soil of our experiences, and these will inform our next steps – our decision making. The years of decisions will carve our lives into distinct seasons ...."
   ~ Jo-Ellen A. Darling

Questions for Journaling

1. What season of the lifecycle are you in now? Which stage have you just relinquished? How did it prepare you for what is happening now or coming next? What strengths have you gained? What did you have to let go of to be here now? Is there anything else that you need?

2. Which metaphors in nature can you use to write a parable or description of what is happening to you? Write that story.

3. What do you need to let go of now? Can you make space for something new to emerge? What does that look like? Can you be patient with yourself, yet gently persistent and faithful in your seeking?

4.   To whom, what or where are you being called now?

5.   To whom do you truly belong?

6.   Where does love want to take you? Where is the spark of new life leading you?

Exercises

1.   Spend some time in nature this week.

2.   Afterward, recall the sounds and sights as you journal. Were your senses able to take in the nurture of nature?

3.   If not, what was your experience? Can you do something different in nature that aligns more with who you are – such as sitting by a creek reading a good book, doing yoga poses on the beach, or taking an early morning run or walk?

Sowing and Reaping

"Watch your thoughts, they become your words; watch your words, they become your actions; watch your actions, they become your habits; watch your habits, they become your character; watch your character, it becomes your destiny."

~ LAO TZU

"Sowing and reaping" is a spiritual principle I have found to be exceptionally helpful in my spiritual journey. I see this as a metaphor of natural law. This idea is pronounced in Buddhist and Taoist teachings as well as in many of the teachings of Jesus in the New Testament. It is a metaphor for life that we can use as a tool for living in the world, or even as a prayer. The premise around sowing and reaping is: what we do with our thoughts, words, and actions (sowing), comes back to us in return (reaping).

We can think of thoughts, words, and actions in both the sowing and reaping process as primarily forms of powerful energy that fuel our choices. The premise around *sowing* is that we release the energy from these thoughts, words and actions, depending on how attached we are to them or our held belief in them. That's why it's crucial to pay attention to our thoughts: our defensiveness, self-justification, or lack of compassion toward others always begins in the inner life. Self-reflection becomes key because our perceptions cannot change if we do not question them, study them, and release them for a greater good.

For example, we may be defending our hurt feelings and this may feel delicious for quite a while. In our own defense, we make the other person wrong, see them without compassion, and then act on that by holding a judgment or resentment. This may fuel our unhealthy egos, making us feel better about ourselves for a while. But in the end, this is all about sowing judgment toward others. When we judge others for not living up to our expectations, we build two walls within: one that splits ourselves, and the other that stands between us and the other person. We fail to see them as equal human beings in different places on life's journey. The result is that the wall within ourselves weakens our true self, but gives more power to the false self.

The premise around *reaping* is that we receive back the energy of the thoughts, words, and actions that we have sown. In the case above, this judgment toward someone else comes back on us, through our own feelings of guilt, self-judgment, a lack of compassion, and maybe an attitude of arrogance that actually boomerangs. If we are wise, we come to realize that we have also hurt ourselves. When we contemplate what we are reaping concerning the judgments we have made about others, we hopefully see the crack in our perceptions and follow a different path to transcendence. This path will include understanding, forgiveness, and acceptance – for those we have judged *and* for ourselves.

I was once asked to do a journaling workshop for a church that was going through a schism. The church was splitting over the ordination of gays in their denomination, and other disagreements with the ruling body of the church. As the schism unfolded, there was obvious judgment on both sides of this issue: finger pointing, underhandedness, accusations, and blame, all played out in the local press. Little did I know that their event, titled the "Language of Lament," would have several members present that were dealing with the effects of this schism as well as other unrelated, broken circumstances in people's lives.

As I prepared for the workshop, I read and contemplated Jesus' parables on sowing and reaping. I was again reminded to see our thoughts and feelings as seeds that eventually turn into a harvest. Where do our thoughts and feelings come from? Obviously, they can come from different places, such as our conscience, our beliefs, or from past memories. Some come directly from the negative ego – our pride, our woundedness, and our need to be right – even when part of us may have a good reason to object to the ego's demands.

Let's say you disagree with someone or a group of people about an issue. Have you ever found yourself thinking or speaking about them in a negative way, then stopping yourself to confront it? Don't they have a right to disagree with you? We may have automated responses in life from prior experiences. Yet, if we listen carefully, the Inner Teacher speaks within us. When we are in touch with that, we will find ourselves less defensive and more willing to see things from another point of view.

When we are conflicted, we still feel emotionally negative, in a lot of pain, or angry and resentful. We should not dismiss these negative thoughts and emotions. Rather, we can ask the Inner Teacher to guide us about the matter at hand. Perhaps we need to uncover something we have sown toward someone else: negative thoughts, criticisms, or jealousy. We are now reaping the discomfort of our own thoughts and beliefs, and if we persist in our defense of ourselves, we will only find the self-justifications that support these continued feelings. Sometimes this will point to beliefs, attitudes and feelings that we have about ourselves. This translates into projecting our ills onto others. Still, we need to be honest and examine these thoughts and feelings.

Quite possibly it is only a matter of changing our attitude toward someone or toward our self. Why do we believe *what* we believe about another or ourselves? Whether we discover an answer quickly or not, we can decide how we shall change our mind in this moment. We can remain angry or allow ourselves to see the good *and* the brokenness that is in them. Instead of berating ourselves, we can choose to accept, love, and forgive ourselves, despite our current tendency to blame others. We can stop blaming others or ourselves for our failures, critical thoughts, or bad behavior because taking responsibility is different than blaming. When we change our minds, our hearts will follow. We can then move through the important decision to make specific apologies or living amends.

Although we *can* do something in the moment to change our situation, the more difficult questions or resolutions may take time. The answer to "What can do I now?" may initially be to simply reflect more in our journals and in our prayer and meditation time about our awareness. Trusting the process will be key, and this takes practice. We can ask for the grace to trust and have patience.

I remember offending people at work more than once in my life. How I treated others was often sporadic and self-centered. I often lacked respect and sensitivity. When I understood this through the journaling I did each time it happened, I found it helpful to apologize through my attitudes and actions. I then felt in alignment with my true self and what I really wanted in life that had seemed out of reach:

to treat others the way I wanted to be treated, whether they treated me the same way or not. It was a tough lesson. Yet, I mostly found that my attempts to directly apologize or make amends – however painful to my ego – changed the energy between myself and others for the better. Richard Rohr captures this idea in one of his Daily Meditations. In essence, he says that deep love and suffering are sometimes the only things that can supercede the ego's defiance and bring us to a place of deep spiritual surrender.

Meditations

"You remain unaware of your freedom to change how you think. When your thinking is locked in false certainty or negativity, it puts so many interesting and vital areas of life out of your reach. You live impoverished and hungry in the midst of your own abundance."
~ John O'Donohue, Eternal Echoes

"When we walk toward what is uncomfortable, we increase our capacity to be with difficult experiences... We must wander across the harsh landscape [and be] willing to be changed by it."
~ Christine Valters Paintner, The Soul of a Pilgrim

"We've all experienced thoughts, feelings, and bodily sensations that informed us that something wasn't right and needed to be rectified – even if we ignored taking any action from those cues. Perhaps we need to uncover something we have sown toward someone else: negative thoughts, criticisms, or jealousy. We are now reaping the discomfort of our own thoughts and beliefs, and if we persist in our defense of ourselves, we will only find the self-justifications that support these continued feelings."
~ Jo-Ellen A. Darling

Questions for Journaling

1. What are the changes and transitions happening in your life now?

   a. What are your thoughts about these changes and which emotions surface as you investigate them?

   b. What do you think is the purpose of these changes?

   c. On second look, is there a deeper purpose?

2. Are you sad, depressed, afraid or angry, or having other negative emotions or states of mind because of these changes?

   a. Are there good or valid reasons for these emotions?

   b. Are some from longstanding misperceptions in general? If so, what do you think the misperceptions might be?

3. What in life distracts you from being present to these changes and moving forward?

   a. Where do you hide?

   b. What can you change or do to be more present – to come out of hiding?

   c. Is there a risk you need to take?

4. Who are the mentors in your life? (These can be authors, poets, therapists/psychologists, inspirational figures in history, sponsors, religious or spiritual figures, spiritual directors, life coaches, friends, or common people like you and I who have overcome great obstacles.)

   a. Journal your thoughts and feelings and your spiritual sense of each one of your mentors – their qualities that you might adopt and strengthen *in yourself*.

5. If you don't have any mentors right now, per se, to whom can you commit to let speak into your life? Can you risk asking them for time to share honestly about what you are discovering?

6. Try journaling some of your thoughts about sowing and reaping.

   a. Is there a situation that you can apply this principle to?

   b. To what truths does your reflection ultimately lead?

Exercises

1. After journaling the questions above, explore a significant issue you are having or are anticipating, and find a new mentor or trusted friend/person that you think may help. This process could entail:

   - Using prayer and meditation to truly see the issue: perhaps it is a change of job, changes in relationship(s), change in some major perspective of your life, such as how you view and relate to yourself, someone else, or your Higher Power.

   - Following the "thread" of revelation to the issue you're exploring: you can search the topic online, in libraries, on bookseller websites or on YouTube to begin the search.

   - Talk to a trusted person about the issue: what is their experience with the issue? Ask and search for book titles about it.

   - After you decide with whom or what resources to engage in, journal about it:
     - Is it someone or something you encountered positively in the past, or is it someone or something new? (Rereading favorite books and seeing favorite movies often inspires me again. On the other hand, a new author, movie, or person to talk to may be what is needed.)
     - Is it a spiritual program, a philosophical or religious entity, or a person?
     - Why are you choosing them, and how does this feel?

- What thoughts and feelings does this bring up for you?
- What are your hopes for engaging with this new guide/mentor in your life?

2. Journal a list of thoughts that you have around the particular issue.

- Include your feelings as well. For example, "I feel that he/she is unable to understand how I feel because their life is so good/perfect/wise and they could not possibly see this from my viewpoint," etc.

- Now counter each thought with an opposite or different viewpoint. For example, "How do I really know this? Have I judged this person; have I not spoken with them to let them know how I think and feel about this? If so, why am I afraid to reveal my struggle or truth, or to be open and hear their thoughts on this?"

Reading to Feed Our Souls

"This is one of the great gifts of pilgrimage: an invitation to discern what is essential."

~ CHRISTINE VALTERS PAINTNER, THE SOUL OF A PILGRIM

Several years ago, I read a few articles and book reviews about introverts and extroverts. In my reading, I was led to Susan Cain's book, *Quiet: The Power of Introverts in a World That Can't Stop Talking*. This book validated my needs as an introvert, which I had often carried with some guilt and shame about not fitting into a more extroverted personality type. But this book not only grounded an essential part of who I was, it helped challenge me to stretch in areas where I felt invisible and disconnected, especially in social situations. I found I could risk being more hospitable around people with whom

I had nothing much in common, including our personality types. This has helped me to appreciate differences and be less anxious, and at the same time to be more accepting and gentle with myself.

Whether you are alone or partnered – unemployed, attending college, working, raising children, retired, caring for grandchildren or elderly parents, or live in assisted living or a nursing home – it's important to continue to feed your soul. This can be done in so many ways, but whatever life stage you are in, one of the best ways to do this is to read continuously. For those who resist this suggestion, it is not how quickly you read or the number of books you read. Rather, it is the lifelong benefits of reading that can help sustain and support our change and growth. A lifetime reader will be spiritually formed by what she or he reads. Reading is as important as following a spiritual path because reading will always inform that path. In large and small ways, it will shape your outlook on life: your spiritual beliefs, the philosophical principles and values that you decide are important to you, and the way you will interact with the world. Reading spiritually inspiring books, such as biographies and books about human accomplishment, faith, history, philosophy, and artistic expression may lead you to make major decisions in your own life that you might not make if you do not read them.

Writers of all kinds can be mentors and teachers in our lives who will inform – and thus influence – our life choices. Discovering these beautiful voices of the human spirit can lift us out of the spiritual poverty of our own lives. When I left a dead-end job in 2012 that had depleted my spirit, I came upon several writers who led me to great inner healing. I was paying my dues at the time: a year's salary to be out of work so that I could find a new position – and more importantly without even knowing it – a turn in the road that would bring me on a new inner path.

During those years, my relationship with one of these writers grew strong, and I have thanked the Universe many times over for his companionship, wisdom, and the great gift of his books, particularly *Anam*

Cara and *Eternal Echoes*. Early on, I learned that John O'Donohue had passed away at the young age of 54, and I actually grieved his passing. I wrote a poem dedicated to him during this period of unemployment. The poem encompassed all that I felt in the early weeks and months during which my soul opened more fully in deep resonance to my new friend, as well as the heart of a loving God.

In those years, O'Donohue became a mentor, friend, and true spiritual guide through his writings. His healing words and perspectives were soothing to my soul, and he has gently challenged many long-held beliefs I have had about myself. Many other subsequent writers, as mentioned throughout this text, have continued to enrich my life.

Over the years, I was often led to books that caused me to change direction slightly or greatly at critical junctures of my life. As a high schooler I loved the quirky, creative, and truth-telling novels in my modern literature class with Mr. Black, such as *One Flew Over the Cuckoo's Nest* and *Animal Farm,* which inspired me to work toward a college degree in English and later to become a writer. In college, my English and writing professor, Neil Bruss, gave us the great gift of developing our critical thinking and writing skills by watching films like *Citizen Kane* and reading biographies such as *The Power Broker: Robert Moses and the Fall of New York.* During my twenties, it was the books of Ayn Rand that attracted me to explore and embrace – and then ultimately discard – her philosophy of Objectivism; it lacked compassion. When I turned 31 and greatly struggled with my relationship to alcohol, *The Road Less Traveled* by M. Scott Peck arrived in my hands at my sister-in-law's home as I peered through the bags of books she had just purchased. Peck's book gave me the impetus and drive I needed to begin the long journey of recovery. Contemplating the benefits of entering therapy, I became willing to examine my life choices up to that point, and the even harder journey of making the necessary changes that would allow me to begin healing and to move forward. This included doing the difficult work of psychotherapy and leading a sober life.

Continuing into my thirties, I was introduced to Victor Frankl's classic book, *Man's Search for Meaning*, a book largely about finding meaning despite circumstances of great personal – and collective – pain and suffering. Frankl came to this understanding long before he was a prisoner in the Nazi's concentration camp at Auschwitz. What I learned from Frankl – what he validated for me as I entered the difficult decade of my thirties – was that if he could survive a Nazi concentration camp and continue a life without bitterness and losing his way, I could survive the pain of my own past, including the pain of divorce, the consequences of an addiction, the hurt that I had caused others, and the hurt that others had done to me. Not only could I survive, but I could thrive and continue the search for a God that had shown himself to me when I was a child. This thriving would lead to making choices that mattered to me, that increased my ability to help not only myself, but also others with my time, gifts, and resources. Reading Frankl's book helped me become a citizen of the world.

In 2019 my husband and I were taking extended time away in an RV camper and for the first few weeks, the atmosphere was frequently contentious and stressful. On top of this, I wasn't sleeping well. My father had died a rather traumatic death four months prior, and I had spent a good part of the previous year making trips to my parents' home to assist them. I was still grieving during our trip, though it seemed like I should have been doing better. In one of my journal entries during an interrupted night of sleep, I recorded a quote by writer Martha Whitmore Hickman *Healing After Loss*. It essentially said that even though we want to help others, sometimes it is time to take care of ourselves. We should not feel guilty about this, she wrote, but give ourselves what we need until we are strong enough to carry the burdens of others again. We can trust that we will know when it's time.

This quote helped me see that I clearly had not seen or valued my own needs in the early days of my grief. If I had identified them, maybe I would have communicated them to my husband. In reality, I was expecting him to know what they were. Yet, how could he know what was going on with me if I did not know this myself? When I then realized I could not expect myself to be in normal travel mode, and that this was clearly unfair to my husband, we began to talk. I asked for his patience and understanding that I may not be up to everything he had hoped we would do on our trip, and that we would need to take it one day at a time. A conversation unfolded about the death of his own parents and how he had responded to those events. My husband had dealt with his loss very differently than I had. He was far more accepting of his parents' deaths, and his grief was not as prolonged. As I continued to journal and write creatively during this difficult trip, the chaotic, painful, and stressful memories of losing my father were comforted through the process of my own compassionate journaling practice – a way of taking care of myself.

As you read, it's important to journal about the ideas that inspire you, and the things you resist or disagree with and that trigger an internal response, such as quotes, stories and experiences that you can relate to. If you need more structure with reading, you can join or form a book group with others, or you can do a self-study. Either way, journaling your internal responses will facilitate a breakdown of the author's ideas and insights so that you can reflect on them. Those of us who love to read can forget what is in a book as soon as we pick up another, because maybe we're reading only to escape. The point is to savor the moments that mean something and then break them down to see why they mean so much. As you commit to this process of integration, you begin to trust your own instincts and come to know your own self – how you feel, what you believe, what you value, what you know, and also what you don't know.

Today when I read, I highlight the most important or striking ideas of the text. Sometimes I enter these ideas into my journal and respond to them by writing my thoughts, freely and without editing them as much as possible. This meditative journaling enables me to more deeply see how the writer's perspective is being rooted in my life.

Meditations

"A lifetime reader will be spiritually formed by what she or he reads. Reading is as important as following a spiritual path because reading will always inform that path. In large and small ways, it will shape your outlook on life: your spiritual beliefs, the philosophical principles and values that you decide are important to you, and the way you will interact with the world. Reading spiritually inspiring books, such as biographies and books about human accomplishment, faith, history, philosophy, and artistic expression may lead you to make major decisions in your own life that you might not make if you do not read them."

~ *Jo-Ellen A. Darling*

"When you face your aloneness, something begins to happen...You no longer need to covertly scrape affirmation from others or from projects outside yourself. This is slow work; it takes years to bring your mind home."

~ *John O'Donohue, Eternal Echoes*

"Humans cannot live happily without meaning – and ever deeper meaning. Symbols have the power to give meaning – the meaning we wake up for each morning."

~ *Richard Rohr, Immortal Diamond*

For John O'Donohue

Beloved poet
ancestral roots we share;
I mourn your passing.

Like a great shock
your words meet my soul
at the door, waiting …

… a threshold I crossed,
not knowing your kindred spirit
would be there to guide.

In your *Book of Blessings*
my own experience is uttered;
I weep in gratitude.

They say, "Read good books" –
but no one said a thing
about shooting stars –

stars so bright they hurt.
The comet of your life soars……
crosses my horizon

triggering sparks of
tears and creativity,
extreme hope, and love.

How can I thank you
from this side, dear poet?

I trust you have heard.

~ By Jo-Ellen A. Darling

Questions for Journaling

1. Which authors are you drawn to and why? What themes do they write about that nourish your awareness of life?

2. What are some important books that you have read? Why were they important?

3. What book (or articles, magazines, online material, etc.) are you now reading?

   a. Is the reading inspiring or deepening your perspective, feelings, or hopefulness about life? Or is it taking you away from a reality that you are having difficulty facing at this time?

   b. Is your thinking being challenged? What are your intentions to follow through, i.e., how will you practice the concepts that are offered in the reading, in your own life?

   c. If you read fiction, such as mysteries, romance, or sci-fi, can you balance this reading with other reading? Which books will you read? Check out GoodReads.com, Amazon's "100 Books to Read in a Lifetime" and other reading lists.

4. Journal about the process of being "led to" or finding a book in your past which impacted your life in some way. Perhaps it had a profound effect on your thinking – in particular or in general – perhaps a book that opened up new paths to self-knowledge, philosophical truth, spiritual connection, or creative inspiration. Where did it lead you? What were the fruits in your life from this reading?

Exercises

1. Make an intention to be led to a book that will inspire you. Go to a bookstore or library where you can touch and hold

and read the books themselves (rather than online). Look at titles and hold one that attracts you. Open it and read something on the page. Is it speaking to you in some way? Is your interest held? Try a few more pages, or scan the chapter titles for one that speaks to you. If nothing resonates, put it down and move on.

2. Read a book in a different field or genre about something or someone that you would not necessarily be drawn to, such as physics, short stories, travelogues, poetry, a novel, a biography, history of a people or time period, world events or global issues. (Ask your friends and acquaintances what they are reading for ideas, or browse through books online.)

    a. Name something important that you have learned from its reading.

    b. How does it connect to your own life?

    c. How has your heart opened?

    d. How does it play out in your life, i.e., are there any actions you want to take because of the knowledge you have acquired?

Healing Our Wounds Through the Practice of Tending

"These cuts at the core of your identity cannot be healed by the world or medicine, nor by the externals of religion or psychology. It is only by letting in the divine light to bathe these wounds that healing will come."

~ JOHN O'DONOHUE, ETERNAL ECHOES

Healing is not head work – it is soul work. As much as we can participate in healing our wounds by consciously changing our thinking, we must continue to move into unknown territory to access a deeper level of the subconscious. I have found this level of healing and self-knowledge to truly be the "slow work of God." Oftentimes in doing this work, a feeling of self-empowerment emerges: our healing may bring new confidence, bliss, joy, and a feeling of aliveness. Yet, self-empowerment sometimes arrives in ways we do not expect, such as through humility. Often, humility comes from disempowerment that seeks no need to fight back. Instead, a part of us – such as the controlling negative ego – is ready to surrender, to accept that we are not the center of the universe or someone else's life. Journaling provides a way to continue this journey inward each day, even in some small way. We give ourselves time, make intentions, and practice rituals if that helps. We need to arrive eventually at a place of *compassionate awareness* – not only for others, but also for ourselves.

O'Donohue's opening quote does not necessarily mean that religion or psychology are not essential to our healing. Perhaps it more so suggests that while these can play an amazing role in healing our ego – which is necessary to survive in the world we live in – it is the divine energy that reaches into the deepest recesses of the heart and soul, where the roots of our wounds often hide in darkness.

It's difficult to be loving and caring toward those we don't like. This is one of the reasons it's so hard for us to love others and ourselves. The small self has its long list of likes and dislikes: I don't like rude people; I don't like needy people or those who are honest about what they see in me; I don't like Republicans or Democrats; Catholics or Evangelicals; Latinos, Blacks or Whites. On and on.

I used to cringe when reading any author who talked about self-hate. It seemed so extreme. "I don't hate myself," I told myself when reading such nonsense. But in truth, I disparaged myself often in my thoughts, in my words, and in my self-neglect and other actions. If I think and act in these ways toward myself, then I will think and act in these ways toward others. The cycle was difficult to break. I still do this on occasion, and I probably always will. For me, the ticket to freedom is to remember to keep loving myself in all my brokenness, character flaws, errors, and sins when these rise to the surface. To see even myself as "other ..." this other that needs my compassionate awareness.

The fact that I've been wounded in life is a human trait I share with all people. Our vulnerable places are the true self, wounded by life, by love, by unintended failures. The true self holds these wounds, like an egg holding the yoke. The divine Light will make a new creation – whole, untouched, the deepest kind of beauty. It is healing and new life, created in the image of the Source of Life – the someone or something greater in this universe than me.

John O'Donohue's powerful opening quote has been true for me. I can do all the psycho-spiritual work of creating an external life that I love and even feel passionate about, but the invisible super-reality of a loving power that I call God – whom you may describe and name differently – is the ultimate healer of my wounds. Yet, it is also me doing my part, as Goddess is doing hers. When this work of the divine is happening, sometimes I see it and know it, and yet so much of the time I don't.

The Spirit's part can look like wisdom coming from others, or through the healing realm of nature. It can manifest as the power of goodness working miracles in politics, science, and medicine through human endeavor. It can arrive unexpectedly as mercy, opening my eyes to the suffering of others. I can only say that the energy of divine love has properties that I do not yet fully possess, but that I trust will be shared with me on this journey, as needed. Placing myself in the hands of love and compassion, the adventure unfolds.

I am surprised continuously by the faithfulness of the Divine Presence, the help that is available when my weak and vulnerable self – as well as my prideful and defensive self – is in need of healing and direction. When we are young, we must learn right and wrong so we can learn to live with other human beings. Knowing right and wrong is the first step. Sometimes we take that teaching, however, as though it is written in stone. We become judges of everything and everyone, including ourselves. But in time, I begin to see my errors without judging them. One reason is that I've learned a new clue: that even my search for Spirit is the Spirit inviting me and desiring *my presence*.

Over time, it may feel like the wounds do not fully heal, but all that is needed is to be willing to receive the Spirit's guidance. We can be sure to almost always find a life-giving direction that leads to the next right thought, feeling, attitude or action step. And in that moment, I am fully healed. In other words, I continue to begin again – and again and again – with every interaction of my day reaching for, or receiving, a divine connection. To me, all of what I have just described is a way of praying.

Meditations

"What might it mean for you to mature by entering the painful reality of your losses rather than avoiding them?"
~ *Peter Scazzero, Emotionally Healthy Spirituality Day by Day*

"As we grow more intimate with our own places of exile and woundedness, we discover a deep well of compassion for the strangeness of others."
~ *Christine Valters Paintner, A Love Note from Your Online Abbess*

"Often, humility comes from disempowerment that seeks no need to fight back. Instead, a part of us – such as the controlling negative ego

– is ready to surrender, to accept that we are not the center of the universe or someone else's life. Journaling provides a way to continue this journey inward each day, even in some small way."

~ *Jo-Ellen A. Darling*

Questions for Journaling

1. Select one or more of the meditation quotes and gently contemplate them in your quiet time. Which words or phrases stand out? How do these relate to any of the relationships in your life? With whom do you need to find the path of compassion?

2. Do you have a sense of where you are overall in your compassion and love levels? These are easy to overlook. As an example, I had an old acquaintance come back into my life, and I realized I lacked even a willingness to see her with compassion. It was an eye-opener. I was asked to be led to the path of compassion and gently it came to me. Do you have a similar experience going on? Is there anyone you are avoiding, even in prayer?

3. Where do you need to practice self-compassion the most? Think of situations where you feel an unease, such as in a relationship, when you are in a group, or when you are confronted with other people's needs, requests or wishes. Dialog with your true self to find the clues that can show you what it is that you need from a power greater than yourself.

4. Write a prayer, poem, or psalm about self-compassion. Let it speak!

Exercises

1. Can you take a step today that leads to self-compassion? What will you do? Journal about it later on.

2. Create a collage using the theme of self-compassion or compassionate awareness. Be creative.

3. Create a collage of your compassion for others. Add the faces of people for whom you feel compassion. What will you do at some point to express your compassion for them?

Further Along the Path to Wholeness

"There are no manuals for the construction of the individual you would like to become. You are the only one who can decide this and take up the lifetime of work that it demands."

~ JOHN O'DONOHUE, ETERNAL ECHOES

New to journaling or not, we may still view ourselves as primarily fractured or broken in some fundamental way, and without hope of ever being cured or whole. Or we may tend to avoid the wounded areas and choose not to go there in hopes of staying above the fray, or away from opening Pandora's box. I propose that just for this moment, may you see yourself as whole, not because you are perfect, fixed, or no longer wounded or broken in any way, but because you are now willing to be in touch with these many aspects of who you are. These parts often exist without your awareness of them – the positive *and* negative aspects, the stuck *and* thriving parts, the true self *and* the false self in you.

The figure on the next page is a visual of the many aspects that comprise the wholeness of who we are. This is not a complete representation by any means, but what I see as the major areas of life that we can consciously address in our journaling efforts. We can journal to be free, to love ourselves, and become agents of love in our own lives and the lives of others – even while doing it a little at a time. Add your own areas of wholeness that may be missing from this figure as well.

Aspects of Wholeness – Chart

Sit with the Aspects of Wholeness chart for 10 or 15 minutes. Journal your thoughts for each aspect represented, if you wish. Meditations, Questions for Journaling, and Exercises follow.

Meditations

"I propose that just for this moment, may you see yourself as "whole," not because you are perfect, fixed, or no longer wounded or broken in any way, but because you are now willing to be in touch with these many aspects of who you are."

~ Jo-Ellen A. Darling

"In the great economy of grace, all is used and transformed, and nothing is wasted. God uses your various False Selves to lead you beyond them."

~ Richard Rohr, Immortal Diamond

"I work a spiritual program. I go to God for all the tools and information I need. God, to me, is a higher level of consciousness. Every day in prayer and meditation I go deep within myself to a quiet place where there's peace, love, light, hope and joy. I honestly take my daily inventory, I release all my self-will, I turn over my will, and I ask God to lessen my nonfunctional character traits. I commit myself to correcting my previous mistakes. This gives me a conscious contact with my Higher Power."

~ Anonymous

Questions for Journaling

1. **My Needs** – What are the one or two areas of your greatest needs at this time? Ask, "What am I needing?"

My Needs

Physical, mental, emotional, social, and spiritual.

My Healthy Ego/ Character Strengths

My ability to love, care, and get along with others. The unconditional love and acceptance I have for self and others.

My Desires and Longings

My deepest wants and yearnings: those I've identified that are life-giving and in line with my deepest values; those that are addictive and destructive and lead to "death."

My Unhealthy Ego/ Character Defects

The conditional love and acceptance I have for self and others; my survival traits from wounds from the past; my unwillingness to change and grow; my need to be "right."

My Shadow Self/False Self

How I have hurt self and others by not choosing to be honest with and true to myself.

What I Do

My job, roles, hobbies, and interests.

My Past Experiences of Wounding

How I've been hurt by self and others, intentionally or not.

My Body

How I perceive my physical self and take care of my physical needs.

My Wholeness

My Unconscious Self

My night dreams and all that has not yet been brought to my conscious awareness.

My Feelings

These include those that I am able to feel and learn from and those that are blocked or unconscious.

My Inner Light / True Self

The true person I am and was born with beneath all social and cultural conditioning; all that is good in me, does good, and lives in unity with Spirit. The one in me that seeks and knows "truth."

Gender Energies

The ability to balance my doing and my being at appropriate times (taking action and waiting, seeking and waiting, roles, etc.).

My Conscious Self

My longings and desires and all that has been brought to my conscious awareness through the intentional work of noticing, reflecting, meditating and contemplating.

My Thoughts

Those that are unconscious, or those I fail to acknowledge out of fear; those that are conscious and help me "see" and live a healthy life; or those that are wise and revealed from the conscious work that I do.

2. **My Body** – What thing do you most need to do for your body at this time?

3. **My Feelings** – What feelings are affecting your daily life in a negative way? Which positive feelings are sustaining you as a result of the hard work you have done/are doing to change?

4. **My Thoughts** – What thoughts are sabotaging your efforts for an emotionally healthy life? Make a list of these thoughts for a couple of days and see what shows up.

5. **What I Do** – Are your job and extracurricular activities life-giving? In other words, does this work or activity feed your soul in some way, even though it may primarily benefit others? If not, what can you change?

6. **My Desires and Longings** – The positive, joyful, and hopeful things in life you would love to become, do, or accomplish, including the quiet spiritual longings you are in touch with when you take time for silence, solitude, prayer, meditation, and journaling.

7. **My Unhealthy Ego/Character Defects** – What character flaw is currently showing up? How do you handle it? Do you need help? Notice new opportunities to sidestep it when it appears in your thoughts or behavior.

8. **My Healthy Ego/Personality** – What are my positive character traits? If you aren't sure, ask your friends to tell you. It is a great way to receive feedback about how others experience you in a "healthy way" when you have no idea of your positive effect on others.

9. **My Shadow Self/False Self** – What are the areas of your personality that trip you up? Do an inventory over a week or a month, journaling the difficulties in your responses to others

and to your own self when you make a mistake, aren't being perfect, are feeling resentful or jealous, etc.

10. **My Inner Light / True Self** – What are the areas of your personality that you feel grounded in? You may never speak to anyone about these areas, but you know deeply that your true self, or your inner light, is a good thing when you are "in it." Do an inventory over a week or a month, journaling about these joyful or grounded feelings in your responses to others and to your own self, such as when you make a deep connection, when things flow serendipitously, or when you have deep magnanimity or gratitude for self, others, and your Higher Power.

11. **My Unconscious Self** – What *tip of the iceberg* are you noticing these days, that if you pay more attention to, can lead you to an undiscovered but important aspect of yourself?

12. **My Conscious Self** – What are you really conscious of, on a daily basis? Scan the happenings of your day, several days in a row, making note of your conscious awareness by finishing this sentence stem: "Today I was conscious of ...."

13. **My Past Experiences of Wounding** – When you experience a reaction that is deeply painful, uncomfortable, or intensely negative in a relationship, think about it as a wound that needs to be dialogued with: ask it questions and respond with your *nondominant* hand. Keep writing. (See "The Power of Finishing a Sentence Stem" in Chapter 1, and Appendix B for writing prompt examples.)

14. **Gender Energies** – What are your definitions of gender energies? Although there are many gender identities, what are the energies behind them? Which ones feel more or less comfortable or uncomfortable to you? What roles do you

"wear" that have traits you feel at home with or not, and how can you be more authentically yourself in these roles (parent, child, wife, husband, friend, spouse, partner, leader, victim, peacemaker, hero, servant, provider etc.)?

Exercises

1. To explore your desires and longings – the positive, joyful, hopeful things in life you would love to become, do, or accomplish, including the quiet spiritual longings you are in touch with when you take time for silence, solitude, and journaling – complete these sentence stems over a week-long period (refer to Chapter 1 for instructions). When you've completed this exercise, go back and highlight anything that stands out to you. Take these to your times of prayer and meditation over several weeks. What is rising to the surface? What will you do next?

   "I want ..." "I yearn to ..." "I've noticed I have a desire to ..." "The deep longing in my soul is ..." "Since I was a child, I've wanted ..." "I've always wanted ...." "My Higher Power could be leading me to ..." "My heart longs to ..."

2. Create a collage that represents your current state of wholeness. Be compassionate and gentle with yourself as you add cutouts of magazine images or other pictures, photos, words, symbols, prayers, quotes, or anything that creates a picture of the complex human that you are. This would include all the graces you have received, the gifts, the gratitude and perhaps the hope you have for your future, as well as the current struggles that are still in process – such as wounds that you are currently aware of.

Note: See the chart of my "Rule of Life" on the next page. Follow the instructions to create one in your journal.

3. A *Rule of Life* is used in many organized groups and religious orders to define the activities they do to stay close to their higher power and grow spiritually. If you are not interested in the God part of this exercise, you can still do a rule of life that includes non-religious spiritual practices that are meaningful to you and that bring you peace and joy. These could include things you do that make you feel connected to yourself, your life, others, and the world.

    a. Use a landscape piece of paper and make six rows.

    b. Label each row: 1) Daily/Regularly, 2) Weekly, 3) Monthly, 4) Quarterly/Seasonally, 5) Annually.

    c. Think about the things that you need, that you desire for good, that you want to do for self or others: things that bring you joy, that bring deep satisfaction, that nurture you, that stir your passion and creativity, or that connect you to a higher power and the experiences of inner peace, joy, lovingkindness, etc.

    d. Next, you may want to journal briefly or at length on each of the things you wrote for each column.

    e. When you finish, go back and highlight one or two new things in each row that you feel you can explore this year, and make an effort to commit to at least one or two of them.

    f. Journal daily about the steps you are taking to explore – and eventually commit to – new habits and changes in your life. Celebrate each one!

    g. Schedule these things into your calendar for the year, beginning today.

Rule of Life (Example)

Daily/ Regularly	Weekly	Monthly	Quarterly or Seasonal	Annually
Journaling – enhances my awareness, keeps me emotionally and spiritually balanced	Time in nature – connects me to a higher power, nurtures a creative mindset	Attend a writers' group – provides support, fun and opportunities for community	Day at a retreat house, natural preserve, or park – gets me away from the routines and renews me	Weeklong silent retreat – opens my heart, time to unload, rest, connect with Spirit and identify and release the obstacles that keep me stuck
Prayer and meditation – connects me to Spirit, to awareness of others' needs and self needs.	12-step meeting – keeps me honest and open-hearted, and an ongoing member of a group	Celtic Spirituality Night at our local cathedral – a sacred space to connect with God of my understanding and friends for dinner afterward	Camping – connects me to nature, gives me a break, good for my marriage	Something to do with writing – set goals for projects, facilitate or attend a writers' retreat, or attend a writers' conference
Read – passages from spiritual books, daily meditation books – informs and supports my desire to be on a spiritual path	Attend religious services – provides opportunities for fellowship, spiritual growth and service	Meet with spiritual director – increases awareness to see where the Spirit is found and leading me in my life	Weekend retreat – topics that interest and challenge me to grow	Pilgrimage – local or far. A day or more to visit local, regional, or distant landscapes with the intention to reflect, pray, journal, and spend time in nature and sacred awareness

Rule of Life (Example), continued

Daily/ Regularly	Weekly	Monthly	Quarterly or Seasonal	Annually
	Yoga – connects my body to my soul by practicing compassion toward the body	Contra Dancing – music, friends and food, as often as we can		Donations - to worthy causes
	Volunteering - anything that helps others	Book Group online – opening myself to others' perspectives		Adult Education class – something fun, creative, or hobby/interest related

Spiritual Awakenings

"When we say we are contemplating God's "mystery" or willingly practicing unknowing, we are also saying that not-knowing is the necessary portal through which everything in this universe manifests."

~ BRIE STONER, ONEING: AN ALTERNATIVE ORTHODOXY

A spiritual awakening can be defined as an experience of being illuminated or enlightened in some way. It is often an extrasensory experience in which your true self knows – beyond the workings of your own mind and the visible world – a deep truth about self, life, or the divine. Spiritual awakenings come in many forms and can be great or small. They are often difficult to describe to someone else. They mostly come unbidden, but they are life-changing. They are important experiences that give us hope and renewed energy to live well and beyond the limited expectations of our socially-conditioned

221

minds and limited egos. They move us from life's routines, apathy, and distractedness to the heightened experience of knowing that which cannot be known with only our five senses. Small or large, these experiences "en-courage" us in the true sense of the word. These awakenings provide a fearless opening to experience life's deepest possibilities, fueling our spirits to continue the journey at hand – even through difficulty and encounters that sometimes require great risk and vulnerability.

A spiritual awakening can be as simple as feeling joyful or intensely connected while watching a brilliant sunrise or reading a book that offers an insight that is just what was needed. It could be the kind of awakening that changes the direction of your entire life, like a prolonged-felt visitation of the Spirit, or a chance meeting with someone who brings heightened meaning and purpose into your world. It can be a group experience where you learn something fundamentally true about yourself, someone else, universal human nature, or the divine Presence.

Many years ago, I had a non-religious spiritual awakening after attending a program on sexuality. During the 5-day workshop, we explored Jungian archetypes, allowing ourselves to express them through the art of dance. Some of these archetypes were male, female and gender neutral. We wrote and spoke about our sexual histories and journeys. We talked about how childhood had influenced our sexuality, and we created collages that expressed what we had learned since then. On the last day, the staff led us on a guided meditation during which we picked up something shiny and beautiful on the beach that had been brought to shore by the ocean waves, tailored to each one of us. It was a sort of final gift of the retreat.

When I returned home, I went to the YMCA and swam laps, as I have done for many years. During my swims, I often meditate or pray if something comes to mind. That day, I wondered what it meant that I had not seen a shiny gift on the beach during the meditation, but instead, something tiny and squirming – like an inch worm. I had to admit I was not happy that a shiny and beautiful image had not appeared to me. I wondered for several days what the image I had received could mean for me.

As I held it and wondered about it, I realized that many of the distortions – the negative messages, experiences, and images that had informed my self-concept of sexuality – had been loosened during the workshop. I sensed the past had been erased and the birth of self-acceptance regarding my sexuality had been given – with the company of the inch worm symbolizing this new beginning. This fragile, vulnerable, and perfect symbol seemed to suggest an aliveness, a healing, a transformation – from the wounds, the negativity, and the baggage of the past – to something deeply good, beautiful, sacred and alive.

I have also experienced awakenings in my life that I consider to be religious. More recently, I came to see with my heart and understand in my mind the truth of systemic racism in our country. The Black Lives Matter (BLM) movement actually began in 2013, a year after the acquittal of the shooter and death of an African American teen named Trayvon Martin. At that time, I considered BLM just another organization. The BLM movement gained momentum in 2014, however, after Michael Brown and Eric Garner were fatally wounded by police officers in Ferguson, Missouri, and in New York City, respectively. During those killings, I remember at one point realizing how the group's name – *Black Lives Matter* – resonated with me as raw truth, and I felt convicted. Then in 2020, the death of George Floyd was a watershed moment as our country took to the streets in protest of regular police brutality against African Americans.

Before the media began to highlight these fatal and unlawful incidences, I had difficulty grasping what systemic racism was really about. I thought Blacks had come a long way and wondered why there were still voices crying out for justice. The terrible fate of these Black men was the most serious claim that could be made – the unjust killing of human beings – and it finally got the attention of my heart. Yet in story after story, we began to hear how African Americans were denied equal access to healthcare, employment, housing, certain fields of work, equal pay, quality education, and on and on. I also realized that I could not really understand these hardships because I had never lived in their shoes. I did not grow up being afraid of the police or tolerating sneers and hateful remarks at work because of my skin color. Nor did I know even a tenth of the facts about African American history.

When the shootings began to get national coverage, I was *intellectually* concerned, but my heart did not necessarily respond to these events. When I saw the video of Eric Garner being killed by New York City police officers, I finally felt enraged. In that moment, I realized that social justice had become a movement of the divine Spirit, just as Civil Rights had become a movement of the Spirit in the 1960s.

When BLM's national wakeup call came during the Covid-19 pandemic in 2020, I was ecstatic and deeply moved by the nonviolent protestors from all walks of life and races who took to the streets. I began to learn more about my own white privilege and racist attitudes by listening to the experiences of Black Americans and reading and educating myself about slavery, Reconstruction, and the ongoing challenges of racist policies and attitudes in our country told by people of color. I was astounded to learn how many facts in African American history and blatant injustices toward Black Americans were either left out or grossly understated in my primary, secondary, and college history classes. To educate future generations and remember one's dark history is the only way to prevent repeating it, as the Holocaust remembrance movement has so faithfully done. I am forever grateful for the upcoming generations and activists that are now leading a momentum of change for *all* Americans – for full equality under the law.

Reflection, Meditation and Contemplation

There are three practices we can do throughout our lives to deepen our mindfulness as we make daily decisions to stay the road of our spiritual growth. These are *reflection*, *meditation*, and *contemplation*.

Reflection keeps us aware and current in our own lives: our thoughts, feelings, interactions with the world, the things we say and do, and the disruptive things from the past that may need tending. Although we may not immediately understand the deeper meaning of our initial reflections, it provides a necessary first draft of all that is happening – and has happened – in our lives.

Meditation grounds us to a place of knowing what is and is not important in the events of our lives. We begin to savor some of our experiences, gleaning from them the wisdom we need to move forward. We become aware of our false self, and the things we think, say, and do that do not move us in a spiritual direction of thriving and trans-formation. Those things might include holding onto outdated beliefs and some of the ways we respond in the world. If we're committed to meditation, we become more in touch with our true self and the things we do feel called to be and do.

Contemplation is a form of meditation or prayer that helps us discern where we are, what is possible, and where we may be headed. Contemplation inspires us to make changes in our lives that reflect our deepest values and longings. If we are tuned-in to life, truly pay-ing attention as well as taking time for solitude and applying these three practices that ultimately connect body, mind, heart, and spirit, we are given graces and insights that may surprise us, often generating joy and a deep gratitude for the gift of life.

When we look back many years or just a year ago, we may see that something new has continuously emerged on the horizon. We see and feel and live the changes that have slowly occurred as we do the inner work of deepening. If it is true that our outer world simultaneously reflects or parallels our inner world and ongoing choices in life, the needed and wanted changes in us will become a reality, if we remain committed to this process.

The table below can be used throughout the journaling process to remind us of the deeper and broader questions that can lead us in living into the more specific, desired areas of our lives. Refer to these methods often.

Reflection, Meditation and Contemplation: Where are You?

Methods:	Question	Goal	Example
1. Reflection	What has happened and is happening in my life that is meaningful?	I carefully consider my life, as it has progressed and how it is still being lived, in detail and in its totality	I look at my life in depth and detail to see if where, why, and how I'm spending my time is deeply meaningful to me, or not
2. Meditation	Is how I'm living – how I'm being and what I'm doing – fulfilling some of the deepest longings and values in my soul?	As I search for the meaning in my life, I surrender my time to that which deepens my discernment of both the past and present, where I begin to discover my deepest longings and values	I surrender control and thoughtfully observe what life might be saying to me and how I am being drawn. As I savor what I am noticing, I become willing to release the false self/ negative ego, and become more energized to make the changes that reflect my deepest longings and values

Reflection, Meditation and Contemplation: Where are You? (continued)

Methods:	Question	Goal	Example
3. Contemplation	How do I live my life now that I have understood its meaning and have discovered new meaning to be possible?	I take seriously the dreams and new visions for my life that are being revealed, and I begin to trust and regard my life as a great "possibility"	I consider the spiritual practices and path I am on now, how I can continue to open myself to new possibilities, and to truly discover and experience what is possible and most meaningful and in line with my true self

A Personal Story

When pain surfaced in 2013, it was as if a door in me wanted to open. I started to understand the importance of accepting the wounded parts of myself. The child and adult in me began to voice the words of pain, struggle, and healing in poem after poem in the many months afterward. In turn, I experienced a new level of freedom that had escaped me for decades. By avoiding the deeply broken pieces in my life, I had failed to see and honor the whole of my life. It seemed I often forgave others by giving them the benefit of the doubt, but when it came to myself, something held me back.

A linear way of thinking led me to believe I needed to be healed in order to experience wholeness, greater freedom, and peace. While this may be partly true, I came to see I did not need to be fully healed to experience the amazing freedom that the soul work of self-acceptance and self-love would bring. What was missing was my compassion toward myself, toward the unconscious wounds, character issues, and judgments from the past – my failures and sins, as some call them. When the threshold of pain in my life became an invitation to journey *through* rather than around it – and my willingness was aligned with that invitation – 1 began to practice love and acceptance on myself more regularly. Once I committed to this work, a wounded self began to emerge as a transformed self.

Meditations

"We don't need to work on the higher Self; there is nothing to do with this Self other than make contact with it, listen to it, and become aware of its guidance. It is the personality that needs help and training, but it can be trained only by the higher Self."

~ *Kabir Helminski, Living Presence*

"Thresholds are challenging because they demand that we step into the in-between place of letting go of what has been while awaiting what is still to come. When we are able to fully release our need to control the outcome, thresholds become rich and graced places of transformation. We can only become something new when we have released the old faces we have been wearing, even if it means not knowing quite who we are in the space between."

~ *Christine Valters Paintner, The Soul's Slow Ripening*

"I began to see the fears that drove my ego, which in turn fed my need to defend myself... These fears not only began to lose their power, but beneath them the butterfly of vulnerability began to emerge and guide me to an authentic way of being."

~ *Jo-Ellen A. Daring*

Questions for Journaling

1. What is your personal story? What are the most powerful spiritual dynamics of your story?

2. Were you aware of a higher power working throughout your life, or was it something else? How would you describe it now?

Exercises

---

1. Think about some aspect of your personal story that you want to savor: a lesson you learned, a relationship you had, a "mountaintop experience," a great grief that you not only survived but strengthened you and led to many positive changes in your life. Write a list of the aspects of that experience you want to savor, meditate on them, and remember them with gratitude.

2. Write a narrative about the experience in the previous step, as if you were sharing it with a friend. Reread it tomorrow or next week during a time of meditation or prayer.

3. Create a collage of the wounded self-image. Add magazine images or other pictures, photos, words, symbols, prayers, quotes, or anything that creates a picture of the complex human that you are. As you select items to add to the collage, be aware of the connection being made as the spirit inside you (the true self that seeks truth) engages with each item and what it represents as you add it to the collage. Journal your experience.

4. Repeat step 3, only this time create a collage of the transformed self-image as you are now.

Finding the Good in Religion

"The Sabbath," as Jesus said, "was made to benefit people, and not people to benefit the Sabbath."

~ GOSPEL OF MARK, THE NEW LIVING TRANSLATION

While religion is most often thought to be divinely inspired, it is humans – prone to much error – who create the container and shape of religion. As we know, the power of religious institutions can be healthy or unhealthy, and used for good or bad. Hopefully, we are awake to moral and ethical principles – awakened to the potential shadows, the dangerous and negative aspects of religious power. Each generation must seriously reflect upon the abuse of religious and other institutional power to be able to speak truth to that power. Now more than ever, through our reflection of recent history and the on-set of social media, we see the ongoing consequences of the abuse of religious power over time, including how it has:

- Enabled systemic slavery and apartheid;
- Perpetuated bigotry and exclusion in society;
- Sometimes ignored the genocide of members of other religions and groups;
- Been used for terrorism, war, and the oppression of women and other groups;
- Covered up the systemic sexual abuse of children;
- Aligned itself with destructive political forces that perpetu-ate marginalization of the poor and the powerless.

If all these abuses can be found in both religious institutions and the secular culture, then we might ask, how do we find the good in religion?

In fairness to most religions, it is these very institutions and their charities, ministries, and congregations which have supported much-needed economic development, food, clothing, medicine, and education for many the world over. This has also occurred through their partnerships with non-governmental organizations (NGOs) and inter-governmental organizations (IGOs), such as the United Nations, the International Human Rights Commission, and the Child in Need Institute. Nonetheless, it is always important to educate ourselves and question institutional systems of thought – political, religious, or philosophical – to which we subscribe. Specifically, we need to know if a religious entity has truly made restitution from its past mistakes and abuses. We oftentimes see the same problem with institutions as with individuals: if institutions fail to admit wrong-doing, make restitutions, and educate its members about these errors from the past or present, institutions are also doomed to repeat them. As someone famously said: the coverup is worse than the crime.

All of us can have a deeper spiritual or religious life – if we open ourselves to it. Opening ourselves is essential to the process. As we grow in our spirituality and/or our religious faith, we will find that opportunities to deepen a spiritual connection can take many forms. The bottom line for many of us is to search for signs that can lead us to an authentic faith – both inwardly and outwardly – versus a false faith that never leads us to the heart of who we, and the divine, really are.

In Buddhism, a beginner's mind is essential for allowing wisdom to be revealed in any moment, as we let go of what we already know to receive something new. It is similar to the path of mindfulness, which is a practice of bringing one's attention to the present moment, gently and without judgment. If we follow no religion, or were damaged by religious associations in the past, 12-step groups are a place to authentically explore our concept of a higher power, which is described brilliantly in the *Twelve Steps and Twelve Traditions of Alcoholics Anonymous* and many other Twelve Step books. For Christians searching for renewal, Christian mysticism, also known as Christian contemplative spirituality, provides a rich heritage of paths to intimacy and wisdom, loving service to our neighbors, and deep connection with a God of love. Like other mystical sects of the main religions – such as Sufism in Islam, Kabbalism in Judaism, and Vedanta in Hinduism – finding a higher power and the mystical in the ordinary, day-to-day aspects of our lives is a common thread. Reading religious and non-religious altruistic texts and authors, attending religious and spiritually-based services and group events, and working for peace and justice and the greater good via religious and secular communities, are ways we give back from all that we have learned from these paths.

Spiritual writers and poets of all traditions – from the Sufi Muslim poet Rumi to Mary Oliver and Joy Harjo, from William Blake to David Whyte, from Rilke to Maya Angelou, from Hafiz to Clark Strand – can provide pathways to spiritual experiences that can be a beginning point for many in search of a higher power. For those who acknowledge a higher power, these poets and writers will revitalize one's understanding and experience of God, as well as for many who are disillusioned by passive, uninspiring, and ritualistic religious experience.

Opening myself to religious expressions outside of my tradition has led to a beautiful deepening of my own religious convictions. Learning from other traditions has opened me to new practices that have led to a deeper peace, a wider consciousness, and more profound depth and understanding of the Great Spirit's love for the entire creation. For example, practicing yoga has given me a beautiful way to practice balance and lovingly treat my body as the sacred temple that it is. Reading and listening to the words of the Dalai Lama and Thich Nhat Hanh has inspired me to work for peace in my own heart, and to pass that on to others through nonjudgment and acceptance. Christian Mysticism's practice of silence and solitude has helped me be a more grounded and gentle person in my responses to life.

Several years ago, I began reading *Autobiography of a Yogi* by Paramahansa Yogananda. (I admit, I am still not done reading it.) This Hindu yogi's experience of his search for God is inspiring. I eventually made the Hindu connection to the music of ex-Beatle George Harrison, whose music and life were highly impacted by his exposure to Hinduism and his embracement of Hindu beliefs. Seeing Harrison's strong connection to God through Hinduism (listen to Harrison's music) only validated my view that the Spirit manifests itself through many paths of enlightenment. Harrison was raised as a Christian but felt disillusioned by the Christian culture that surrounded him. Yet he never denounced his roots but told his mother in a letter that what he'd found only made more sense of his Christian roots. His spiritual path led him to be the first to raise money through benefit rock concerts to feed the starving people of Bangladesh. He promoted Yogananda's book for the rest of his life to share with others the freedom he had found.

My own exploration of other religions has not made me a Hindu or a Buddhist, or to stray from my Christian faith. In contrast, it has had the opposite effect of leading me to a more genuine faith. This exploration has also led me to a deep respect for the freedom of other people and cultures to follow their own religious paths that offer God's good to the world. Many of our religious and spiritual practices can be shared – or left at the door – as we're invited to a new movement of spirit among believers and seekers of all religions. We can unite with others around the world in the common goodwill found in all love-based, authentic religion.

As the Covid-19 pandemic showed us in 2020, religious and political systems have more at stake than their own survival and their own beliefs and interests. All religions share common ground in efforts to create sustainable economies as well as cooperative ventures in medicine, the environment, trade, education, agriculture, and peace-keeping, to name a few.

Our most important mission is to be aware, to know what our own conscience tells us – not just what is good and evil – but what is good and better. Knowing the histories of our religious institutions and spiritual traditions and staying abreast of what is happening in these institutions today is crucial to speaking truth to power. Ensuring our religious communities continue working for human rights, the environment, and social justice for the peoples of all nations, depends on all of us.

Meditations

"Everything that exists is the manifestation of a single source of Life and Being."

~ Kabir Helminski, Living Presence

"The religious False Self can even justify racism, slavery, war, and total denial or deception and feel no guilt whatsoever, because "they think they are doing a holy duty for God" (John 16:2). The ego has found its cover, so be quite careful about being religious. If your religion does not transform your consciousness to one of compassion, it is more a part of the problem than any solution."

~ Richard Rohr, Immortal Diamond

"As we grow in our spirituality and/or our religious faith, we will find that opportunities to deepen a spiritual connection can take many forms. The bottom line for many of us is to search for signs that can lead us to an authentic faith – both inwardly and outwardly – versus a false faith that never leads us to the heart of who we, and the divine, really are."

~ Jo-Ellen Darling

Questions for Journaling

Religious Experience:

1. Were you raised in a particular religion? What was it like?

    a. Do you still value this religion or not? If yes, what is the good you have found? How has it changed, grown, or shaped your worldview?

    b. If not, do you have a spirituality for life? What is the good you have found? How has it changed, grown, or shaped your worldview?

2. If you were not raised in a religion or religious household, are there any religions or philosophies that have attracted you as an adult?

   a. What do you value about them?

   b. What is the shadow side in the history of the religion that you now follow? Do some research.

   c. Have there been renewals in the history of this religion or philosophy? When and what were they?

3. Some people remain religiously affiliated in spite of all the bad press about their religion. They still benefit or have managed to find the good that still exists within the institution; some also say they are "working for change on the inside."

   a. If you are one of these people, journal how you are participating/working for change on the inside.

   b. Journal your own feelings and thoughts, including your hopes and dreams as to how your engagement on the inside continues to feed your soul and offers opportunities for transformation, for not only yourself, but for others and the world.

Exercises

1. Attend a spiritual or religious event in your area. Journal your experiences. What speaks to you or enlivens you about them?

2. Find and read a spiritual book that draws your attention. Join or form a book circle and read it with others to reflect on how the concepts of the book can inform and change lives.

3. Alone, with friends, or an intentional group, watch documentaries on various denominations or religious experiences. What stays with you after you've seen them? What personal enlightenment are you gaining from them?

4. Watch films about the plights of other people. Movies like *The Killing Fields (1984)*, *Schindler's List* (1993), *Amistad* (1997), *Lion* (2017), *Indian Horse* (2017), and *Harriet (2019)* bring the world to us in ways reading about them cannot. How are you moved by what you have watched? Are you invited to make a change in your own life as a result?

Journaling as Pilgrimage

> *"When we commit to a contemplative path, we begin to let go of the things that aren't important anymore... Our pilgrimage might lead us to a place of deep peace and joy at not "fitting in" anymore. We can be true outcasts in the world. We might experience a sense of delight that our ways are not the world's ways, but a path rooted in a deeper kind of wisdom."*
>
> ~ CHRISTINE VALTERS PAINTNER, THE SOUL OF A PILGRIM

Most often we think of pilgrimage as a journey of travel to a sacred, religious, or historically significant site. But pilgrimage can also be a nonreligious experience. Either way, a pilgrimage may be an intentional search for insight, self-knowledge, or healing in a life situation. Going on a pilgrimage may be a way to honor one's God, find an answer to prayer, or simply seek an open-ended blessing of renewal from the divine. What this suggests is that a pilgrimage can be simultaneously an outer *and* an inner journey of discovery, whether taking a single day or several weeks. Pilgrimage can also be when we are companions to another in some way, such as through a friend's illness or grief, where we have our own unique, inner experience of spiritual discovery.

Journaling can be a companion to the outer and inner pilgrimages we make. We search and find meaning as we write about our experiences and find the nuggets of wisdom and insight into ourselves that we can then savor. Savoring is an important aspect of spiritual experience: it helps our souls to integrate our experiences as wisdom, which often becomes our deepest truth.

We may make a specific intention for our inner pilgrimage, such as when we ask for a spiritual awakening or express a desire for the direction of our life to be revealed or transformed. Often, events surrounding these transformational changes are burned into our hearts and souls as we remember the sacred places we journeyed to.

The most important time in any person's life is the present moment. It is in the present moments in which life-giving insights are given, and in the present moment that we make life-changing choices. Perhaps we cannot change the circumstances of our lives, but we can change our minds and hearts in any moment we choose to do so.

Pilgrimage is one of the ways we can practice and experience living in the moment. A vacation approached and lived as a pilgrimage moves us out of the routine ways of thinking, feeling, and sensing. Because we are more relaxed, we eventually cross the threshold to the unconscious. We are given an opportunity to see, moment-by-moment, that we are traveling in a time of meaningful discovery. Phil Cousineau writes in *The Art*

CAIRNS

Eternal pilgrims we,
on the sometimes broken
sometimes silken
path
we call our lives.
Longing pilgrims we,
hungrily seeking
stones and rocks
all shapes and sizes
to point the way.
Blessed pilgrims we,
when the stories of our
lives
sometimes broken
sometimes silken
are deemed cairns
by the one who truly
listens.
Grateful pilgrims we,
gathering stones and
rocks, and with the one
who truly listens
patiently creating
a cairn of balance
that stretches toward
heaven.
Wise pilgrims we,
as we bless the cairn
bless the
sometimes
broken
sometimes silken
path
we call our lives,
and know that
heaven is the gift
of welcoming
the broken and the silken
with equal measure.

By Jennifer (Jinks) Hoffman

of Pilgrimage that when we visit ancient ruins or landscapes, it is a voice *inside of us* that "beckons" us to the experience.

Likewise, the experience of journaling as pilgrimage offers enlightenment, whether we have yet learned to see well or not. All it takes is a willingness to notice, feel, sense, acknowledge, pause, breathe deeply, and surrender from living on autopilot and a self-made schedule. When we take the time to journal – and perhaps, just as importantly, to review our journal pages at a later date – we reconnect with important experiences that have changed us.

Vacation, Pilgrimage or Retreat?

> *"A journey (vacation) asks: what will you take with you?*
> *A pilgrimage asks: what will you leave behind?"*
>
> ~ BARB MILLER, SPIRITUAL DIRECTOR

Vacation, retreat, and pilgrimage are, outwardly, three very different kinds of events. What is common in our lived experience of them, however, is how they can generate much creativity, joy, and insight that can profoundly affect the journey of our life. These three ways to spend time away also gives us a way to look forward to something special in our lives that takes us away from long periods of routine and working. Going on vacation, retreat, or pilgrimage can transform a stale outlook on life to one of appreciation, gratitude, and creative living. However, getting the most from these periods of travel and retreat time will be impossible if we do not spend some time in reflection and journaling our conscious thoughts and feelings as we prepare, undergo, and later savor these experiences.

If we review a memorable vacation, retreat, or pilgrimage in our past, we may discover an internal process that led us to make the decision to go in the first place. We may notice that we were initially attracted to a certain place. We may ask ourselves questions as to why this place drew us to itself. Soon, we may find ourselves going to a deeper level of awareness, recognizing that a longing had existed in us. What was the nature of this longing, and why did we want to go there? Recognizing that longing or desire may take us to another level of reflection: how does this longing connect to knowing ourselves more fully? What is the hidden meaning in the longing or desire that caught our initial attention?

As I prepared to make a trip in the early 2000s, I wasn't fully aware that I was really searching or longing for something deeply spiritual. I made plans to participate in a trip to the Austrian Alps. Hiking had become a favorite local pastime and I was drawn to the beauty of the Austrian countryside. (That seed was planted in my childhood viewing of the *Sound of Music*.) Although I loved spending time in nature for many years and knew, on some level, that it supported my spiritual life, I hadn't necessarily seen a *longing for beauty* as having spiritual origins. It was only later – in 2009 – that I began to honor and value experiences of beauty as a necessary spiritual practice.

In early 2002, I booked a hiking trip to Zillertal in the Tyrolean Valley of Austria, where I would spend a week dining, picnicking, socializing and climbing mountains with perfect strangers. As the June date for departure approached, it was a trip I almost did not make. With the attacks of September 11, 2001 the year before, the travel jitters were still wreaking havoc on the traveling public, and no less on me. I seriously considered canceling the trip. After journaling and praying through my fears for several days and discussing them with my therapist, I was finally calm and trusting enough to go – no matter what would happen.

On the one free day allotted to us at the end of the week, I boarded a local train to Innsbruck, a city I had visited 20 years prior with a friend. This time, I explored many places on my own while also experiencing the joy of my own company. After a visit to the Cathedral of St. James, I relished a walk through the lovely flower gardens in Old Town. I later sat at an outdoor café in view of the City Tower clock, drinking Austrian-grown coffee as the Innsbruck Stadtturm (as the clock is called), struck noon into the ever-pleasant day. Later,

I caught the Nordkette gondola – the first time I rode in one – high into the Austrian alps, where afterward I sat perched on top of the Hungerburg overlooking the "bowl" which the surrounding Karwendel mountain range had formed around Innsbruck. At the top of the Hungerburg, I turned around to face the shocking and harshly beautiful mountain peaks stretching as far as I could see. I wept involuntarily in those moments, which had given me a humbling yet exalted view of creation and the mystery of the divine, who I felt had mysteriously brought it all into being. The trip was, in its own way, a vacation, a retreat, and a pilgrimage rolled into one.

The most lasting effect was a profound experience of dwelling in the physical beauty that Austria offered, and a desire to create more beauty in my life and in my living spaces when I returned home. Back in the States, I reread my journal entries from the trip and savored the experiences by creating a collage and adding my photographs to it. Remembering the gorgeous flower boxes attached to homes in the magnificent countryside and on sidewalks and buildings in the towns and cities, I created a flower box garden on my city apartment steps and indulged myself daily in its beauty, which forged a lasting desire for gardening. I journaled much after my return, expressing gratitude that I could make such a voyage in the first place, as well as return with memories and gifts that have sustained me, in one way or another, ever since.

Longings for travel that you may experience in the present, but which cannot be pursued or fulfilled now, are important to explore. These "seeds of desire" may serve a purpose for the future that could be an important part of your life.

One such unfulfilled longing occurred after my divorce in the 1990s. For a long period of time, I did not travel due to finances. However, I found myself deeply attracted to Rick Steves' European travelogues on PBS and his book *Europe Through the Back Door*. As I watched his program, I felt a palpable hunger in my soul, but it wasn't clear why or where in Europe I wanted to travel. Although I did not make that particular trip until 2016 – nearly 20 years after that time of deep longing while watching Steves' program – I realized the seeds of that desire had become clear: to connect more intimately with the place and time of my ancestors, particularly my Irish heritage on my father's side of the family.

Before that trip with my husband, I arranged to visit the church where my great grandmother and her nine siblings were baptized in the village of Aughavas in County Leitrim, Ireland. After visiting St. Joseph's – which replaced the original St. Mary's church – we enjoyed a wonderful meal and conversation with Fr. Peter Tiernan. We later walked the old cemetery adjacent to the ruins of St. Mary's. There I found a very faded tombstone of another relative born two generations prior to the births of my great-great grandmother's children. To this day, I look forward to working on this side of my family tree. When the time is right, I know it will bring new energy and vitality to my life.

Meditations

"By staying present to the discomfort of life, we grow in our resilience and our ability to recover from the deep wounds that life will offer us. We grow in our compassion for ourselves as we learn to embrace all of the vulnerable places inside of us."

~ *Christine Valters Paintner, The Soul of a Pilgrim*

"'Don't push the river,'" says my friend Richard Rohr. Don't get ahead of your soul. The goal isn't to get somewhere. This isn't about forcing something to happen. The goal is to be in harmony with the gifts that are already given. The goal is to fall in love with your life."

~ *Paula D'Arcy, Sacred Threshold*

"Pilgrimage is one of the ways we can practice and experience living in the moment. A vacation approached and lived as a pilgrimage moves us out of the routine ways of thinking, feeling, and sensing. Because we are more relaxed, we eventually cross the threshold to the unconscious. We are given an opportunity to see, moment-by-moment, that we are traveling in a time of meaningful discovery."

~ Jo-Ellen A. Darling

Questions for Journaling

1. Journal about a travel experience you had in a faraway place, or one very different from home that changed you in some way. What were your longings before you departed from home? Now in retrospect, what were the gifts you received during and after the trip? Did they lead to any major changes in your life?

2. What are the current longings in your heart? Try writing this sentence stem and write for as long as you need to become clear about what is going on inside of you: "I have this longing to...." Later, come back to this question and repeat it throughout the week or month. See what emerges.

3. Like tending a garden, how can you tend to one of your longings? One way is to journal about it, to honor it in some way, or perhaps to make peace with it if it does not seem as though the timing is right. I once had a friend who longed to marry. She waited a long time, and the waiting became painful for her. She made a decision to find deep gratitude for all that was happening in her life, but to also continue to meet and spend time with new people with whom she shared interests. She eventually met someone who brought much joy to her life, but he was afraid to remarry after a painful divorce. In her heart she knew it was unprocessed fear that held him back, but

she decided to let go. After time apart, he had worked through his fear and they were eventually married. That "friend" was me.

4. What will you do with your life now? What major changes or minor shifts have you discovered that bring you contentment and joy?

Exercises

1. Do you have a favorite local place you go where your spirit feels nourished? If not, make a plan to explore some nearby spaces that could be places of refuge when your soul is needing time apart from where you work or live. Make it a point to take time out and explore them once a week, perhaps on your way home from work or some other time you can find. If your life is busy, schedule it so you won't skip over this exercise. Journal about your "sense of things" after you spend time in these places.

2. Plan a vacation, retreat, or pilgrimage for yourself. It is best to do this solo, but doing it with a partner who respects your space, or going with a group of strangers with like-minded intentions, can be fruitful experiences as well. See "Guidelines for a Pilgrimage or Retreat," which can also be used for a vacation by adjusting some of the guideline parameters.

A Retreat Story

I was required to design my own retreat for a class in 2013. I realized after the retreat that I had also made a pilgrimage. As I traveled to the retreat house more than an hour from home, heading west through the beautiful farm country of southeastern Pennsylvania, I listened to sacred music and stopped at Blue Marsh Lake. I gazed at the body of water and trees on a hill from my car, allowing nature to provide the metaphors I needed that would prepare me to receive the wisdom I was seeking in those precious hours. I had gone on that retreat intending to lay down anxiety and fear around being out of work. At Blue Marsh Lake, I wrote the following reflection before continuing on:

> "At the boat ramp I sit in my car, perched in the lot overlooking the lake. Eventually I notice a perfectly balanced tree directly in front of me, a good 100 yards away. It had five main branches, spread out perfectly like a fan in front of me. Jesus' parable of the fig tree comes to my mind.

My journal continued when I began to settle in at the retreat house:

> "If something isn't producing fruit, get rid of it; let it go. I see the connection to the chapter I've also chosen to read ("How Do I Get Free, How Do I Stay Free? The Practice of Letting Go" in Jeremy Langford's book, *Seeds of Faith*). I've chosen 'letting go' as my theme for the next two days: let go and be open to God; let go of job worries and anxiety; and let go of any specific agenda here... let go and let God lead. Then a loud and distinct thought came to me as I wrote about these events in my journal: "The tree of anxiety/fear is not producing any fruit in my life – cut it down!"

Then, before I unpacked my bags, more insight arrived:

> "While walking the labyrinth, I felt free, opening my heart to hear the divine. I soon saw a bright green inchworm in one of the circuits on the labyrinth. I picked up a small branch of pine needles and placed them near him so he would climb on. I then raised the branch to my palm, where the inchworm then fell off and wriggled frantically on its back, trying to get

back on its feet. ("Oh, I am like that,' I thought, 'tiny, frail, in God's hands… always trying to do things my way.") Again, I offered the pine needles and slowly lifted them toward my face to get a better look but the inchworm flipped off the needles and onto the ground again. ("Don't I do this sometimes – practically jumping out of God's hands when he comes close? Instead of receiving his gift of grace – don't I insist on handling it solo? 'Gee, God of the Universe, no thanks. I can manage.' But is it really possible? Don't I just become blind and fearful and think I'm no longer in his palm or presence?"

The retreat continued to provide much wisdom through nature:

"I go to my room and open the large window overlooking the west lawn. A red-tailed hawk quickly catches my eye as she soars close to the building in the billowing airwaves that rattle through clumps of leaves on the trees. The hawk was totally playing, I could tell. She wasn't looking for food, or anything, just enjoying the ride: letting go and doing what she's made to do – enjoying the currents that God had created for her! I wonder why I don't do this more? Why I don't let go and let the flow of God move me naturally, like the wind lifts the hawk without any effort on her part, except to a) spread her wings, and b) be willing to go up. I decide that I want to trust God more, like Red-tail trusts the wind!"

During and after the retreat, I realized that moving from one place to the next – from my home an hour away to the park, to the labyrinth, and then to my room on the third floor – had been a mini-pilgrimage that prepared me for the next 24 hours of solitude. It became apparent to me that walking from room to room in the 1930's English Renaissance style house I would stay in for the night – from leaving my cloistered room and stepping into the hallway, from making my way down the stairwell to the dining room, from being inside the building to stepping into the outside courtyard centered around a lovely fountain, and taking the many paths on the property which led to many special places – *this* had all become a pilgrimage within a time of retreat. To this day, the quality of mindfulness that I experienced that day is something I tap into often when I am in deep need of coming back into the present.

Questions for Journaling

1. Where are your favorite landscapes? What spiritual qualities do they possess?

2. Do you long to travel? Where and why?

3. Can you trace these longings and love of landscapes back to your childhood or another time of life?

4. Sit quietly for several minutes and meditate. Think of a couple of your personal pilgrimages through life, such as a time of joy or sadness, of great achievement or longing, or whatever it is that stands out in your memory right now. Make a list or journal your thoughts as to what was essential in each of those journeys.

Exercise

1. If you are able to plan a short one-day retreat or pilgrimage, journal about the possibilities of where and why you would go. Journal your thoughts before, during, and after your experience. Throughout the next week, savor the moments that were significant. What is the story about *you* that these moments are telling?

2. If you desire, create a mini collage on a page in your journal. Cut out pictures and words from magazines and paste them. Use colored pencils or markers to draw or doodle anything that comes to mind. Gaze on what emerges, then savor what you see.

Thresholds and Liminal Spaces

Often when we take a vacation, go on retreat, or make a pilgrimage, we cross several thresholds. These thresholds mark the moments of beginnings and endings, such as the present hope or joy that accompanies the anticipation of our travel plans. Later, they may mark a time of remembering and savoring our experiences when our adventure ends – the feelings of renewal and the promise of new beginnings after we arrive home.

Sometimes threshold places are fast and furious, such as when someone dies suddenly, and our lives change forever. During these times of unexpected and unwanted experiences, we are forced to the next place, unprepared, jarred, and disoriented by the experience. Many who have survived the pandemic of 2020 lost their jobs and loved ones with no choice but to carry on. It's important to remember that life will continue to offer us a healing path through the wilderness if we can stay committed to a spiritual focus and make choices that support an authentic path. We must, in these cases, ask ourselves what it is that we really need and want.

Liminal spaces – also known as thin places – are times when we dwell in a shared space with Spirit. Liminal spaces are usually when things aren't clear and decisions are often on hold – they can be like long hallways of pacing, of waiting and discernment, even after we arrive home from a fruitful time of being away to travel or rest. Perhaps we are waiting for the right timing for a life-changing decision to be made, such as choosing a vocational direction, or a decision to marry or not after much soul searching. Perhaps the significance of our time spent on pilgrimage or retreat is a feeling, thought, or desire we had about our lives that deserves our attention upon return. Instead of dismissing it, we stay with it in our journals and reflection time, holding it in our hearts. This liminal space may last a while, until we are fully ready to make a decision in regard to what our feeling, thought, or desire is pointing us to.

Ultimately, we can find some willingness to wait with trust. In doing so, we will have interrupted making impulsive and costly choices that could set us back. We will have learned to trust the right timing of things – including choices made by others – and receive the gift, perhaps not *when* we wanted it, but a gift nonetheless.

Meditations

"This journey of crossing the threshold is about what leads to life, and yet remarkably, few choose it."
   ~ Christine Valters Paintner, The Soul of a Pilgrim

"Liminal spaces are usually when things aren't clear and decisions are often on hold – they can be like long hallways of pacing, of waiting and discernment, even after we arrive home from a fruitful time of being away to travel or rest."
   ~ Jo-Ellen A. Darling

"May you listen to your longing to be free."
   ~ John O'Donohue, Eternal Echoes

Questions for Journaling Before and After Vacation, Pilgrimage or Retreat

1. What question do you need answered, or gift do you need to receive presently in your life from this vacation, pilgrimage, or retreat? If nothing specific comes to mind, can you make an intention to be truly open to receive the wisdom that is waiting to be given for your life?

2. Spend at least a short amount of time in daily solitude for two weeks before your departure, whether it's taking a walk on your lunch hour, sitting quietly in a place of beauty, or connecting with yourself in ways that work for you (hot bath, meditation, physical workouts, fasting, yoga, etc.). Be gentle with yourself and expect to receive something good from the experience.

3. When you return from your time away, reread your journal entries and highlight the things that stand out to you as you journaled throughout your vacation, pilgrimage, or retreat. During your first week home, take some time each day to review these highlights. You may want to summarize them, so they all appear on one page. What are these highlighted words saying to you? How are your thoughts, feelings, and desires for change being informed? Respond to these questions in your journal.

4. Name one or more action steps that seem to be a natural progression from the insights you have received about yourself and your life journey. Come back to these steps on another day and clarify any questions as to how you will go about integrating the spiritual or practical insights you have been given.

5. What decisions have you made as a result of your journey through your recent vacation, pilgrimage, or retreat? What have you let go? What are you moving toward?

Exercises

1. Plan a vacation, pilgrimage, or retreat that fits your budget. It can be as short as a day or weekend, or for as long as a month or more. Journal the highs and lows, the excitement, the anticipation, and the fears. (Are you afraid of flying or going solo? Write it all down!)

2. Turn a vacation into a pilgrimage by framing it as one before you go. Have a plan. Include which books, music, or other media you will take – and just as importantly – not take. Think about planned time alone and with others, but be flexible. Research places to see and experiences that would be important or desirable for you. Bring an open heart and mind, all your feelings, your journal, and an awareness of trust that Spirit will show up.

3. See "Guidelines for a Pilgrimage or Retreat" in this chapter for more guidelines.

4. Slowly read "Through God's Eyes," a poem below written by Kathy Koval after she attended a retreat. Read it again and circle the words and phrases that capture your attention. Reflect and respond to them in your journal. What is the personal, authentic invitation to you in this poem?

Through God's Eyes[6]

If you would see yourself through God's eyes
there would be nothing to fear.
No doubt, no consternation, no complaint.
There is no room for that in God's vision of you.
Only love –
wild, raw, abundant, freely flowing,
light upon light upon light
permeating, splashing.
Nothing needs to, nor can be hidden from this love.
So dance the dance of your heart
wildly, unapologetically.
Allow yourself to move freely within the circle
knowing all places are open to you.
You belong anywhere.

---

6 "Through God's Eyes," Copyright © Kathy Koval. Used with permission.

The dance floor is open.
Be wild, be tender, be outrageous.
Laugh, cry, shout, sing, or be silent.
Be you as God sees you.
Don't keep the world waiting.
Move with God, move in God.
Move.

By Kathy Koval

Guidelines for a Pilgrimage or Retreat

For a retreat, here are guidelines written by a member of my spiritual community, Jane Williams, Ph.D. You can modify these guidelines for a vacation, as well. You may need to remove or replace the words "Spirit" or "God" to make it more relatable to you.

A Brief Guide for a Retreat[7]

Allow a **minimum** of 6 hours for your retreat (a full day is best).

1. Go alone.

    *   Take only what you need; leave behind your phone (or turn it to **silent** and do not check it), camera, iPod, computer, and any other electronic gear; if you are driving to your retreat site, do not turn on the car radio or CD player; take a small amount of food, your journal and pen, and a water bottle.

2. You may select a chapter from a book, a poem, a piece of music (if you choose this, you may bring a CD or iPod, but only to listen to that selection), a particular scripture passage, or a picture on which to meditate/contemplate and journal; **OR** you might want to take materials for you to use to create

---

7 Adapted from "A Brief Guide for a Retreat," Copyright © Jane Williams, Ph.D. Used with permission.

something (watercolors, mandalas to color, clay, etc.); **OR** you may want to be on retreat at a place where the labyrinth is available; **OR** you may want to use the retreat as silent meditation time – time to focus on the present and be mindful.

3. To begin your retreat, take time to center yourself in silence, to pray for the God of your understanding's guidance for your retreat time, and to ask the Spirit to help you to be present and aware of each moment.

4. Alternate between:

   • Moments of taking something in (walking in nature, reading scripture or a spiritual passage, listening to music, etc.);

   • Sitting with what you have received (meditate, close your eyes, do mindful breathwork, walking meditation, etc.);

   • Expressing what you have taken in (journal, sing, use art materials). Let each portion of the three movements be for at least 20 minutes – take your time – this is not something to "accomplish" or a task to finish, but rather a meal for your soul which requires tasting and savoring slowly. You may do this several times with the same or different readings, music, etc. If you re-use the same materials, you may begin to discover deeper meaning and different details than you did with your initial examination.

5. Follow the Spirit's leading such that if you feel the need to change where you are sitting or walking, do so, and do it mindfully. If you feel tears, let them come. If you feel deep joy, express it. If you feel tired, let yourself rest (but do not use the whole retreat to sleep!).

6. As your retreat time comes to a close, take time to express your gratitude to God for the opportunity to retreat, and ask God's

guidance and protection as you prepare to re-enter the world. End your time with 10 minutes of silence, imagining that God is holding you in God's hands – securely, lovingly, comfortingly.

7. As you walk or drive back to where you live, refrain from filling the space around you with music, a phone call, or the radio. Use the travel time to be mindful and pay attention to what you notice on this part of your retreat – what do you see, sense, hear, etc., that you did not notice before; what inner feelings are you aware of?

8. Before you enter your home, apartment, or room, pause at the threshold and pray a prayer of gratitude for the gift of this time and for whatever Spirit is leading you toward.

    *   Return home determined to notice and not forget the impact of your experience. Retreat can be a life renewing experience, yet it is easy to forget the nuances of your experience. Reviewing your journal after several weeks or months will help keep your perspective fresh."

The Journey to Self-Love

"I invite you to abandon your efforts to fix yourself and instead reclaim your innate beauty and worth as a luminous cell in the body of Mother Earth."

~ MIRABAI STARR, WILD MERCY

The journey to self-love begins by being true to ourselves in the circumstances of our lives. Sometimes it involves making controversial choices or decisions that others disagree with. At other times it is choosing ourself over others in the spirit of self-care when we are in deep need and exhaustion. At other points in our lives, self-love will entail an important decision to pursue a work life that mysteriously calls us to something different and less practical than what everyone else is suggesting that we do. Yet as we give ourselves time to sift, discern, and pray about how to handle the various aspects of our lives, a choice will appear that will feel more right than not. Or, after contemplating our choice for days, weeks or months, it may be something that we will not be able to live with after all. Perhaps the timing will not be right, so we will table it. If the choice arises later, we will know we are not finished with it. We will want to reconsider its invitation, or let it go once and for all. All of these choices will lead us to becoming more true to ourselves.

Self-love is one of the more difficult terrains I have ever navigated. For years, loving myself was often a patchwork of moments of deep self-knowing, held together by a tiny thread of yearning for more. Today when they occur, these moments often have a strong emotional connection, such as deep self-compassion. Very often, this journey requires a change of beliefs about myself and others. We may not be able to progress without first opening our hearts and lives to others with a new level of honesty. We may not get there without the company of friends, teachers, and spiritual guides – including writers and poets – all of whom can help us explore our own inner lives.

Yet, I've come to realize that no one else can do the work of self-love for me. Only I can make that journey.

For several years, I have read the writers and poets who point to the importance of knowing oneself, caring for oneself, and learning to be oneself. I've meditated upon their prayerful and mystical insights about the value of the human heart and the nature of the benevolent Spirit alive in this universe. I've then pursued the practices I've shared in this book to help me stay focused in my spiritual life.

In addition, I wouldn't have ever begun to grasp or experience the depth and breadth of my Higher Power had I limited myself to the traditional paths of my religious affiliation. Only when I began to read and then join contemplative and spiritually growing communities who were seeking something deeper and truer than what many of the more traditional churches and other spiritual communities in the wider secular culture had to offer, did my journey open wide and deepen. Thanks to the shared experiences of these amazing teachers, poets, writers, translators and program facilitators, I rediscovered the longing inside that was always there.

Gunilla Norris writes eloquently about this in her book, *Inviting Silence*. She says in essence that we tend to think that what we do is who we are. Yet, overidentifying with what we do actually moves us further away from the true self – who we really are and who we've always been. All we need to do, she says, is "stop, feel, and grow silent to receive the gift of ourselves."

Prior to finding these mostly modern communities and scribes who have reinterpreted much of what I learned about God growing up, I lived a life trying to do and be enough for others from a false sense of self. By confronting the discomfort and fear that negative feelings and experiences generated – and identifying and experiencing the ungrieved losses in my life – this self-regard has grown into a compassionate awareness that I now know to be a path to self-love. As we do this, we may also experience a deeper connection with the God of our understanding.

Something to ask ourselves when we hear the critical voice that points out our negative attributes, character flaws, or a time of failure from our past, is: how do I take this to the next level? Am I able to dialog with this part of myself and see an earlier version of myself with compassion? Can I begin to forgive myself and see my errors without condemning my value as a precious creature entrusted to this universe? Can I trust and be loved – even partially – by a power greater than myself that may lead me to the deepest level of security I may ever know? If I can say yes – or even "possibly" to any of these questions – I believe self-compassion and self-forgiveness can eventually lead to a right sense of self-love.

The Spirit of love has given me hope after much relationship error and trying to heal my life on my own. If the adage "You cannot give what you do not have" is true, then the fact that I think I am loving others cannot stand if I continue to lack self-compassion, self-forgiveness, and self-love. These three essential qualities of loving others – compassion, forgiveness, and love – are the rose petals of authentic love that can and must be practiced on ourselves.

And if the journey to love includes the path to self-love so that we can experience our wholeness, then how are we loving others? Do we cut them a break often and give tough love, or gentle but frank honesty when needed? Do we take the high road and respect their freedom to make their own choices without interfering or criticizing them when they do not meet our expectations? How do we really treat others? Are we kind to them – or sarcastic, suspicious, undermining? Turning these questions around to ourselves, we will find the answer to our own level of self-love.

One of the important ways we love others is by making amends to them – whether a daily apology over a moody response to someone who doesn't deserve it, or a more serious infraction that has required much prayer, meditation, and consultation with others. Unlike the sixties' movie, *Love Story*, real love is saying you're sorry, because when you do so with sincerity, you are saying you care. Our feelings are to soul like the nervous system is to the body: they can tell us when something is off and when all is well. Likewise, self-compassion will grow when we notice – with compassionate awareness – how we berate ourselves for making mistakes, how we judge ourselves for not being enough, or when we beat ourselves up for our insensitivity and carelessness with others. Just as we need sincerity and humility to move in the direction of forgiving others, this same approach is what we need to begin to truly love ourselves.

Yet, the process of loving ourselves is less about fixing ourselves and more about allowing grace into our lives. There are many definitions of grace: clemency, mercy, reprieve. My favorite is: "a disposition to be generous or helpful; *goodwill*." The practice of compassionate awareness begins to pay off. Eventually, one begins to truly accept that one has faulty perceptions and character flaws, and yet discovers that a natural self-forgiveness begins to flow. The fruit of all this is a renewed mind-set toward ourselves and others – and a more stable and lasting grace.

To start over with a fresh perspective, we sometimes think we have to go all the way back to the beginning of our life, or to our previous relationship, or to that assault, or whatever it was that knocked us down. Maybe so. Yet, if we have already addressed these issues in any depth, it may not be necessary to keep going back if it keeps us in chains. Instead, we can decide to let it go, or mine it for more treasure. Either way, we can move forward. Wherever we are, we can begin where we are: in the present moment.

Meditations

"Love is both who you are and who you are still becoming, like a sunflower seed that becomes its own sunflower."

~ *Richard Rohr, Immortal Diamond*

"The self is not an object or a field point of reference. It is a diverse inner landscape too rich to be grasped in any one concept. There is a plurality of divine echoes within you."

~ *John O'Donohue, Eternal Echoes*

257

"Our feelings are to soul like the nervous system is to the body: they can tell us when something is off and when all is well."
~ *Jo-Ellen A. Darling*

Questions for Journaling

1. What has been your journey to self-love up to this moment in time?

2. As you begin to think about letting yourself receive the gifts of self-compassion, self-forgiveness and self-love from your Higher Power, what do you notice? Do you have resistance? Or are you inclined toward acceptance? Journal what both resistance and acceptance look like for you.

3. How do you feel and think about yourself when you are around other people? This week, notice and journal your thoughts and feelings when you gather with others.

4. In the next few days, how do you think and feel about yourself when you are alone, doing something you enjoy? How about when you're doing something that might be necessary, but that you *don't* enjoy? How can you bring *compassionate awareness* into this area of your life?

5. "Well-ordered self-love is right and natural," wrote Thomas Aquinas, a medieval philosopher and priest. Although his quote is affirming, for many of us the attributes of self-love have not been "well-ordered, right and natural." Yet his words are powerful and worth contemplating. Write about them whether you resist or embrace his ideas.

Exercises

1. Meditate on a quote above that attracts your spirit. Respond to it in your journal. Tell yourself what the words mean to you and how the quote is important to your journey at this moment in time. Repeat this exercise for any of the words, phrases, or quotes you can relate to.

2. Reflect on the concepts of self-compassion, self-forgiveness and self-love. What do these three ways of being with yourself look like? They might be: "impossible, unnatural, daunting…" Or they may be: "desired, necessary, but wishful thinking…" Or they could be: "a blessing, a long-awaited gift, a work in progress…"

3. Reflect again on self-compassion, self-forgiveness and self-love. Take some time to think and journal about how you want to love yourself. Be specific.

4. On a large sheet of paper, write "Self-Love" in the center. Draw spokes all around this phrase. Add all the words and phrases that are true for you now; try not to edit your words as you do this. Go back and add more as you think of them during the week. Or, use the sentence stem, "Self-love is …" and repeat this stem over and over with all that comes to mind associated with what self-love means to you.

5. If you feel wounded, sad, angry, or depressed when a memory arises, see if you can name the ungrieved loss. This loss or wound may be covered by negative experiences, shame, or guilt. Get beneath them in your journal and see what it is you need to grieve. Share this with someone you trust.

6. How will you begin a commitment to love yourself starting today – right now? Be concrete in your thinking. For example,

whenever you are around a family member or other person you do not get along with or feel safe with (inwardly or outwardly), lean into your Higher Power. Be intentional. Ask for what you need to be your true self. Ask for wisdom, humility, and peace in your own soul. See the other person as a wounded child. Send them thoughts of healing and hope. Then ...... let go and live your life!

Epilogue

D ear Reader,
> We are living in difficult times. It may be more important than ever to be gentle with yourself, to find the quiet moments, and to still your heart. Start with five minutes a day. A little silence and solitude go a long way.

I encourage you to study your own life as laid out in these pages and elsewhere. You need only be present to your own life to discover the precious jewel that you are on this earth, and to live the most meaningful life possible. Journaling will take you far along that path.

Each day is a new beginning. Keep an open mind, and try not to overanalyze what is happening – in your life or in anyone else's. You have a right to be here, and so do they. Yet, one cannot or should not trust just anyone – so ask to be guided to those teachers and examples who hold the qualities that you want to become in yourself. Choose wisely.

Remember that you need not do life alone. In truth, you are never alone. The Spirit is *always* available to you. Do whatever you must do to still your heart – and then listen: to the birds and crickets, the rivers and streams, the mountains and meadows. Listen to your life: to whoever and whatever is coming at you on a daily basis. Listen to your own soul. Then decide what you need and want to do.

Now gather whatever it is you need in your spiritual backpack. Grab your hat and walking stick and continue on the path – of life, of love, of compassion, and forgiveness. You just might be astonished by what you find.

P.S. You can connect with me and other readers on my *Journaling as a Spiritual Path* website: www.journalingasaspiritualpath.com

Acknowledgements

I wish to acknowledge the following people, both living and deceased:

Thanks to my family and friends who encouraged me along the way, especially my parents, Jacqueline Darling and J. Walter Darling, and my sister Jeanne Darling, for their enthusiasm and support. I am grateful to friends for their encouragement and interest: Del DeLaurentis, Lynne Anthony, Sue Martinelli, George Maunz, Linda Klopp, Georgia Earp, Cathy Campanaro, Katherine Ferrara, Greg Cook, Regina Bogle, and many others along the way.

Thanks to those who contributed to the creation and completion of this book: Bobbi Benson at Wild Ginger Press, for bringing your patience, expertise and artistic beauty to the pages of this book; my readers, Sue Martinelli and George Maunz, for your excellent feedback and encouragement; my dear friend Susan Boskette, and Jane Williams, Ph.D., for valuable feedback at the rewriting stage; Gina Bogle for recommending Wild Ginger Press; and Eric R. Strauss for your legal guidance.

Thanks to all the authors, poets, publishers, and others who generously allowed me to use some or all of their material freely: Paula D'Arcy (Orbis Books and The Crossroad Publishing Company), Christine Valters Painter (Abbey of the Arts), Kabir Helminski, Clark Strand, Parker Palmer (Berrett-Koehler Publishers), Richard Rohr (Center for Action and Contemplation (CAC) and John Wiley & Sons), Brie Stoner (Center for Action and Contemplation (CAC), Kathy Koval, Christine Labrum, Doug Wysockey-Johnson (Lumunos), Ken Burns (Florentine Films), Jennifer (Jinks) Hoffman, Peter Scazzero (Zondervan), Kay Lindahl (SkyLight Paths), Mirabai Starr (Sounds

True®), Nancy L. Bieber (Turner Publishing), Philip Simmons (Penguin Random House), Alan D. Wolfelt, Ph.D. (Companion Press), Eugene Peterson (Wm. B. Eerdmans Publishing), Barb Miller, LuAnn Sgrecci O'Connell, and Tyndale House Publishers. A big thanks to Sorin Books® for use of much material by Christine Valters Paintner, Joyce Rupp, Macrina Wiederkehr, and James Finley.

A special thanks to Donna Wood and Doug Wood and their families for their gracious willingness to let me include my personal recollections of Richie Wood in this book.

Abundant thanks to all who have been mentors throughout my years in Pennsylvania – you know who you are. To the many teachers and professors over my life who have inspired my love of writing, especially Paula D'Arcy, Neal Bruss, Ph.D., and Sherry Blackman. Special thanks to the Kairos School of Spiritual Formation, Oasis Ministries, Shalem Institute for Spiritual Formation, the Lehigh Valley Chapter of Spiritual Directors International (SDI), Northeast Wisdom, Jesuit Center for Spiritual Growth, Saint Francis Center for Renewal, and Saint Francis Retreat House, for being the Lighthouses of God's love, compassion, and grace.

With much love and gratitude, I thank my dear husband, Mike Jendzeizyk, for his love and support of this project, for being a great listener, and for getting me out of "the cave" each week to have some fun. Our adventure continues....

ENDNOTES

Rohr, Richard. Richard Rohr's Daily Meditation, July 2, 2019. Copyright © 2019 by Center for Action and Contemplation. Used by permission of CAC. All rights reserved worldwide. References: [1] Adapted from Richard Rohr, Way of the Prophet (Center for Action and Contemplation: 1994); [2] Prophets Then, Prophets Now (Center for Action and Contemplation: 2006), MP3 download; and [3] Rebuilding from the Bottom Up: A Reflection Following the Election (November 11, 2016) (https://cac.org/rebuilding-bottom-re-flection-following-election/)

_____ *Creation is the Primary Cathedral.* Copyright © 2016 by Center for Action and Contemplation. Used by permission of CAC. All rights reserved worldwide. References: [1] "Legend of Perugia," St. Francis of Assisi: Omnibus of Sources, 1055-1056. [2] My work with men's spirituality is now carried by Illuman. Visit Illuman.org for information about male initiation rites and other resources. Adapted from Richard Rohr, *Eager to Love: The Alternative Way of Francis of Assisi* (Franciscan Media, 2014), 47-48. (https://cac.org/creation-primary-cathedral-2016-11-15/)

Stoner, Brie. "Becoming Christ" from *Oneing: An Alternative Orthodoxy* (Volume 7, No. 1) (Albuquerque, NM: The Center for Action and Contemplation). Copyright © 2019 by CAC. Used by permission of CAC. All rights reserved worldwide. References: [1] Teilhard de Chardin, *Christianity and Evolution: Reflections on Science and Religion* (New York: Harcourt, 1971), 180. [2] Richard Rohr, *The Universal Christ: How a Forgotten Reality Can Change Everything We See, Hope For, and Believe* (New York: Convergent, 2019), 16. [3] Beatrice Bruteau, *God's Ecstasy: The Creation of a Self-Creating World* (New York: Crossroad, 1997), 39.

APPENDIX A:
Tools for Journaling

Choosing a Journal and Protecting Your Privacy

If you decide to write by hand, buy a journal that suits you. For example, I tried some of the fancy journals you can buy at the local bookstores and pharmacies (which might work for you), but I didn't like the bindings on them – they didn't lie flat enough. I settled upon using a "steno pad" because it is smaller than larger notebooks (6"x9") and easy to carry in a purse, knapsack, or briefcase. The smaller-sized pages are a little less intimidating than an 8"x11" sheet of paper. The steno pads lie flat when opened and I can easily stack and store them for future review. You can try a couple of types of notebooks until you decide which one is the most comfortable for you to use.

   a.   Buy a box of your favorite pens that are easy to write with and that don't blot the pages. Invest in a couple of yellow or other bright colored highlighters for highlighting areas of your journal that you want to go back to.

   b.   Place a return address or name and phone number on the front or back of the journal in case you leave it somewhere and it can be returned to you.

   c.   Don't leave your journal lying around the house if you live with others. I recommend always keeping it in your purse, bag, knapsack, or briefcase both for privacy and so you have it with you wherever you go for longer periods, such as work or school. That way when something important comes up, you can record it, if only to make a note of it so you can journal about it later.

d. Try a little art deco on the cover of your journal if you use a plain pad. Last year, I cut out stars and other figures from my Christmas cards before I recycled them and taped them to the cover of my steno pad. It gave it a feel of authenticity and reminds me of how important and special my journal is to me.

Online Journaling

If you decide to journal online, on your tablet, or on your laptop, make sure you back it up (not just on the iCloud™), and make sure no one has access to it. I'm of the generation that does not trust the Internet with my personal thoughts and feelings, so I suggest you talk to people your own age about how and where they journal. There is a lot of new and good journaling software and websites out there that might be the right match for you. But be sure to check out these companies thoroughly and review their privacy policies before signing up. A good place to start would be to search "journaling apps online".

APPENDIX B:
Writing Prompts for Tending the Soul

Add your own sentence stems/writing prompts to this list. Use them to get you going when you feel stuck or need to explore an issue.

I've been …

I should be …

I'm surprised by …

I want to …

I'm willing to …

I'm not willing to …

I don't see how …

I'm upset by …

I desire …

I wish …

My biggest challenge is …

I need more …

My biggest struggle is …

The turning point recently was …

My worst enemy is …

I want to …

I want to give …

I want to give up …

I need to …

I'm sad when …

I like …

I like listening to …

I love …

I love it when …

I wish I could …

I feel lonely when …

My greatest gift is …

I truly feel comforted by …

My greatest gift to others is …

I still need to work on …

Lately I haven't received …

I am anxious about …

I am totally at peace when …

I'm looking forward to …

I'm finding it difficult to forgive …

Honestly, I feel as if …

An invitation from God came recently when …

I noticed a seed was planted that might be taking root in …

I sense your presence most powerfully when …

What I need from you now is …

My heart longs for your …

I really need help with …

I accept my God-given humanity most when …

I still reject the part of me that …

An image of you that feeds my soul is …

I have gratitude right now for your …

I see you in …

I hear you in …

I feel your touch in …

I don't believe you are …

I really struggle with …

I'm grieving my …

I'm surprised by your …

I felt so emotional when …

God, I wish you would take this thought …

My daily routines are …

One of my "attachments" is …

I can detach from this by …

The next step for me could be …

The rhythm of my contemplative practice is …

The last time I felt spiritually nourished was …

I truly need to let go of …

I see how attached I am to …

I sense I am approaching a threshold that …

My relationship with the God of my understanding is …

I resist the Divine when …

My deepest desire for a relationship with a Higher Power is …

Questions for Journaling

Add your own questions to this list – and questions who others pose in articles, podcasts, conversations, etc.

1. What do I no longer have?

2. What do I no longer want?

3. What has changed the most, recently in my life?

4. What have I been thinking a lot about lately?

5. What do I want to be doing a year from now?

6. What is the most difficult thing going on right now?

7. How can I make my daily life more fulfilling?

8. What spiritual practices or healing arts am I drawn to, and why?

9. What do I really want for myself?

10. What do I want to really *know*?

11. What have I heard or read lately that I keep thinking about?

12. What is the still small voice saying inside about a problem I'm having?

13. What area(s) of my life are being neglected?

14. Is there a journey I want to make in the next two years?

15. What did I love to do in my childhood?

16. What is my number one intention for today?

17. If I could do anything in my life, what would that be?

18. Why do my dreams seem so unattainable?

19. Is there a more attainable gift I can give myself in the meantime?

20. Who are my closest friends and confidants?

21. What or who am I missing in my social network?

22. Is there something about myself that others may not know?

23. What am I deeply disappointed in?

24. What am I most unhappy about, and what can I do about it?

25. Who can I ask for help?

26. What are my favorite things to do in my spare time?

27. What am I going to do about _____?

28. What are the ways I connect with my Higher Power?

29. What is my Higher Power like?

30. What ways have I experienced my Higher Power's love today?

31. When did I feel disconnected today from my Higher Power? What happened?

32. What are some metaphors that I love to use?

33. For what things am I most grateful?

34. What grace do I need for tomorrow?

35. What is the most important thing anyone ever told me?

APPENDIX C:

Guidelines for Journaling Groups & Writers' Groups

There's a time for us to join a community of people who share our interest in writing and our love of words. The focus of the group can range from spiritual to professional growth. These can be any number of writing groups or book study groups that meet with a focus ranging from self-exploration to improving creative expression, to writing a book or publishing in some way. You can check online (Meet-Ups, Facebook, etc.) or your local library to see if there are existing groups or annual events where people come together to share and explore creative ways that inspire the creative process in your area. Because this book and chapter has focused on spiritual growth and the creative process, I recommend the following guidelines.

Guidelines for Journaling Groups and Writers' Groups

Begin with a small group of people. Invite those who have a desire and can make a commitment to meet for a few weeks or months. Do a trial period to see if people want to continue.

1. Meet for an hour or two. If working online, perhaps keep the time shorter. See how the members feel about the period of time you will meet.

2. The leader (or members can take turns) opens the session with a reading from a meditation book, a quote from a book, a poem, or an excerpt from a sacred text. Make it relevant or connected in some way to the reasons you are meeting. Say a few words about it and why it was meaningful to you (5 minutes).

3. Do a few writing exercises together, such as writing off a line from a poem, writing a haiku, responding to a question, brainstorming a word, using sentence stems/writing prompts to dig beneath the surface of our normal way of thinking. See Appendix B for a list of prompts and questions for doing these exercises.

4. Ask members to share about their experience of writing as well as the content of what they wrote. How might it relate to their spiritual or creative journey?

5. Allow time for one or more members to share what they discovered or wrote since the last meeting, either in their journals, creative writing projects, or other creative pursuits. What inspired them?

6. End the meeting with each member naming a word or symbol that speaks to their true self. What are they taking with them from this shared time today?

7. Try to keep a lot of commentary to a minimum. No comparing and overanalyzing. Unless you have designated the group to be a *critique group*, commentary should **not include** what could have been done better, what members "could not relate to," or negative comments in general. Keep it positive and affirming.

8. Keep a list of recommended reading by members of the group, and update and distribute it frequently.

APPENDIX D:

Time Tables for How You Spend Your Time

TABLE 1: "Doing Time" Activity Table – Daily

(TABLE 1) Based on hours awake: (24 - X hours of sleep = hours awake)	SUN.	MON.	TUES.	WED.	THUR.	FRI.	SAT.	KEEP, CHANGE OR LET GO
DOING TIME - Daily								
Meals								
Daily Hygiene/ Dressing								
Commuting (RT)								
Working or Volunteering								
Family Time								
Read/TV/ Internet								
Exercise/Health								
Other								
SUBTOTAL TIME (Table 1)								

TABLE 2: "Doing Time" Activity Table — Weekly

(TABLE 2) DOING TIME - WEEKLY	SUN.	MON.	TUES.	WED.	THUR.	FRI.	SAT.	KEEP, CHANGE OR LET GO
Laundry/House								
Bills/Finances								
Shopping/ Errands								
Date Night(s)/ Social Time								
Hobbies								
Volunteering								
Friendships								
Recreation								
Group Activities								
Subtotal Time (From Table 2)								
Subtotal Time (From Table 1)								
TOTAL DOING								
Less Hours Awake = Free Time Left for BEING TIME								

TABLE 3: "Being Time" Activity Table — Daily/Weekly

(TABLE 3) **BEING TIME**	SUN.	MON.	TUES.	WED.	THUR.	FRI.	SAT.	KEEP, CHANGE OR LET GO
Reflection Time/ Journaling								
Relaxing/ Napping								
Spiritual Practices								
Time in Nature								
Other								
Other								
Other								
TOTAL BEING (Table 3)								
TOTAL DOING (From Table 2)								
SUBTOTAL — Add Total Being & Total Doing Time								
Less Hours Awake = Personal Time Left in the Day								

Author's Notes
All definitions are taken from The Free Dictionary
www.thefreedictionary.com

Preface

1. Carl Jung (https://owlcation.com/humanities/The-Difference-Between-Carl-Jungs-and-Sigmund-Freuds-Views-on-Religion).

Introduction

1. Teilhard de Chardin famously said: "We are not human beings having a spiritual experience. We are spiritual beings having a human experience."

2. "A fixed mental attitude or disposition that predetermines a person's responses to and interpretations of situations." (https://www.thefreedictionary.com/mindset).

Chapter 1

1. Oftentimes we can share these experiences with loved ones, friends or members of groups or communities to which we may belong and whose members we trust. However, we may need the help of a spiritual advisor, psychotherapist or other *professional* for these memories, so it is important to contact one if you become overwhelmed, anxious, depressed, etc.

2. No offense to garbage collectors, they are essential workers. What a difficult job it must be to collect everyone else's waste. They're extremely important for keeping our environment clean for all of us – in heat, rain, snow and ice.

Chapter 2

1. Marianne Spitzform was our companion during a "Monk in the World Ireland Pilgrimage" with Christine Valters Paintner in 2016. She said the original story (modified here as I interpreted its significance to my own life) came from Matthew Wright, an Episcopal priest who received the story from his Sufi teacher.

2. See these books for more about the "true self": Richard Rohr's *Immortal Diamond: The Search for Our True Self* (Jossey-Bass: 2013), Thomas Merton's *New Seeds of Contemplation* (New Directions, 1961), Kabir Helminski's *Living Presence: A Sufi Way to Mindfulness & the Essential Self* (Penguin-Putnam: 1992), Margaret Silf's *Inner Compass: An Invitation to Ignatian Spirituality* (Loyola Press, 2007), James Finley's *Merton's Palace of Nowhere: A Search for God through Awareness of the True Self* (Ave Maria Press, 1978), and Joyce Rupp's *Open the Door: A Journey to the True Self* (Sorin Books, 2008).

3. Exercise offered by Donna Holstein and Linda Witmer during a Sacred Rhythms Silent Retreat in February, 2020 (https://www.practicingsacredrhythms.com).

Chapter 3

1. Loss of soul in our corporate culture is exquisitely explored in David Whyte's hopeful book *The Heart Aroused, Poetry and the Preservation of the Soul in Corporate America*.

2. From the USFDA website (https://www.fs.usda.gov/detail/dbnf/home/?cid=stelprdb5281464).

3. Human needs are more thoroughly explored in "Figuring Out What You Need" in Chapter 3.

4. Saul McLeod, MRes, Ph.D., Teaching Assistant and Researcher for The University of Manchester, Division of Neuroscience & Experimental Psychology, Manchester, United Kingdom. (https://www.simplypsychology.org/maslow.html).

5. Spiritual Directors International (https://www.sdicompanions.org/what-is-spiritual-companionship).

6. Narcissism and its personality disorder (https://www.thefreedictionary.com/narcissism).

Chapter 4

1. I often find a deep connection with my Higher Power in the process of regaining my balance.

2. Sherry Blackman is the author of *Call to Witness*, Broad Street Publishing (2013).

3. If you are unable to get outside or near a window for time in nature, try watching nature films on PBS, The Discovery Channel, Animal Planet, Netflix, YouTube or National Geographic. Or, purchase large photography books of different countries that show the beauty of the land, or photographic nature books.

4. Question 7 under "Journaling Reflections from Nature" was posed by Sharon Clymer Landis, co-author of *The Spacious Heart: Room for Spiritual Awakening*, Herald Press, 2014.

5. The second half of life typically begins in our forties or later, but some people may experience this shift earlier.

Chapter 5

1. For more information about clearing committees, see "Coming to Light, Cultivating Discernment through the Quaker

Clearness Committee" by Valerie Brown, Pendle Hill Publications.

2. LuAnn Sgrecci O'Connell, Spiritual Director. Quote used with permission.

3. Panentheism is the belief that God is a part of the universe as well as transcending it.

4. My understanding of unitive consciousness is seeing not only from our limited knowledge and experience, but seeing ourselves and others within the wholeness or oneness of all humanity, God, and the universe.

5. St. Catherine of Genoa penned the famous quote, "My deepest self is God."

6. Lao Tzu was an ancient Chinese philosopher and poet, well-known for penning the book *Tao Te Ching*. He was the founder of the philosophy of Taoism, a religious and ethical custom of ancient China.

7. When I'm out of synch with my journaling, I normally know to use rituals and spiritual practices to help me become receptive to the wisdom needed for an issue or situation. Just know this restless thing can still happen, even after 35 years of journaling.

8. Living amends means making genuine changes toward ourselves and others that are not tainted with the negativity of our thoughts or feelings. It is a renewed attitude, perhaps by keeping an open mind and accepting others for who they are, and extending these qualities to ourselves by practicing self-compassion and self-forgiveness. It is living in a way that reflects our true self. Our behavior has changed because we – our heart, our soul, our deepest self – has changed.

9. "The slow work of God…" is from "Patient Trust" by Pierre Teilhard de Chardin, from *Hearts on Fire,* edited by Michael Horter, SJ (Chicago, IL: Loyola Press, 1993).

10. Joy Harjo was the Poet Laureate for the U.S. in 2019, 2020, and 2021.

11. Many religious groups are offering more and more wholistic offerings, including those that feed body, mind, emotion, *and* spirit. Seek and you shall find them.

12. Barb Miller, Spiritual Director. Quote used with permission.

13. Adapted from "A Brief Guide for a Retreat" by Jane Williams, Ph.D. Used with permission.

14. Thomas Aquinas, theologian, philosopher, and apologist of the medieval church.

Note: Website links provided in this book may change without notice.

References

Baker, Karle Wilson. "Three Small Poems," *Poetry: A Magazine of Verse*, (Poetry Foundation, October 1921)

Cain, Susan. *Quiet: The Power of Introverts in a World That Can't Stop Talking* (Crown Publishing Group, 2013)

Cameron, Julia. *The Artist's Way: A Spiritual Path to Higher Creativity*, 1992, (New York: G.P. Putnam's Sons, 1992)

Cousineau, Phil. *The Art of Pilgrimage: The Seeker's Guide to Making Travel Sacred* (Berkeley, CA: Conari Press, 1998)

D'Arcy, Paula. *Gift of the Redbird: The Story of a Divine Encounter* (New York: Crossroad Publishing Company, 1996)

Eichenbaum, Luise, and Susie Orbach. *What Do Women Want: Exploding the Myth of Dependency*. Copyright © 1983, 1999, 2014 by Luise Eichenbaum and Susie Orbach.

Hickman, Martha Whitmore. *Healing After Loss: Daily Meditations for Working Through Grief* (New York: William Morrow, HarperCollins® Publishers, 1994)

Landis, Sharon Clymer. *On the Journey: Meditations and Reflections by Fellow Travelers from the Kairos Community*, Copyright © 2016 by the Members of the Kairos Community. (Landisville, PA: Yurchak Printing, 2016)

Langford, Jeremy. "The Practice of Letting Go" from *Seeds of Faith: Practices to Grow a Healthy Spiritual Life* (Brewster, MA: Paraclete Press, 2007)

May, Gerald G., MD. *The Awakened Heart: Opening Yourself to the Love You Need* (HarperCollins® Publishers, 1993)

Norris, Gunilla. *Inviting Silence: Universal Principles of Meditation* (New York: BlueBridge, an imprint of United Tribes Media, Inc., 2004)

Peck, Scott M. *The Road Less Traveled: A New Psychology of Love*, Traditional Values and Spiritual Growth (New York: Touchstone/Simon & Schuster, 1985)

Ramakrishna, Sri. *The Gospel of Sri Ramakrishna*, 465 (https://www.vedantany.org/sayings-of-sri-ramakrishna/

Whyte, David. "Self Portrait" from *Fire in the Earth* (Langley, WA: Many Rivers Press, 1992)

Wohlleben, Peter. *The Hidden Life of Trees: What They Feel, How They Communicate – Discoveries from a Secret World* (Vancouver: Greystone Books, 2016)

About the Author

Jo-Ellen Darling is a creative nonfiction writer, spiritual seeker, occasional retreat leader, and pilgrim on the Christian Contemplative path. She began to journal at age 30, after an intense episode of spiritual awakening. Leaving alcohol and substances behind following a "dark night of the soul," her journaling soon became an amazing inner journey of self-reflection, self-knowledge, creative expression, and continued spiritual growth. Besides regular journaling for nearly 35 years, she attributes her search for the Divine and her True Self to be the foundation of the sustaining growth in her life and writing. Reading books with a spiritual focus, meditating on poetry and sacred texts, and spending time in nature and with kindred spirits have been the gifts that have nourished her journey through a lifetime of struggle and grace, pain and joy. Jo-Ellen received a B.A. in English from the University of Massachusetts at Boston, and an M.S. in Communications Management from Simmons University. She is also a 2011 graduate of the Kairos School of Spiritual Formation. Jo-Ellen and her husband live in the Lehigh Valley, Pennsylvania. *Journaling as a Spiritual Path* is her first book.

Readers can connect with the author, read her blog, and watch for events at www.journalingasaspiritualpath.com and on Facebook https://www.facebook.com/Journaling-as-a-Spiritual-Path

Made in United States
North Haven, CT
21 January 2022

15088892R00176